Donated by
James L. Johnston
to The Heartland Institute
2015

A Cato Institute Book

South Africa's War against Capitalism

WALTER E. WILLIAMS

PRAEGER

New York
Westport, Connecticut
London

Library of Congress Cataloging-in-Publication Data

Williams, Walter E. (Walter Edward), 1936–
 South Africa's war against capitalism / Walter E. Williams.
  p. cm.
 Bibliography: p.
 Includes index.
 ISBN 0–275–93179–X (alk. paper)
  1. South Africa—Economic policy. 2. Industry and state—South
 Africa. 3. Capitalism—South Africa. 4. Apartheid—South Africa.
 5. Blacks—Legal status, laws, etc.—South Africa. I. Title.
 HC905.W55   1989
 338.968—dc19   88-34028

Copyright © 1989 by Walter E. Williams

All rights reserved. No portion of this book may be
reproduced, by any process or technique, without the
express written consent of the publisher.

Library of Congress Catalog Card Number: 88-34028
ISBN: 0–275–93179–X

First published in 1989

Praeger Publishers, One Madison Avenue, New York, NY 10010
A division of Greenwood Press, Inc.

Printed in the United States of America

The paper used in this book complies with the Permanent
Paper Standard issued by the National Information Standards
Organization (Z39.48–1984).

10 9 8 7 6 5 4 3 2 1

*To South Africa's decent people of all races and
ethnic groups who are seeking a human rights–enhancing
solution to its thorny problems*

Contents

Illustrations		ix
Preface		xi
Acknowledgments		xiii
Introduction		xv
1	**The Evolution of Apartheid**	1
2	**The South African Legal Structure**	23
3	**The Drive for Racial Labor Laws**	45
4	**Market Manipulation to Support Apartheid**	67
5	**Apartheid: Rhetoric versus Reality**	97
6	**Apartheid: A Triumph over Capitalism**	125
7	**Postscript for South Africans**	145
Selected Bibliography		151
Index		157

Illustrations

MAP

1	Early Migration Patterns	6

TABLES

3.1	Selected Mine Employees by Race	59
4.1	Profit Maximization without Taxes	83
4.2	Profit Maximization with Taxes	84
4.3	Optimization with Profit Tax	84
5.1	A Comparison between South Africa and Other Industrial Countries in Annual Percent Growth of Gross Domestic Product at Market Prices, 1964–74	98
5.2	Employment of Whites and Blacks on South African Railways and Harbors, for Selected Years, 1926–75	104
5.3	Black Urban Population, 1936–70	111
5.4	Employment on Gold Mines	116

6.1 Approximate Work Time Required for Average Manufacturing Employees to Buy Selected Commodities in Retail Stores in Washington, D.C., and London and at State-fixed Prices in Moscow and Johannesburg during May 1976   133

6.2 Surveys on Disinvestment and Sanctions   137

Preface

South Africa has become the world's pariah nation for its denial of the political franchise to most of its nonwhite population and for having one of the most highly codified systems of racial discrimination, known as "apartheid." For this, South Africa deserves the moral condemnation that it has received from most of the world. However, while post–World War II moral condemnation did possibly speed up the demise of colonialism on the African continent, decades later it is readily apparent to any observer that the mere elimination of colonialism was not a sufficient guarantee for the personal liberty and higher standard of living hoped for by the African common man and woman.

The author feels that the experiences of postcolonialism should serve as a caution for postapartheid South Africa. Compassion requires that we seriously entertain questions and thoughts about what kind of system is going to replace apartheid. Will such a system promote the kind of liberties and standards of living hoped for by both South African and Western opponents of apartheid?

My purpose in writing this book is several fold. For one thing, I want to provide the average Western layperson with a sketch of South Africa. All too often, the conflict there is seen as a struggle between blacks and whites. The reality is quite different. South Africa's black population consists of several major ethnic groups, who have developed different customs and values. When people casually use the phrase "the blacks of South Africa," it has just about the same meaning as the phrase "the whites of Europe." We would all acknowledge that the latter conceals tremendous ethnic, cultural, and religious differences among peoples of the same racial group. The same is the case with "the blacks of South Africa." There is just as much diversity among South African's blacks as there is among its European population. Afrikaners and Britishers can hardly be said to be of one mind. Moreover, there is a lingering mutual suspicion and distrust stemming from the Boer War and the fact that Britishers carry the option of being welcomed in Commonwealth countries.

Then there is South Africa's Asian (mostly Indian) population who have stood in periodic conflict with the black ethnic groups and with the Europeans, too.

All these factors lead the thoughtful observer to the conclusion that, even if whites were to pick up and leave South Africa, there would still remain a great potential for human conflict, just as we have witnessed in parts of postcolonial Africa. Therefore, any solutions to South Africa's stubborn dilemma must recognize and accommodate its racial and ethnic diversity.

A more important purpose in writing this book is to address what has become an all-too-popular theme among the oppressed in South Africa and their Western supporters: that apartheid is a result of capitalism. If capitalism can be described as the unfettered operation of the market in the allocation of society's scarce resources, then apartheid is the antithesis of capitalism. Therefore, I devote many pages to making the argument that apartheid is indeed a struggle *against* capitalism—and hence the title of the book. While recognizing that apartheid affects many areas of economic life, the major emphasis here is placed on South Africa's labor markets in the development of apartheid. Hopefully, by fully understanding what apartheid is, we can fully eliminate it in such a way that it does not reemerge in another guise.

South African scholars will no doubt find faults of omission, commission, and emphasis. However, I would be more than pleased if this publication were to pique the interest of a more general audience and therefore contribute to the enrichment of popular debate. As an adjunct to that goal, there is also my hope that the ideas presented here will make a small contribution to a lasting set of solutions by pointing to questions lost in the emotional war being waged against apartheid, both in South Africa and abroad.

Acknowledgments

Insomuch as racism has been a dominant feature of South Africa, the country provides an excellent laboratory to examine various economic hypotheses. Like most Americans, my knowledge of South Africa had been limited to vague glimpses from news clippings; and it was not until 1978 that I met a real live South African—albeit in Hong Kong—in the person of Leon Louw, director of the Free Market Foundation of South Africa.

After our meeting, Mr. Louw helped arrange for my first visit to South Africa in 1979, to participate in a one-week conference sponsored by the University of Witwatersrand in Johannesburg. Having had my interest piqued by that experience, I accepted an engagement in 1980 to speak before most of South Africa's universities, business groups, student groups, clubs, and local organizations. This was a chance to meet and exchange views with nearly all of South Africa's divergent factions.

It was not until 1986, when I accepted an invitation by Professor Duncan Reekie of the University of the Witwatersrand to attend his conference on "How Business Transcends Politics" that I came up with the idea of writing this book.

Therefore, I owe a major debt of gratitude to Leon Louw—a lawyer by training—and his wife, Frances Kendall, for whetting my interest in South Africa and providing the many introductions that have assisted me in understanding some of the actual issues of the situation.

My gratitude also goes to Michael Schewitz, a student at Witwatersrand University, who served as my overseas research assistant in tracking publications and other materials necessary for the later chapters.

Marion Friedlander, my assistant/secretary, cheerfully typed numerous versions and updates of this manuscript, traced down data and publications, and brought my attention to matters of syntax, clarity, and style—for which I owe many thanks.

The John M. Olin Foundation, through their general support of my academic efforts, made it possible for me to have the time and financial resources to do the research for this manuscript.

A final debt of gratitude must be acknowledged to Connie and Devon Williams, my wife and my daughter, who gave me the moral support and toleration (of my absence) that ultimately made the manuscript possible.

Introduction

South Africa's apartheid—a pervasive system of legalized racial discrimination—has made it the focus of worldwide revulsion. The international attack on this morally offensive system has forced the South African government into a defensive posture—so much so that, unlike the past, no government official would now even dream of attempting to justify traditional apartheid principles in the international arena of opinion.

But long before the international climate made apartheid an untenable proposition, South Africa's legalized system of racial discrimination was under attack from within. A small part of the internal battle against apartheid was waged on moral grounds by South Africa's decent people, both white and nonwhite. A much larger part of the battle was waged not for decency or the brotherhood of man, but on economic grounds where the stakes were profits and losses.

In any government policy—including legal discrimination—to create special privileges for one group, those special privileges show up as special disadvantages to some other group. In South Africa, those disadvantages were felt mostly by its nonwhite population. But part of the disadvantage was felt by members of its white population. This produced widespread tension leading to resistance, evasion, and contravention of racially discriminatory laws, by people who shared the same white supremacy ideology as the government officials and politicians who made the laws. That kind of opposition to apartheid continues today and has become more open, pervasive, and effective.

Albeit at a skirmish level, the economic assault against legalized racial discrimination began even before South Africa was granted responsible government by England in the early twentieth century. It grew in strength and precipitated a national crisis—the 1922 Rand Rebellion—when the white managers of South Africa's mining companies broke their racially discriminatory labor agreements, which included quotas for hiring whites, and began replacing white miners with black miners. The strike that followed—the most violent in South African history;

it had to be put down with tanks, artillery, and warplanes—cost the lives of hundreds of white miners and government soldiers and caused injuries to hundreds more. Its political fallout among white voters drove the prime minister and his party from office. The new prime minister, and his party, came to office on the promise to make white businesspeople, who for the most part were believers in white supremacy, acknowledge this belief in their hiring policy, or—in the phraseology of the time—maintain a "civilised labour policy." Part of this so-called civilized labor policy called for minimum wages, rate for the job—whereby employers were to pay all employees the same way, regardless of race—and punishment for companies that did not hire enough whites.

Apartheid and its many contrasts, contradictions, and cruelties has already been extensively examined and analyzed in political, moral, and sociological terms. This book analyzes South Africa's apartheid in economic terms, mostly in its labor markets. Hopefully the analysis will help provide insights that cannot be obtained using the standard tools of political science and sociology, and thus contribute to the framework for conflict resolution among all of South Africa's racial and ethnic groups. Moreover, a better understanding of apartheid in South Africa can also contribute to a greater understanding of racial issues elsewhere.

Finally, we hope that a better understanding of the economic workings of apartheid will provide the West with a better basis to form an appropriate response in its international relations with South Africa.

The plan of the book is as follows: Chapter 1 provides a brief—and by no means complete—early history of South Africa, with focus on the racial and ethnic diversity of its peoples and the evolution of its thinking about apartheid. Chapter 2 highlights some of South Africa's legal institutions, with primary emphasis on its racially discriminatory laws and some of the challenges that the government has faced in getting those laws established. Chapter 3 focuses primarily on the historical forces behind the development of South Africa's racially discriminatory labor law. Chapter 4 applies standard economic analysis to apartheid in business and the labor market. Chapter 5 continues the analysis of the previous chapter, bringing to light the market challenges to apartheid and the government's response to these challenges. Since many apartheid laws have recently been repealed, relaxed, or unenforced, Chapter 6 provides a summary of these changes and a general discussion of what can be learned about racial relations from the South African experience. Finally, Chapter 7 is a postscripted suggestion to all people of goodwill in South Africa who want to bury apartheid completely and not see it reemerge in another guise.

1
The Evolution of Apartheid

South Africa is a beautiful country that occupies the southern portion of the African continent, from latitude 22°S to 35°S. To the east, west, and south, South Africa borders on the Indian and Atlantic oceans. To the north, it shares borders with Namibia, Zimbabwe, Botswana, Swaziland, and Mozambique. Completely enclosed by South Africa are the "independent" states of Transkei, Ciskei, Lesotho, Venda, and Bophuthatswana—parts of which share a border with Botswana.

South Africa is a country rich in mineral wealth. It possesses the world's largest known deposits of precious minerals such as gold, platinum, diamonds, and semiprecious gemstones. It also contains the world's largest deposits of strategic industrial minerals such as chromite, manganese, vanadium, flourspar, and andalusite. Moreover, it is richly endowed with coal, iron ore, antimony, copper, titanium, uranium, zinc, nickel, lead, and phosphates. Most of these minerals are exported. In 1980, their export value was nearly 15 billion rand (at US$ 0.76 = 1 rand; its value in U.S. dollars was over 11 billion).

South Africa's population of nearly 28 million lives within its four provinces: Natal, Cape, the Orange Free State, and the Transvaal. According to the 1985 census, that population consisted of roughly 19 million blacks, nearly 5 million whites, 2.8 million coloreds, and 861,000 Asians. As of 1985, 88 percent of whites, 91 percent of Asians, 77 percent of coloreds, and 38 percent of blacks were urbanized. None of these different racial groups are homogeneous; they are all distinguished within themselves by intraracial language and/or ethnic diversity.

While blacks are roughly 72 percent of the population, they actually consist of several major ethnic groups. The Zulus, estimated to number 6.4 million, are the largest single ethnic group—followed by 2.9 million Xhosas, 2.9 million Northern Sothos, 1.9 million Southern Sothos, 1.4 million Tswanas, and 1.1 million Tsonga. The balance are the Ndebeles, Swazis, and Vendas. The native language of the black population can be divided into four major language groups: Nguni, Sotho, Tsonga, and Venda. Nguni is by far the most prevalent language and is spoken by at least 9 million blacks belonging mostly to Zulus and Xhosa. Sotho is the next largest spoken language, belonging to the Northern, Eastern, and Western Sotho. Despite the fact that black language can be broken down into four major groups, there are numerous dialects within each language group, such as Nguni spoken by the Ndebele and that spoken by the Zulu.

In 1985 the white population (4.9 million) was 18 percent of the total. Like the black population, it is ethnically diverse. The ethnic composition of Afrikaners—formerly called *Boers*, the Dutch term for farmers— is a mix of Dutch, German, French Huguenot, and English; and they are the largest component of the white population. South Africans of English ancestry are the second largest component. A negligible part of the white population consists of Jews (117,000), Italians (23,000), Germans (59,000), Greeks (23,000), French (11,000), Dutch (24,000), and Portuguese (56,000). Sixty percent of the white population identify themselves as Afrikaans speaking, while the remainder identify as English speaking.

Coloreds are roughly 10 percent of the total population. They are mixed-race people who find their antecedents among Malays from Indonesia, Cape Hottentots (Khoi-Khoi), Europeans of many nationalities, Bushmen, Indians, and Africans. The language of 90 percent of the coloreds is Afrikaans; the rest are English or Arabic speaking. There are about 150,000 coloreds who are Cape Malays, representing a mixture of Indians, Cingolese, Chinese, Indonesians, and Malagasy, and belonging to the Islamic faith.

Asians—numbering 861,000—are slightly more than 3 percent of the total population. Living mostly in Natal, Indians account for 99 percent of the Asian population. Chinese—numbering 9,000—are only about 1 percent of the Asian population. Within the Indian population there are significant ethnic/language/religious differences. The mix consists of combinations of Hindu, who are divided into four basic language groups, (Tamil, Telugu, Hindi, and Gujariti) and Muslim, who speak Urdu and Gujarati. In terms of religion, the Indians are Hindu, Muslim, Christian, and Zoroastrian. In 1985, eighty-one percent of Indians lived within 90 miles of South Africa's port city of Durban.

While it is true that South Africa of the nineteenth and twentieth centuries has been home to a wide variety of languages, ethnic populations, and cultures, it was not so at the time of the first European contact. South Africa's Cape Province was discovered by a Portuguese maritime expedition headed by Bartholomew Diaz, who was searching for a sea route to the East. Diaz spent only a few days at Algoa Bay before returning to report to King John II of Portugal.

In July 7, 1497, King John dispatched a second expedition under Vasco da Gama. Da Gama rounded the Cape of Good Hope on November 22, 1498, and cast anchor in Mossel Bay. On reaching shore, the crew was greeted by friendly Khoi-Khoi natives (a Hamitic people who, along with Bushmen, were the original inhabitants of South Africa); they were willing to barter cattle for Western ornaments and trifles. After spending several days on shore, da Gama set sail and reached his ultimate destination—India—on May 16, 1498.

Once a sea route to the East had been established, the Portuguese lost interest in the Cape area of the continent. Instead they concentrated their interests in the gold-mining activities of the Makalanga Africans in what is now Zimbabwe and Mozambique, and then later in Angola in search of silver and slaves to send to South America. It was now up to Holland and England—which were in ascendancy—to settle Africa's Cape, through the Dutch East India Company and the English East India Company.

Jan van Riebeeck, a company official of the Dutch East India Company, established the first white settlement in the Cape on April 6, 1652. The natives that the whites encountered were the Khoi-Khoi and the Bushmen, whose estimated populations at that time were 15,000 and 10,000, respectively. The natives lived by hunting and raising large herds of cattle and sheep. The Dutch traded copper wire and beads with the natives, but disputes broke out over cattle stealing and land. The natives resented Dutch occupation of their grazing lands near Table Mountain. Reprisals, attacks, and theft led to the First Hottentot War in 1659. A peace treaty was reached the following year, with the indigenous people realizing that they were no match for the Europeans.

The victory established a permanent presence of Europeans to service the ships en route to India. Even with increased white settlement, which included the arrival of 200 French Huguenots between 1688 and 1700, there were not enough whites to raise vegetables, tend herds, erect buildings, and do all the other work. Numerous attempts to persuade the Hottentots and Bushmen to work for the Dutch East India Company failed. Therefore, van Riebeeck's attention turned to importing slaves from the eastern, northern, and central parts of Africa. Soon there were more slaves in the Cape than whites.

British involvement in South Africa resulted indirectly when France invaded Holland in order to help the Patriot party proclaim a republic. The prince of Orange, the ruler of Holland, fled to England. Believing his plight to be temporary, the prince asked the British government to take over Holland's colonial possessions until he could be restored to power.

In 1795, nine British warships sailed into Richard's Bay in the Cape of Good Hope. They encountered brief resistance from the governor and the colonists, who were already in rebellion against the Dutch East India Company. The governor surrendered, and the British occupation began. It lasted until France and Britain made peace by signing the Treaty of Amiens in 1802. The terms of the treaty required the transfer of the Cape to the Republic of Bavaria, which Holland was then to be called.

Peace in Europe did not last very long, and in 1803 war broke out between France and Britain. To protect its sea routes, England dispatched 63 ships with 7,000 soldiers on board to retake the Cape. A surrender was signed on January 10, 1806, making the Cape inhabitants once again subjects of the king of England. At the end of the war in Europe (1814), the Cape Province became a British colony by formal cession.

EARLY RACIAL PROBLEMS

Hottentots and Slaves

The Hottentots and Bushmen had little desire to work as laborers for the settlers. Van Riebeeck obtained permission from the Dutch East India Company to import slaves. The first slaves arrived from the west coast of Africa in 1658. More slaves were brought in from East Africa, the East Indies, and Madagascar. By the time slavery was abolished in 1834, there were nearly 30,000 of these imported peoples, who mixed with Hottentots and Europeans and became what is now known as the "Cape Coloureds." Relying on slaves for labor, the Dutch East India Company "pursued a policy of nonintercourse with the tribes in the hinterland."[1]

In the early years of Dutch East India Company rule, under Christian influence, a baptized black had rights and privileges similar to the European. During the first 20 years of Dutch settlement (1652–72), 75 percent of children born to slaves had European fathers. Some of the "coloured" children who emerged from the Dutch/slave/Hottentot union were similar in appearance to southern Italians. In fact, there were also marriages between Europeans and Hottentots. With the increased use of slaves, such practice soon became disgraced; and in 1685, the marriage of Europeans with slaves of full color was banned. But European marriages to half-breeds were still permitted.

According to Neame, by the middle of the eighteenth century, whites in South Africa regarded color just like whites in America. Abraham Lincoln said, "What next? Free them and make them politically and socially our equals? My own feelings will not permit this... Whether this feeling accords with justice and sound judgment is not the whole question, if indeed it is any part of it. A universal feeling, whether well or ill-founded, cannot safely be disregarded. We cannot make them our equal."[2]

Modern South African racial policy saw its early beginnings soon after 1807 when the British outlawed slave trade in the colony and no more slaves could be brought to the Cape. Since Hottentots were not willing to work for the Europeans, a clamor for a replacement work force arose. The Earl of Caledon, the Cape's first civil governor, introduced a pass law for Hottentots, which held that all males not working for whites would be classified as vagrants. A Hottentot would be punished as a vagrant unless he was carrying a pass. The only way to obtain a pass was by entering into a labor agreement with a white employer. Hottentots without passes would be arrested and hired out to a farmer. The Cape's Council of Policy expressed a strong preference for colored labor—condemning white labor as lazy, incompetent, and much more expensive.

Discriminatory laws against the Hottentots drew strong protest from the missionary churches in the Cape. As a result, in 1828, the government passed Ordinance 50, which abolished its earlier restrictive laws against the Hottentots.

While Ordinance 50 did not apply to slaves, it applied to other nonwhites and read:

As it has been the custom of this colony for Hottentots and other free persons of colour to be subject to certain hindrances as to their place of living, way of life and employment, and to certain forced services which do not apply to other subjects of His Majesty, be it therefore made law that from and after the passing of this Ordinance no Hottentot or other free person of colour lawfully living in this colony shall be subject to any forced service which does not apply to others of His Majesty's subjects, nor to any hindrances, interference, fine or punishment of any kind whatever under the pretence that such person has been guilty of vagrancy or any other offence unless after trial in the due course of law, any custom or usage to the contrary notwithstanding.[3]

By 1834, slavery was abolished within the British Empire. By law all non-Europeans were then granted the same rights as Europeans.

European Contact with the Northern Natives

According to Fagan, "It was not til near the end of the eighteenth century [that] the European settlers came into contact with Bantu tribes."[4] (See Map 1.) The Afrikaners had no desire to have anything to do with the Kaffirs (Bantu). "Governor van Plettenburg, in 1774, issued an edict threatening to fine, or even condemn to death, anyone who persisted in trafficking with the Natives."[5] In 1788, the governor's Council of Policy ratified a treaty with the Xhosa to make a dividing line between the whites and the natives at the Fish River, some 600 miles away from Cape Town. The treaty was broken by Xhosa incursions across the Fish River—which led to no less than nine so-called Kaffir Wars until they were finally defeated in 1878.

The British broke the Dutch policy of nonintercourse with the Bantu, and by 1834 there were 17,000 Fingoes farming the area between the Fish and Kei rivers. The Dutch—resentful of British interference—began to move out of the Cape colony. Sir Benjamin D'Urban, governor of the Cape from 1834 to 1838, said that what came to be known as the "Great Trek" was caused by the "insecurity of life and property occasioned by the recent measures, inadequate [government] compensation for the loss of slaves, and despair of obtaining recompense for ruinous losses of the Kaffir invasion."[6] One of the leaders of the Trek considered the chief reason for the exodus to be that slaves "were placed on an equal footing with Christians contrary to the laws of God and the natural distinction of race and colour, so that it was intolerable for any decent Christian to bow down beneath such a yoke; therefore we rather withdrew in order to preserve our doctrines in purity."[7]

Thus, some of the basis was laid for later British–Boer conflicts. The Boers, who settled in the interior, established republics and fashioned constitutions based on the notion of no equality between black and whites and, above all, resistance

Map 1
Early Migration Patterns

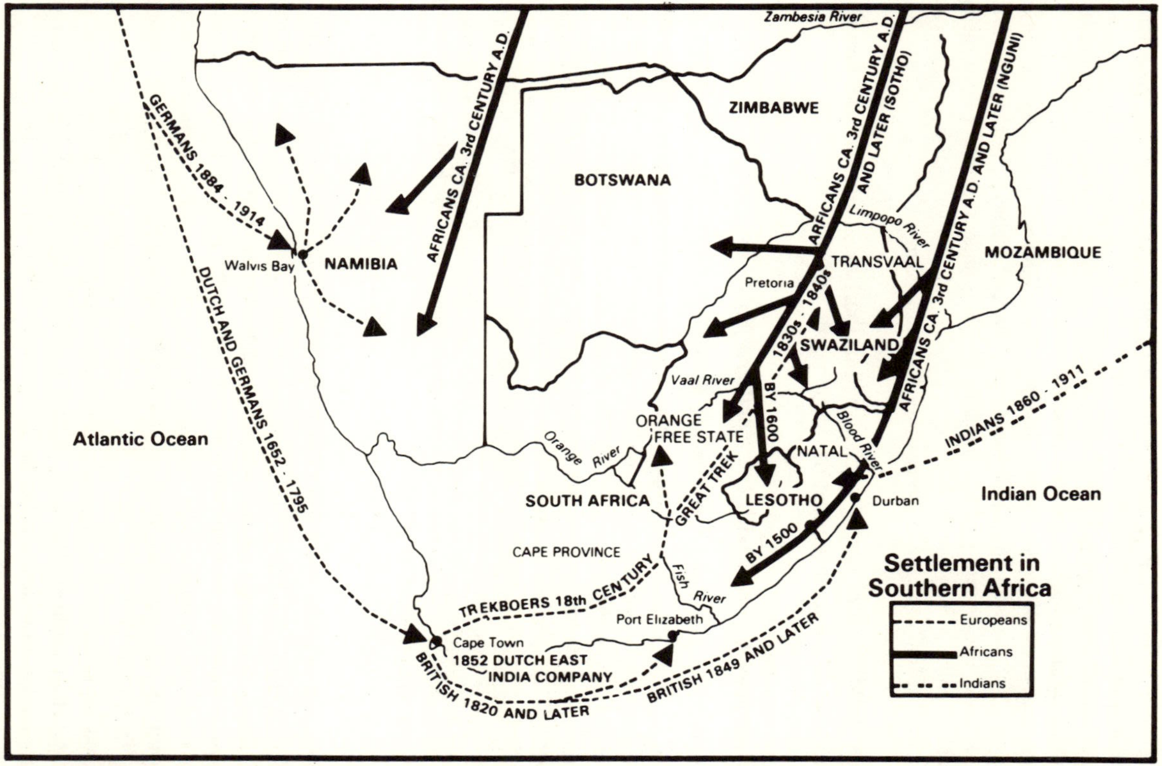

Adapted from: Foreign Policy Study Foundation, Inc., *South Africa: Time Running Out* (Berkeley, California: University of California Press, 1981), p. 24.

to British rule. The Cape that they left behind was at the same time repealing the color bar and giving nonwhites a voice in its political life.

When the Boers established the Republic of Natal, its Volkraad (legislative assembly) ordered that all natives found in the Republic were to be removed as a measure to "avoid collisions of different races, which would inevitably result from the continued residence of themselves and the Natives."[8] The order was set aside by the British secretary of state for the colonies, who declared that the Boers would be allowed to stay in Natal on condition "there shall not be in the eyes of the law any distinction of colour, origin, language or creed."[9] Ultimately, in 1845 when the British annexed Natal, most of the Boers left for the Boer republics. By 1856, Natal had a legislative council to which twelve members were elected. Any person—irrespective of color—had the vote franchise. In 1865, this was changed; a new law excluded from the franchise all natives who were governed by special laws. While not disenfranchising Coloureds and other non-Europeans, the measure practically excluded all natives from voting.

Having trekked north, the Boers would have nothing to do with the liberal ideas of the Cape and Natal. When the Orange Free State was granted responsible government in 1854, it adopted a constitution giving the franchise to whites only. In addition, its laws declared: "No Arab, Chinaman or Coolie or other Asiatic Coloured person may settle in the State for longer than two months without permission."[10] The Boers in the Transvaal adopted similar policy and a constitution that permitted no equality between Europeans and non-Europeans. Indians in Natal, who had migrated from Madras and southern India to work in the sugar and tea plantations, were cleverly denied the franchise by a law saying that people from countries without a parliamentary franchise would not be included on the voted roles.

The Indians who entered the Transvaal as merchants encountered resistance from the predominantly English chambers of commerce. White shopkeepers did not wish to face increased competition, and prevailed on President Paul Kruger to pass legislation halting the further infiltration of Indians. The Kruger government passed Law 3 of 1885, which made Asiatic registration compulsory, prohibited Asiatic land ownership except in certain designated places, and denied Asians the franchise. While Law 3 was in fact the law, it was never actually enforced. India itself joined South African Indians in protesting loudly against it.

While the treatment of non-Europeans was not the primary cause of the Boer War, it played an important role. In the Boer republics, Britain practiced intervention on behalf of the natives, seeking to secure them access to courts of law and freedom of movement. The more fundamental issue turned out to be the poor treatment of Englishmen in the Boer republics.

SOUTH AFRICAN THINKING ON RACE

Apartheid (pronounced "apart-hate") means literally "apart-ness"—the state of being apart—"separateness," or "separation." Use of the term did not appear until relatively late in South Africa's racial history: in a lead article in *Die Burger* on March 26, 1943.[11]

South Africa's apartheid contains some of the same features as U.S. segregationist history, but it also contains features that make it unique: A South African white could be an advocate of apartheid without also being a "racist" or "white supremacist," in the traditional usage of these terms.

There were indeed differences between Europeans and Africans. Often these differences were explained by racist theories referring to innate racial inferiority or by "enlightened" theories of cultural, historical, biological, and environmental differences. Dudley Kidd argued that initiation rites and the intensely sexual life in the Kraal (enclosed native village) distracted the African child.[12]

Charles Loram, Yale University's Sterling Professor of Education, and historian Edgar Brookes welcomed the segregationist program of South African Prime Minister James B. M. Hertzog and they helped him to draft speeches defending it. Both Loram and Brookes were acting as what might be called "humane paternalists," who—with positive motives—thought they were promoting the best interests of the black African.

This kind of segregationist differed from the many Christian missionaries who saw African customs and institutions as ignorant, superstitious, and evil. There were some missionaries, however, who revered and respected the African tradition.[13] They were the people who originated the term "dual economy," which reflected their belief in a fundamental incompatibility between Western and African economies. Other church people sought to help the natives as reflected in a letter sent by the Church Council of Drakenstein in 1703 to the Convocation at Amsterdam, saying that it wanted to convert the Hottentots "so the children of Ham would no longer be servants of bondsmen."[14]

Inspired by this thinking, Bronislaw Malinowski and A. R. Radcliffe-Brown at the University of Cape Town argued that the institutions of a primitive society were fragile. If they were to come into contact with Western cultures, the native institutions would be shattered and subsumed by the stronger Western culture. Therefore, contact with the West had to be regulated and slowed down.

Whether these arguments had any factual basis or not, they were nonetheless used as a basis for colonist social engineering. In his book *The White Man's Task*, Jan Christiaan Smuts, attorney general of the Transvaal and later South Africa's prime minister (1919–24 and 1939–48) said:

Instead of mixing up white and black in the old haphazard way, which instead of lifting up the black degraded the white, we are now trying to lay down a policy of keeping them apart as much as possible in our institutions. In land ownership, settlement and forms of government we are trying to keep them apart, and in that way laying down in outline a general policy which it may take a hundred years to work out . . . You will have . . . large areas cultivated by blacks, where they will look after themselves in all forms of living and development, while in the rest of the country you will have your white communities which will govern themselves separately according to the accepted European principles. The natives will, of course, be free to go and work in the white areas, but as far as possible the administration of white and black areas will be separated, and such that each will be satisfied and developed according to its own proper lines.[15]

Smuts's view was shared by President Theodore Roosevelt, who said that the British in Uganda "had been particularly well advised in trying to develop the Natives according to their own way of life, instead of trying to make Englishmen out of them."[16]

South Africa's John Cecil Rhodes—founder of the Rhodes scholarships—had another view:

Only one race approached God's ideal type, his own Anglo-Saxon race; God's purpose then was to make the Anglo-Saxon race predominant, and the best way to help on God's work and fulfill His purpose in the world was to contribute to the predominance of the Anglo-Saxon race and so bring nearer the reign of justice, liberty and peace.[17]

There were paternalistic segregationists who were prominent members of the South African Natives Commission, and their recommendations were crucial in the development of native policy in the twentieth century. Ironically, the predecessors to today's Cape Town liberals—the liberals of that day—drafted the first major foundation of apartheid: the Natives Land Act of 1913.

Writing in 1960, Henry Allan Fagan, a liberal judge on South Africa's Appellate Court, said it cannot be overstressed that the early supporters of apartheid

neither intended nor saw in it any injustice towards the Bantu. On the contrary they honestly and positively believed that, while it was the only course which offered sure protection to the White minority, it was also the only way to save the Bantu from the frustration which would only block their progress in direct competition with the Europeans in a mixed society.[18]

Fagan added that apartheid is part of a very strong sense of Afrikaner nationalistic pride. Proud of their own distinctiveness, they are willing to concede the same to other groups. Fagan quoted General J. B. M. Hertzog (later prime minister) as wanting to separate the races "in a manner that will avoid causing ill-feeling or a sense of grievance, and will involve no greater discrimination than the necessities of the case require."[19] Hertzog admonished, "Do not let us take the whole of the Union for ourselves. Let us divide it. Let us give one share to the Bantu, and let them develop there according to their own nature."[20]

While not justifying apartheid laws, Fagan did insist, "I have no hesitation in stating it is my firm conviction that the Government, and also the European population in general, as the ruling group, feel their responsibility for the welfare and happiness of the Bantu people."[21] Fagan accepted conventional and customary segregation, but did not think that government enforcement was justified. This ambivalence is reflected in his comment that:

On the one hand every restriction on a man's activities and on the use and development of his capabilities is unfair and frustrating to the individual concerned and, as regards the community at large, it is economically unsound. On the other hand, people who have a high standard of life may require protection against others whose lower needs make competition unequal and threaten to have a detrimental effect on the way of life of the best portion of the population.[22]

On the basis of protecting "the way of life of the best portion of the population," Fagan agreed that the "rate for the job and reservation was necessary to protect whites, coloured and Asiatics from Bantu."[23]

Many high officials agonized over racial relationships in South Africa in ways that were uniquely different from racial conflict anywhere else. The most unique feature of this agony was the near absence of the racial bitterness and hostility seen elsewhere. Sir Alfred Milner, the British high commissioner for South Africa, in an April 1904 dispatch to Alfred Lyttlton, the British secretary of state of the colonies, wrote:

I think that to attempt to place Coloured people on an equality with Whites in South Africa is wholly impracticable and that moreover it is in principle wrong. But I hold also that when a Coloured man possesses a certain high grade of civilization he ought to obtain what I call "White privileges" irrespective of his colour. I have on more than one occasion given expression to these views. They are very unpopular in the Transvaal at the present time, but I do not despair of their ultimately prevailing.[24]

Milner's sympathetic view was tempered with political expediency: "I personally could win over the Dutch in the [Cape] Colony and indeed all of South Africa dominions in my term of office... without offending the English. You have only to sacrifice the 'nigger' absolutely and the game is easy."[25]

Cape liberals championed a nonwhite policy different from most other Europeans. Liberals felt that the vote should be restricted to civilized men and that all men—regardless of color—should have the opportunity to become civilized. They made it clear, however, that they were not advocating social integration. In 1908, Lord William Selbourne, the South African high commissioner, wrote to Smuts that he accepted the idea of the franchise for those who "have really reached the average level of civilization of the white man," and that he rejected universal suffrage.[26]

Lord Alexander Elgin, the secretary of state for India, told an Indian delegation that, while he opposed restrictions against Indians, "we have to recognize the fact that there are difficulties arising on the part of the White communities and we have to reckon with them."[27] Sir Godfrey Lagden, commissioner of native affairs, said, "I am convinced of the necessity of all Natives being compelled to carry passes as much for the security and protection of themselves as for the White people."[28]

One of the best known missionaries, Reverend Charles Bourquin, saw separation as a way of reducing racial tension:

If we will avoid disaster I think, as many others, that the best thing for Black and White would be for the Natives to live as much as possible their own life, manage their own affairs, and have their independent institutions under the guidance of sympathetic White administrators... But separation, if possible, if it is not too late, should not be carried out without consulting the Natives.[29]

After the 1910 electoral success of Jan Smuts and Louis Botha, Botha recommended "placing of the Native question above party politics and the fair and sympathetic treatment of the Coloured races in a broad and liberal spirit." He correctly anticipated that the native question would become a source for political strife between the white parties.[30]

While a member of Botha's cabinet, General Hertzog spoke to an English audience in 1917 on the subject of South Africa's native policy: "Instead of mixing up Black and White in the old way, confusing everything and not lifting up the Black but degrading the White, we are now trying to keep them apart as much as possible in our institutions."[31] In 1913, the African National Congress presented a protest to Smuts, then acting prime minister, in regard to the pass laws and the new requirement that women carry them, saying they had been passed "for the purpose of slavery." Denying that this was so, Smuts insisted that the laws had been passed for the protection of uncivilized natives and added that he was in favor of granting exemptions to civilized natives.

The official paternalistic sentiments were also extended to Indians. This is seen in the Cape Town Agreement (1927) containing the famous "Uplift Clause," which read:

The Union Government firmly believes in and adheres to the principle that it is the duty of every civilized government to devise ways and means and to take all possible steps for the uplifting of every section of their permanent population to the full extent of their capacity and opportunities. The Union Government accepts the view that in the provision of education and other facilities, the considerable number of Indians who will remain part of the permanent population shall not be allowed to lag behind other sections of the people.[32]

The Cape Town Agreement also provided for a scheme of voluntary emigration of Indians to India. The government offered a cash bonus of £20 ($56) per adult and £10 ($28) per child, in addition to free passage back to India. However, by 1940, only 17,542 Indians had left the country under this scheme.[33]

Soon after assuming the office of prime minister, General Hertzog explained what he saw as the right native policy. Natives should have their own areas. Recognizing the indispensability of black labor, Hertzog declared that natives who wished to work in white areas should be allowed to do so as long as they obeyed the white man's laws. In order to prevent interracial sexual relationships, whites should be kept out of black areas, and vice versa. If there were not enough land for the natives, the government ought to buy more. As it happened, a local outbreak of violence allowed Hertzog to spell out in detail his views on native policy:

We are dealing here with the place of the Native, not in Native territory, but in the land of the White Man where the white man shall rule and have the right to live safely and peacefully. Nobody compels the Native to settle in this territory, but if he does so it is demanded from him that he shall respect the White man and obey the laws of the country... I would again like to assure the native that the White man entertains for him the greatest goodwill and the friendliest feelings, and that the White man is determined to carry out faithfully that fatherly care which he has promised to the Native ever since the foundation of the White man's settlement in South Africa... I would however warn him at the same time that the White man is just as determined as in the days of the pioneers that the control of the country shall be held by the Europeans under the influence of European civilization and that just as little the father in his own house would allow a minor to rule the house, would the white man of the Union allow the government of the Union and its people to be held by the Native, or would the Native be given authority within or over the government of the country. I wish to warn the Natives that whoever is so presumptuous as to claim equal authority with the White man will experience the greatest disappointment and failure.[34]

The Afrikaner mentality is rooted in strong nationalist instincts. In at least this one respect, the Afrikaner is a supporter of black nationalism: Nationalism for the Afrikaner is an exclusive concept, where for the British it is inclusive. Thus, the Afrikaner sees perfect justice and no contradiction in excluding blacks from white society, and granting blacks the same right to exclude whites.

THE EVOLUTION OF NATIONALIST RACIAL POLICY

When Prime Minister Smuts called for South Africa to enter World War II on the side of the Allies, his appearance of being pro-British and against the long-run interests of South Africa, along with his "liberal" ideas on race and native policy, cost the United party and his heir apparent, Jan H. Hofmeyr, the elections in 1948. Daniel Francois Malan's campaign consisted of brutal attacks on the Smuts government. Malan whipped up South African fears concerning the black nationalism that was beginning to sweep the continent, and the spreading communist influence. Europeans in South Africa felt that their supremacy was being threatened, and believed that strong steps ought to be taken to defend it. Dr. Malan was their man.

For more than 30 years, South Africa's native policy had variously borne such names as "segregation" or "separation." It was Malan who—in outlining the National party's native policy—popularized its new name: apartheid. This policy, Malan urged, was to be based on separation and trusteeship:

This means in no way the oppression of the Non-Europeans but the elimination of racial friction through acknowledgment of their right of existence, freedom of development, coupled with the cultivation among them of a spirit of self-respect and self-reliance and the provision to them of the necessary help, but everything in their own sphere and under the sovereignty and leadership of the Europeans. Apartheid must as far as possible also be applied and maintained between the three sections of the Non-Europeans—Coloured, Native and Indian.[35]

The National party's 1948 victory was complete. Malan's cabinet consisted entirely of men who were Afrikaner in descent. When a deputation of 12 blacks presented an address of loyalty to him in October 1948 after his election, Malan said:

I regard the Bantu not as strangers and not as a menace to the white people, but as our children for whose welfare we are responsible, and as an asset to the country. My Government has no intention of depriving you of your rights or oppressing you. Nothing will be taken from you without giving you something better in its place . . . What you want is a rehabilitation of your own national life, and not competition and intermixture and equality with the white man in his particular part of the country.[36]

In 1950, Malan appointed Dr. H. F. Verwoerd—an academic and a brilliantly articulate rhetorician—to be Minister of Native Affairs. Verwoerd agreed that apartheid was not a policy of oppression, but a means for allowing the natives to keep their culture and traditions and to govern themselves to the greatest extent possible. See Appendix 1.A of this chapter for Malan's statement on his government's apartheid policy.

While South Africa's apartheid policy faced bitter criticism overseas, it won acceptance among whites at home. At a 1950 conference held in Bloemfontein, the Action Committee of the Dutch Reformed Churches declared that equality in the economic and political spheres would submerge whites. Europeans could not continue to hire blacks in low-skilled jobs while restricting them from higher skilled jobs. The church prophesied that sooner or later blacks would demand a say in the conduct of affairs. Therefore, the only long-run alternative was to separate the native completely from the white population.

The Nationalist-formed South African Bureau of Race Relations announced that separation and reducing black urbanization, combined with the development of native reserves, needed to be started before it was too late and before trends toward integration could become irreversible.

Addressing the criticisms of his apartheid policy, Malan argued that differences between the European and the non-European populations went beyond color. Color, he asserted, was merely the physical manifestation of two irreconcilable ways of life: barbarism and Christianity. There was also the overwhelming numerical inferiority of the Europeans. Malan added,

May I emphasize, that to consider only the rights of Blacks would be precisely as immoral as to have regard only for the rights of the Whites. I must ask you to give White South Africans credit for not being a nation of scheming reactionaries imbued with base and inhuman motives, nor a nation of fools blind to the gravity of their vital problem . . . To them millions of semi-barbarous Blacks look for guidance, justice and the Christian way of life. Here a tremendous experiment is being tried—not that fraught with the bloodshed of annihilation, nor that coloured with assimilation, but that inspired by a belief in the logical differentiation with the acceptance of the basic human rights and responsibilities.[37]

Malan's reference to the absence of bloodshed may have been meant as a slap in the face to the Western nations who were criticizing South Africa's racial policy. South Africans—unlike colonists in America, Australia, and other places—had not decimated the native population.

Professor Nellie I. Olivier, head of the Department of Bantu Studies at Stellenbosch University, saw the sharp U.S. criticism of South Africa as stemming from an invalid comparison between blacks in South Africa and blacks in the United States. According to Olivier, there is no comparison. Black Americans are American; they have no culture and language of their own, she said. Discrimination against them has been solely on the grounds of color. It is different in South Africa, where blacks and whites are of different cultures. Moreover—Olivier argued—in the United States, whites are numerically superior and have no fear of domination, while the opposite has been the case in South Africa.[38]

Strijdom's Vision of Apartheid

In 1954 when Malan resigned, the National party chose Johannes Gerhardus Strijdom as the new prime minister. Malan's attitude toward apartheid had been nurtured in the more liberal atmosphere of the Cape. By contrast, Strijdom was the leader of the extreme right wing of the Transvaal Nationalists—which was to be seen in his ruthless pursuit of a perfect apartheid.

Strijdom's first order of business—where Malan had failed—was to remove colored voters from the common rolls in the Cape. Strijdom achieved this goal by circumventing the constitution: He packed both the Appellate Division of the Supreme Court (adding five more judges) and the Senate (adding 41 more senators) with loyal Nationalists. Through the power of a packed Senate, Strijdom was able to secure the necessary two-thirds vote required to amend the constitution; and when the measure was taken before the packed Appellate Court in 1955, a majority in the court—10–1—held that the Separate Representation of Voters Act was valid. As a result, 30,000 coloreds, in the Cape, lost their right to vote in Parliamentary elections. Strijdom explained his non-European policy thus:

Call it paramountcy, baaskap or what you will, it is still domination. I am being as blunt as I can. I am making no excuses. Either the White man dominates or the Black man will take over. I say that the Non-European will not accept leadership—if he has a choice. The only way the Europeans can maintain supremacy is by domination . . . And the only way they can maintain domination is by withholding the vote from the Non-Europeans.[39]

In a December 1955 speech, Strijdom said,

In our actions towards the Non-Whites in the application of our traditional policy of separation we shall have to act in such a way as to give proof that we are not hostile towards the Non-Whites; that separation is in the interests of both colour groups; and with this policy clashes and friction are eliminated and coexistence, but not integration, is assured.[40]

Reaffirming South African paternalism, the prime minister said:

The purpose of the apartheid policy is that, by separating the races in every field in so far as it is practically possible, one can prevent clashes and frictions between Whites and non-Whites. At the same time, in fairness to the non-Whites, they must be given the opportunity of developing in their own areas and in accordance with their own nature and abilities under the guardianship of the whites; and, insofar as they develop in accordance with the systems which are best adapted to their nature and traditions, to govern themselves there and serve their community at all the various levels of their national life.[41]

Strijdom's "white baaskap" policy was not without white opposition. J. G. N. Strauss, speaking for the United party, criticized the prime minister for seeing native policy as either baaskap or equality: "As far as this party is concerned, if 'baaskap' means suppression, then we do not stand for 'baaskap.' That kind of 'baaskap' we reject completely. If the Prime Minister means by this 'baaskap' that the non-Europeans, whatever their merits, will always, in all circumstances, be excluded from a share of control of the affairs of this country simply on the basis of their colour, then the United Party rejects that kind of 'baaskap.' " Strauss went on to deny that the United party stood for equality, but maintained "that a door must be left open to the non-Europeans."[42]

Verwoerd's Vision of Apartheid

On the death of Strijdom in 1958, Dr. Hendrick Frensch Verwoerd became prime minister. During his reign, he lived through one unsuccessful assassination attempt, but was stabbed to death on September 6, 1966. Verwoerd had served as minister of native affairs under both the Malan and Strijdom governments. When he assumed the duties of prime minister, Verwoerd made his native policy clear:

Dr. Malan said it, and Mr. Strijdom said it, and I have said it repeatedly and I want to say it again: The policy of Apartheid moves consistently in the direction of more and more separate development with the ideal of total separation in all spheres.[43]

Apartheid rhetoric was one thing, but harsh economic realities made implementation quite another. This was a constant source of frustration, which in turn led to a constant redefinition of apartheid goals. In 1956, Dr. Verwoerd had said,

Apartheid is something which has to be brought about gradually in all spheres of life ... The idea of total apartheid gives one something to aim at ... Everyone realizes that such a thing cannot be attained within the space of a few years, nor even for a long time to come and that South Africa cannot attain that ultimate objective in the near future.[44]

Verwoerd pushed through Parliament a bill that he thought would help to speed up the development of apartheid: the Promotion of Bantu Self-Government Bill (1959). Under its provisions, the government would create eight separate main homelands on the basis of language and culture. In these homelands, administrative authorities (chiefs and headsmen) would be based on the tribal system. Gradually, all European administrative officials, judges, and teachers would be replaced by competent natives. Verwoerd saw these homelands as becoming a community of interests—somewhat like the European Common Market—with white South Africa. No whites would be permitted to live, invest, or do business in black homelands. To facilitate homeland development, the government formed the Bantu Investment Corporation with an initial capitalization of £500,000 ($1,400,000).

The opposition in Parliament and in the public derisively called these homelands *Bantustans*. Verwoerd responded to the criticism by saying that the South African government—like the British government—was training its natives for home rule. Moreover, he said, South Africa was doing it better. In Basutoland (later Lesotho), where Britain was preparing the natives for home rule, whites were allowed to remain in the country—and possibly exploit the natives. Verwoerd said that, if he had his way—like in his South Africa scheme—no whites would be allowed to remain and conduct business that might otherwise be conducted by the natives for their own benefit. At any rate, the Transkei—with about one and a half million natives—was proclaimed the first independent homeland. The territory of the Transkei includes several white towns with numerous white businesses. While promising these businessmen that they could remain as long as they liked, Verwoerd declared that the "white spots" would ultimately have to go. In a London speech (March 1961), Verwoerd described the apartheid policy as follows:

We want each of our population groups to control and govern itself as in the case with other nations. Then all can co-operate as in a Commonwealth—in an economic association with the republic and with each other . . . South Africa will proceed in all honesty and fairness to secure peace, prosperity and justice for all by means of political independence coupled with economic inter-dependence.[45]

Before the House of Assembly in January 1963, Verwoerd elaborated on his vision of grand apartheid:

Reduced to its simplest form the problem is nothing else than this: We want to keep South Africa White . . . "Keeping it White" can only mean one thing, namely White domination, not "leadership," not "guidance," but "control," "supremacy." If we are agreed that it is the desire of the people that the White man should be able to continue to protect himself by retaining White domination, we say that it can be achieved by separate development.[46]

However, Verwoerd did think that whites should be helped in ways not hurtful to the natives.[47] Afrikaner paternalism toward blacks was just the opposite of its antagonism toward Indians, as reflected in the common Afrikaner expression, *Kaffer op sy plek en koelie uit die land*—which translates: "Kaffir in his place and coolie [Indian] out of the country."

The Vorster Vision of Apartheid

Prime Minister Balthazar Johannes Vorster—elected after the assassination of Dr. Verwoerd, who was killed by a mentally ill white messenger on September 6, 1966—explained his own vision of native policy, which differed little from his predecessors:

I believe in the policy of separate development, not only as a philosophy but also as the only practical solution in the interest of everyone to eliminate frictions, and to do justice to every population group as well as every individual. I say to the coloured people, as well as to the Indians and the Bantu, that the policy of separate development is not a policy which rests upon jealousy, fear or hatred. It is not a denial of the human dignity of anyone, nor is it so intended. On the contrary, it gives the opportunity to every individual, within his own sphere, not only to be a man or woman in every sense, but it also creates the opportunity for them to develop and advance without restriction or frustration as circumstances justify, and in accordance with the demands of development achieved.[48]

Vorster served as prime minister until 1978, and then briefly as president—but resigned in 1979 during a scandal involving the misuse of government funds.

The Botha Vision of Apartheid

Addressing the opening of the South African Parliament on January 31, 1986, State President Pieter Willem Botha said, "We believe that the human dignity, life, liberty and property of all must be protected, regardless of colour, race, creed or religion."[49] In the rest of his speech President Botha—who has been in office since 1978—stressed that the South African government is committed to *one* citizenship for all South Africans, within an *undivided* country. Such a statement represents a significant—if not complete—break with the apartheid ideology of the former chief executives of South Africa.

The initial theme of Botha's tenure in office was "adapt or die," meaning that the visions of Malan and Verwoerd were no longer relevant to the realities of South Africa. Botha's initial reform strategy focused on political accommodation for the Coloured and Indian populations—leading to the new constitution of 1983, which was endorsed by two-thirds of the white voters in a countrywide referendum.

When Botha was reelected to office on September 14, 1984, he announced a new cabinet that—for the first time in South African history—would include a Coloured minister and an Indian minister. In 1985, a new three-chamber Parliament—the House of Assembly (whites), the House of Representatives (Coloureds), and the House of Delegates (Indians)—met for its first full session. Among Indians and Coloureds, the new dispensation found only a tepid reception; but among blacks, who were left out of the new dispensation, it helped to trigger the longest period of sustained unrest in South African history. As such, it served notice on Botha that South Africa's major political issue of black representation remained an unsolved problem.

SUMMARY

South Africa's racial policy differs from those in many other places. It is full of contrasts and contradictions. Paternalism toward blacks—considered to be several steps behind Europeans in evolution—has been a dominant feature, rivaled by economics (as we will see in later chapters). While no less offensive to the basic principles of human rights, this paternalism nonetheless produced a racial climate markedly different from the racism of postslavery United States—where hate and violence in the form of lynchings, castration and tar-and-feathering were all-too-common features. For example, the *Encyclopaedia Britannica* reports that, between 1882 and 1951, there were 4,730 lynchings in the United States: 1,293 white persons, and 3,437 blacks. In South Africa, there has been no known case of lynching since 1858 when 42 Bantu prisoners of war were lynched.

South African whites almost boast when they say that their racial problems of today reflect what they see as their humanity in the past: They are quick to claim that—unlike other whites who have come into contact with native populations—they did not exterminate the native blacks. In support of this claim, South Africans point to the white settlers in America who massacred the Indians, and the British in Australia and New Zealand who massacred the Tasmanians and Maori—in some cases for sport.[50]

This brief sketch of South African history should give pause to the erroneous comparison between the situations of blacks in South Africa and blacks in the United States. Culturally, U.S. blacks are identical to the white population. They have no religion or language of their own. This is not the case in South Africa. The black population there—even today, except in urban areas—has a different culture from the white population. For those who seek a comparison between what exists in South Africa and in the United States, it is more appropriate to compare South African blacks to the American Indians. American Indians are a race of peoples on whom an alien European culture was imposed. Official U.S. policy toward them had some of the paternalistic features of South Africa's policy toward its native population—for example, the separation into reservations and homelands. The closest South African equivalent to U.S. blacks are the Coloureds, who are essentially European in culture.

APPENDIX 1.A: MALAN'S APARTHEID POLICY

THE NATIVES

(1) The Native Reserves must be retained and made suitable for carrying a larger population by protecting the soil against erosion and over-cropping and by teaching the Native to make the best use of his soil by applying better agricultural methods. Possible additions must only take place in judicious fashion and after thorough investigation.

(2) In urban areas inside the European areas Natives must be domiciled in their own residential areas with proper attention to good housing and other healthy accommodation conditions. Only Natives who have been assured of work will be admitted, and the detribalized one among them will at all times receive preference. Newcomers from the Native areas or from the European platteland must be regarded as temporary workers and those in excess must be repatriated.

(3) In view of their possession of their own national home in the Reserves, Natives in the European areas can make no claim to political rights. The present representation of Natives in Parliament and in the Cape Provincial Council must therefore be abolished. Representation in the Senate must however continue by the election of three European Senators by different Native councils and further through three others nominated by the Government because of their particular knowledge of Native affairs, as is now the case. These representatives must form a standing and permanent committee on Native Affairs. They must however have no vote on questions of confidence, or on the declaration of war or on measures affecting the political rights of non-Europeans. The present existing Native Affairs Commission must give way to a more effective commission of experts.

(4) The present existing Native Advisory Council must be abolished and in its place a system of self-government on the first-rate and well-tried example of the Transkei Bunga called into being—a system which will keep proper account of the natural groupings among the Natives themselves based on the territorial, historical, racial and linguistic differences between them. This will give to the Natives that opportunity of living out their own aspirations which under the present system are being withheld from them and which in their dissatisfaction makes them willing prey of the Communist agitator.

(5) For higher education separate provision must be made for Natives and their admission to European institutions together with European students must end.

(6) Administratively all Native interests including education must rest with the department of Native Affairs and the necessary sub-departments.

THE COLOURED PEOPLE

(1) The party bases its policy on the fact that the Coloured people form their own separate group between on the one side the Europeans, with whom they share the same

Source: Cited in L. E. Neame, *The History of Apartheid: The Story of the Colour War in South Africa* (New York: London House and Maxwell, 1963), pp. 74–77.

language and cultural interests, and on the other side the Natives, from whom they differ in race, language and standard of civilization and above whom they must hold a privileged position in the European areas.

(2) As against the Europeans the principle of Apartheid must be applied in respect of residential areas, which can only be brought about gradually, and in public transport, recreational areas and as far as possible also in wc k places. Further in urban areas, as well as in the platteland, provision must be made with Government support for better housing for Coloured people, special attention being paid to the requirements of the more civilized ones among them, but in any case separately and at a distance from Native locations.

(3) In territories where the Coloured population is largely resident, their interests, particularly in regard to the provision of employment, must be protected against those of Natives flowing in.

(4) In Coloured residential areas Coloured people must as far as possible be appointed for public positions, and preference must be given to them in granting of business licences.

(5) In the provision of educational facilities for Coloured people special account must be taken of their prospects in the service of their own racial group, as well as in connection with the provision of employment in general. Technical education must be provided for them in accordance with their requirements and they must have their own separate university institutions.

(6) A State department for specially furthering the interests of Coloured people must be called into being in which Coloured people will also serve as civil servants. In this connection a Coloured Advisory Council must also exist, the members of which, apart from a few Government nominees, must be elected by qualified Coloured voters themselves and on the basis of constituencies. The present Coloured Advisory Council, nominated by the Government and dependent on it, must disappear.

(7) In place of their vote as at present exercised—which makes them the playball of the political parties—special representation must be given to the Coloured people in Parliament through a Senator nominated by the Government because of his special knowledge of Coloured affairs, three members of Parliament chosen by the Coloured Advisory Council, and three members of the Cape Provincial Council chosen on the same basis as those in Parliament. The representatives must be Europeans.

THE INDIANS

(1) The party will strive to repatriate or remove elsewhere as many Indians as possible with the co-operation of India and other countries.

(2) The present ban on Indian immigration, inter-provincial movement and penetration must remain and be more stringently maintained.

(3) The Indian must not be allowed to reside among other racial groups.

(4) Trading licences to Indians outside their own residential areas must be reduced.

(5) Family allowances to Indians must be abolished.

NOTES

1. L. E. Neame, *The History of Apartheid: The Story of the Colour War in South Africa* (New York: London House and Maxwell, 1963), p. 13.

2. Ibid.
3. Ibid., p. 18.
4. Henry Allan Fagan, *Our Responsibility: A Discussion of South Africa's Racial Problems* (Stellenbosch: Die Universiteit Uitgewers-En-Boekhandelaars, 1960), p. 11.
5. Neame, *History of Apartheid*, p. 14.
6. Ibid., p. 19.
7. Ibid.
8. Ibid., p. 20.
9. Ibid.
10. Ibid., p. 23.
11. Brian Bunting, "The Origins of Apartheid," in *Apartheid*, edited by Alex LaGuma (New York: International Publishers, 1971), p. 23.
12. John W. Cell, *The Highest Stage of White Supremacy: The Origins of Segregation in South Africa and the American South* (London: Cambridge University Press, 1982), p. 221.
13. Ibid., pp. 221–23.
14. F. A. van Jaarsveld, *The Afrikaner's Interpretation of South African History* (Cape Town: Simondium Publishers, 1964), p. 6.
15. Cell, *Highest Stage*, pp. 224–25.
16. Paul Giniewski, *The Two Faces of Apartheid* (Chicago: Henry Regnery, 1965), p. 123.
17. van Jaarsveld, *Afrikaners' Interpretation*, p. 4.
18. Fagan, *Our Responsibility*, p. 25.
19. Ibid., p. 43.
20. Giniewski, p. 123.
21. Fagan, *Our Responsibility*, p. 35.
22. Ibid., p. 75.
23. Ibid.
24. Neame, *History of Apartheid*, p. 30.
25. Janet Robertson, *Liberalism in South Africa: 1948–1963* (Oxford: Clarendon Press, 1971), p. 1.
26. Ibid., pp. 4–5.
27. Neame, *History of Apartheid*, p. 30.
28. Ibid., p. 31.
29. Ibid., p. 32.
30. Robertson, *Liberalism in South Africa*, pp. 7–8.
31. Neame, *History of Apartheid*, p. 40.
32. Ibid., pp. 52–53.
33. Gavin Maasdorp and Nesen Pillay, "Indians in the Political Economy of South Africa," in *South Africa's Indians: The Evolution of a Minority*, edited by Bridglal Pachi (Washington, D.C.: University Press of America, 1979), p. 301.
34. Neame, *History of Apartheid*, pp 53–54.
35. Ibid., p. 74.
36. Eugene P. Dvorin, *Racial Separation in South Africa: An Analysis of Apartheid Theory* (Chicago: University of Chicago Press, 1952), p. 95.
37. Neame, *History of Apartheid*, p. 81.
38. Ibid., p. 80–83.
39. Ibid., p. 131.

40. Ibid., p. 132.
41. Bunting, "Origins of Apartheid," pp. 25–26.
42. Henry John May, *The South African Constitution* (Westport, Conn.: Greenwood Press, 1970), p. 154.
43. Neame, *History of Apartheid*, p. 157.
44. Fagan, *Our Responsibility*, pp. 41–42.
45. Bunting, "Origins of Apartheid," p. 36.
46. Ibid., p. 28.
47. Alexander Hepple, *Verwoerd* (Baltimore: Penguin Books, 1967), p. 30.
48. Bunting, "Origins of Apartheid," p. 26.
49. Leon Louw and Frances Kendall, *South Africa: The Solution* (Bisho, Ciskei: Amagi Publications, 1986), pp. xv and 50.
50. There are numerous accounts of murders and massacres reported in A. Grenfell Price, *White Settlers and Native Peoples* (Westport, Conn.: Greenwood Press, 1972); "In California the whites killed Indians as 'a sport to enliven Sundays and holidays' " (p. 17). "In Oregon the legislature, politicians, subordinate Indian agents and even Methodist clergy participated in massacres" (p. 17). "In 1871 the kindly Kingsley wrote that he had to use his 38 calibre revolver to shoot children as his 56 calibre rifle 'tore them up so bad' " (p. 17). In Australia, eyewitness accounts reported "the wounded were brained; the infant cast into flames; the bayonet was driven into quivering flesh; the social fire around which the natives gathered to slumber became before morning their funeral pile" (p. 109). Governor Brisbane (1821–25) "proclaimed martial law in the colony west of Cape York and natives were shot like wild beast" (p. 107). In New Zealand, one-third of an estimated 200,000–300,000 Maori died in skirmishes with the white settlers (p. 151). No doubt a large part of the ruthlessness in Australia and New Zealand was due to their use as Britain's criminal colony.

2
The South African Legal Structure

No attempt will be made here to give a full description of South African legal institutions. But to understand how legalized discrimination evolved and was sustained—including challenges to it, and responses—requires at least a cursory review. In this review, there will be no attempt to discuss the current status of South African law, which has undergone many recent changes. A discussion of these changes—made mostly during the Vorster and Botha administrations—will be deferred until Chapter 6.

THE EVOLUTION OF SOUTH AFRICAN CONSTITUTIONAL LAW

South Africa's constitutional history had its beginnings in 1652 when the Cape was settled by the Dutch. As noted in Chapter 1, Dutch rule was replaced by British from 1795 to 1803 when England was protecting its sea route to India against the French. From 1803 to 1806, Netherland rule of the Cape was restored. Then, on the renewal of hostilities between Britain and France, the area was reoccupied by the British and remained a British colony until 1910. During this period the British extended the borders of the Cape, and in 1843 Natal was annexed.

Also in 1834, the Afrikaners—descendants of the Dutch—being dissatisfied with British rule, began their move (the Great Trek) to the interior, where they ultimately formed the Boer republics; the Orange Free State and the Transvaal. The British, however, considered the citizens of the Orange Free State and the Transvaal to be British subjects and rejected their claims of sovereignty. Negotiated settlements failed and the Anglo–Boer War (also known as South Africa's "Second War of Independence"; the first Anglo-Boer War was between 1880 and 1881), broke out in October 1899; the British defeated the Boers in 1902.

The South African government that emerged from all this conflict was modeled on the British Westminster system of parliamentary supremacy—a system in which the constitution is "flexible" in the sense that it provides few entrenched safeguards against arbitrary government. In South Africa, this meant that "Civil liberty and the Rule of Law were [and is] sacrificed on the altar of parliamentary supremacy to the idol of apartheid."[1] In Britain—unlike South Africa—the Rule of Law serves to qualify the supremacy of Parliament and provide protection for the individual.

During the 100-year period of British rule, South Africa was directly subject to the British Parliament. The Colonial Laws Validity Act of 1865 made null and void any colonial act that was offensive to the British Parliament. Then, in 1908–09, delegates to South Africa's National Convention assembled in Durban to draft the South Africa Act, which was passed by the British Parliament and took effect in 1910. This act made South Africa a self-governing dominion within the British Empire, like Canada and Australia.

One of the most difficult problems addressed by the National Convention was the political franchise. Most delegates from the former Boer republics of Transvaal and the Orange Free State, as well as Natal, wanted a whites-only franchise. Only the Cape Province delegates favored a color-blind franchise. The Cape already had colored and black voters, who constituted a significant political force and for whose votes white politicians competed. During the previous 50-year period, Cape whites had become accustomed to sharing the political franchise with nonwhites.

The National Convention finally reached a compromise whereby the former Boer republics were permitted to exclude blacks from their electoral rolls while the Cape was allowed to retain its own franchise qualifications. Membership in the new parliament would be restricted to whites only, however.

This compromise was housed in Section 35 of the South African Constitution, which stipulated that no voter (which only included males) in the Cape could be stripped of his right to vote for reasons of race or color except by approval of a two-thirds vote of both houses of Parliament. Furthermore, Section 137 guaranteed the equal status of Afrikaners and English, and Section 152 provided that neither Section 137 nor Section 35 could be amended except by a two-thirds vote of both houses of Parliament. Sections 35, 137, and 152 became known as the "entrenched clauses" of the South African Constitution.[2]

When the National Convention published its draft constitution, it was greeted by a barrage of criticism from every quarter. The northern provinces criticized the continued nonwhite franchise in the Cape. For its part, the Cape criticized the draft for excluding nonwhites from Parliament and for failing to extend the franchise in all provinces to all "qualified" persons.

Meanwhile—thwarted in South Africa and ignored by the National Convention—the African Political Organization and the Natives Convention sent a delegation to London to protest the South Africa Bill to the British government and its Parliament. British politicians sympathized with the delegation's complaints and said that they wished the bill did not contain a color bar. The dominant feeling in England was expressed by British Prime Minister H. H. Asquith, who said:

> Any control or interference from outside ... is in the very worst interests of the natives themselves ... I anticipate that, as one of the incidental advantages which the Union of South Africa is going to bring about, it will prove to be a harbinger of a native policy more consistent, and ... more enlightened than that which has been pursued by some communities in the past.[3]

In his last speech on the bill, the British prime minister said:

> While we part from this measure without any ... amendment ... I am sure our fellow subjects will not take it in bad part if we respectfully and very earnestly beg them at the same time that they, in the exercise of their undoubted and unfettered freedom should find it possible sooner or later, and sooner rather than later, to modify the provisions.[4]

The British did see the inequities inherent in the South Africa Bill. However, only nine years before, they had fought a costly and unpopular war with the Boers; they were only too anxious to find a way for South Africa to become a self-governing British dominion. Passage of the South Africa Act gave the British Parliament an easy escape from responsibility for the political rights of non-European South Africans.

In 1931, the Statute of Westminster repealed the Colonial Laws Validity Act, and provided that no act of the British Parliament could be extended to a colony without the colony's consent. In effect, the Statute of Westminster granted to South Africa full independence and sovereignty.

South Africa did not wait long before using its new status to accomplish racially discriminatory goals. In 1936, under Prime Minister Hertzog's leadership, the Parliament passed the Representation of Natives Act, which removed African voters from the electoral rolls in the Cape Province and—as compensation—gave them the right to elect three whites to Parliament and two to the Cape Provincial Council. When an African voter challenged this law in *Ndlwana v. Hofmeyr* (1937 A.D. 229), the court held that

> Parliament ... can adopt any procedure it thinks fit; the procedure expressed or implied in the South Africa Act, so far as Courts of Law are concerned, is at the mercy of Parliament like everything else ... Parliament's will ... as expressed in an Act of Parliament cannot now in this country, as it cannot in England, be questioned by a Court of Law, whose function it is to enforce that will, not to question it.[5]

In 1951, the Parliament introduced the Separate Representation of Voters Act. When challenged by a group of colored voters in *Harris v. Minister of the Interior*, the act was found invalid by a unanimous decision of the court. The justices also found that the *Ndlwana v. Hofmeyr* case had been wrongly decided.

In so ruling, the court threw the country into constitutional crisis. The government—not to be outdone by the courts—then increased the size of the Appellate Division from 5 to 11 judges in cases where an act of Parliament was at issue. And in 1955 it passed the Senate Act, which "packed" the Senate by increasing its size from 48 to 89.

Having packed both the court and the Senate, the government was well prepared to have its own way. It introduced the South Africa Act Amendment of 1956, which revalidated the Separation of Voters Act of 1951 and removed Section 35 from the entrenching procedure. This amendment prohibited the courts from invalidating any legislative acts except the entrenched clauses. In February 1956, Cape Coloureds too were finally removed from the common voter rolls.

The Constitution of 1961 emphasized the subordination of the courts to the South African Parliament through its Section 59, which read:

Parliament shall be the sovereign legislative authority in and over the Republic, and shall have full power to make laws for the peace, order and good government of the Republic. No court of law shall be competent to enquire into or to pronounce upon the validity of any Act passed by Parliament, other than an Act which repeals or amends the provisions of section one hundred and eight and one hundred and eighteen.

Parliamentary supremacy was now solidly entrenched in the South African Constitution. To the courts was left the interpretation of Parliament's will, and nothing else. Parliament is free to encroach on absolutely any area of human life, as declared in *Sachs v. Minister of Justice*: "Parliament may make any encroachment it chooses upon the life, liberty or property of any individual subject to its sway, and . . . it is the function of courts of law to enforce its will."[6]

The South African parliamentary system of government leaves little mystery as to how a "civilized" nation can produce an apartheid system that violates the fundamental freedoms of most of its population. Other Western countries have parliamentary systems of government, and yet they maintain a respect for individual rights because their Rule of Law restricts the powers of the legislative and executive arms of government. In South Africa, Parliament's will is absolute.

The Rule of Law holds that all persons are equal before the law; that all persons are subject to the same laws; and that legislative and executive bodies are not above the law and may not engage in arbitrary, capricious, and discriminatory behavior.[7] The Rule of Law is essentially a statement of the legal values necessary for the support and survival of democratic values. As such, it is an instrument for securing individual liberty. In England, the Rule of Law acts as a moral and political restraint on Parliament. But in South Africa, the Rule of Law has shallow roots and is mostly a procedural restraint on executive and legislative actions—ensuring procedural due process, but having little to do with substantive issues of individual freedom. Therefore, South African lawyers qua lawyers confine their criticism of government to instances when it has exercised an arbitrary deprivation of liberty without procedural due process of law.[8]

In *Civil Liberty in South Africa*, Dr. Edgar Brooks and J. B. Macaulay, Q.C., observe,

> Whether or not we agree with the principle of the Rule of Law, we must agree that immense inroads have been made into it in South Africa especially (though by no means solely) during recent years... The rule of law has in fact been challenged extensively on points that affect intimately the lives of thousands of citizens... Almost the whole of the African's life is now governed by administrative decisions, appeal from which to the courts has been deliberately denied by Parliament.[9]

SOUTH AFRICAN CIVIL LAW

The common law of South Africa is a blending of three legal systems: the Roman and Germanic brought by the first settlers in the form of Roman–Dutch law and English law.[10] As such, common law practice in South Africa is similar to that practice in many Western countries.[11] According to Simons, "In spite of the wide range of legal differentiation, mostly of a discriminatory kind, between Europeans and non-Europeans, both are generally subject to the same civil law, though important reservations have been made to meet the special needs of the African people."[12]

South Africa's constitution contains no guarantee of personal freedom such as a bill of rights, but neither is there a guarantee of personal freedom in the constitution of England. However, in England, personal freedom is considered to be a part of—and protected by—English common law. Similarly, personal freedom is a part of Roman–Dutch common law. South Africa's common law is color blind; it reflects the sentiments of the great Dutch jurist, Johannes Voet (1647–1713): "A law has various requisites. In the first place indeed it ought to be just and reasonable—both in its matter, for it prescribes what is honorable and forbids what is base; and in its form, for it preserves equality and binds the citizens equally."[13] Under South African common law, each person—regardless of race—is entitled to basic freedom, with one significant exception (as discussed above) where Parliament has ruled otherwise. This strange dichotomy between South Africa's common law and statutory law was enunciated in 1882 by Chief Justice John Gilbert Kotze: "The court is bound to do equal justice to every individual within the jurisdiction, without regard to color or degree, except where in the particular instance the law expressly provides the contrary."[14] Again, in 1946, South African courts held that "the right of personal liberty ... is always guarded by the courts of law as one of the most cherished parts of our society."[15]

When a person in England or the United States, for example, is arbitrarily deprived of his or her liberty, the writ of habeas corpus may be invoked. Roman–Dutch law recognizes the same remedy: the *interdiction de homme libero exhibendo*. The South African Appellate Court strongly affirms this remedy (for blacks as well as whites) against unlawful interference with personal liberty.[16] Chief Justice Frans Lourens Herwoaf Rumpf said in *Wood and Others v. On-*

dangwa Tribal Authority and Another* (1975) that habeas corpus laws "should always be interpreted in favor of the liberty of the citizen."[17]

SOUTH AFRICAN STATUTORY LAW

The chief source of violations of personal liberty—for blacks and whites—is found in South Africa's statutory laws. Roman–Dutch common law recognizes the writ of habeas corpus in cases of detention.[18] But in South Africa—through acts of Parliament such as the Public Safety Act of 1953—the writ of habeas corpus can be nullified.

The Public Safety Act empowers the government to declare a state of emergency when it considers the public safety to be threatened. A minister, magistrate, or commissioned officer can declare a person to be a threat to public safety. That person can be arrested and detained with no appeal whatsoever. The court cannot substitute its opinion for those of public officials on such substantive issues regarding the arrest and detention as whether the person actually was a threat to public safety. It only matters whether the person was a threat in the opinion of the public official.[19]

Several other South Africa statutes nullify Roman–Dutch common law in the area of civil liberties. These include the frequently amended Riotous Assemblies Act of 1914, the Bantu Administration Act of 1927, and the Internal Security Act of 1976.

The Riotous Assemblies Act empowers the minister of justice to prohibit any person from being in any area if, in the opinion of the minister, that person is promoting feelings of hostility between South African whites and any other segment of the population. Should a person be banished from an area, that person cannot appeal the order in any court of law. He may only request that the minister of justice give a reason for the order. And even this may not be forthcoming if the minister of justice feels that disclosure would be harmful to public policy.

In a 1934 application of the Riotous Assemblies Act—in *Sachs v. Minister of Justice*, involving a left-wing trade unionist named Solly Sachs—the court made it clear that an act of Parliament would supersede any common law protection of personal freedom. The plaintiff held that, prior to his being banned from several magisterial districts for stirring up feelings of racial hostility, he had been denied a hearing in his own defense. The court held:

Once we are satisfied on a construction of the Act, that it gives to the Minister an unfettered discretion, it is no function of a court of law to curtail its scope in the least degree, indeed it would be quite improper to do so. The above observation is, perhaps, so trite that it needs no statement, yet in cases before the courts when the exercise of a statutory discretion is challenged, arguments are sometimes advanced which do seem to me to ignore the plain principle that Parliament may make any encroachment it chooses upon the life, liberty or property of any individual subject to its sway, and it is the function of the court to enforce its will.[20]

The Bantu Administration Act of 1927 contains a provision (Section 29) making it an offense to utter any word or publish anything "with intent to promote any feeling of hostility between Bantu and Europeans." Penalty on conviction is a year or less imprisonment or a £100 fine or both. Another section of the Bantu Administration Act empowers the state president—whenever he deems it expedient to the general public interest—to order the removal of a black African from one place to another, without prior notice and hearing. Because of the power of the Internal Security Act of 1976, bannings under the Bantu Administration Act of 1927 are rare today.

The Internal Security Act of 1976—formerly the Suppression of Communism Act of 1950—empowers the minister of justice to order severe restrictions on the freedom of movement and speech of those persons whom the minister feels are advocating the achievement of any goals of communism, or endangering public safety. The Internal Security Act provides for confining a person to a particular area where he must report periodically to its police station.[21]

This "banned" person may be confined to his house; or else, time away from the house may be restricted to the daylight hours. Typically, the banning order restricts the person from appearing in public places. Moreover, it is illegal for others to quote or show pictures of a banned person.[22] As in the provisions of the Riotous Assemblies Act, the banned person has no appeal to any court. A court may challenge the banning order only if it can determine that the minister of justice acted in bad faith. This is nearly impossible since the minister of justice—by law—is not obliged to give the reason for the banning order.

The South African courts have frequently ruled against these acts of Parliament that violate personal liberties under Roman-Dutch common law. In many of those cases, Parliament merely overruled the courts by modifying the statute in question. It is a major personal liberty problem in South Africa that there is no such thing as judicial review of the legislative acts of Parliament.

NATIVE LAND ACTS

The Native Land Act of 1913—the first major cornerstone of apartheid—sought to accomplish several goals. First, it set aside certain areas as native reserves; second, it aimed to preserve the status quo in areas outside the native reserves; and third (as will be discussed later), it provided for cheap labor. The act said that, except by approval of the governor-general, a native could acquire land only from another native and that no person other than a native could acquire land in a native reserve. This law was to govern the allocation of land "until the Parliament should make other provisions." In the interim, the act authorized a commission under the chairmanship of Sir William Beaumont (the "Beaumont Commission") which was to demarcate areas in which both Europeans and natives would be permitted to acquire land.

No one was satisfied with the Beaumont Commission recommendations; and in the Cape, the land restrictions imposed on the natives were held to be ultra vires—without authority—by the Supreme Court in *Thompson and Stilwell v. Kama* (1917). The court reached this finding by accepting the argument that, since there was a land qualification for suffrage, the restrictions found in the Land Act of 1913 might in effect prevent natives from voting (which they could still do legally in the Cape; see earlier in this chapter).

In 1936, Parliament passed the Native Land and Trust Act in order to provide for "settlement, support, benefit, and material and moral welfare of the Natives of the Union." It set aside, and provided for the purchase of, additional native reserves. It designated land for specific tribes. All told, the land scheduled as native reserves constitutes about 13.7 percent of the total land of South Africa.

One of the provisions of the 1936 act—intended to prevent squatting—was that a native could occupy land that he did not own only if he were a labor tenant rendering at least 122 days work a year.

SOUTH AFRICAN SOCIAL RACIAL LAWS

The observer in South Africa is captured by the thoroughness of its codification of race. The government's extensive regulation of race finds little duplication elsewhere.

The Population Registration Act of 1950

The Population Registration Act empowers the secretary of the interior to classify the entire population of South Africa into three broad categories: white person, colored person, or Bantu person. The colored population is divided into several groups: Cape colored, Chinese, Indian, Cape Malay, Griqua, other colored, and other Asian (puzzlingly, Japanese are defined as white).

South Africa's Parliament has repeatedly tried to lay down uniform racial definitions to deter attempts by people—mostly colored—from crossing the line. For example:

A white person is one who "in appearance is obviously a white person who is generally not accepted as a colored person; or is generally accepted as a white person and is not in appearance obviously not a white person," provided that "a person shall not be classified as a colored person or a Bantu"; a Bantu person is a person "who is, or is generally accepted as, a member of any aboriginal race or tribe of Africa"; and a colored person is one "who is not a white person or a Bantu."[23]

Despite the careful attempts at definition, however, there have been difficulties. A person charged with doing something prohibited to a native might declare that he or she has some white blood, and thus can claim to be a colored. Or if a white person does something prohibited for a white, the person might claim—though this is very rare—that he has traces of colored blood, and is not white.

Under the Population Registration Act, the director of census and statistics may at any time change the classification of any person so long as that person has been notified. A person aggrieved by a racial determination may make an appeal to an administrative tribunal known as the Racial Classification Appeal Board. Its findings may be appealed all the way to the Appellate Court.

The act also provides for third party complaints as to a person's racial classification, concerning which the secretary must investigate and make a determination. To guard against frivolous objections to racial classification, the act demands from the third party a deposit, which is forfeited if the objection is rejected by the Racial Classification Appeal Board. Furthermore, if the board does find the objection to be frivolous, it may require the objector to pay all the cost of the hearing, including those of the "defendant."[24]

The Population Registration Act also requires that an identity number be issued to every individual and that recorded in the registry there be the following particulars: name, sex, residence, racial or ethnic classification, date and place of birth, marital status, and nationality. Racial classification takes on considerable importance because residence, school attendance, jobs, and—up until the recent repeal of the Immorality Act and the Mixed Marriages Act—marriage and sexual partners depended considerably on race.

The Prohibition of Mixed Marriages Act and the Immorality Act

In an attempt to keep its racial classifications unblurred, the South African government passed the Prohibition of Mixed Marriages Act of 1949—even though past records show never more than 100 marriages a year between Europeans and non-Europeans.[25]

Any marriage in contravention of the act would be null and void, and any marriage officer who knowingly performed a mixed marriage would be committing a criminal offense and could be fined. False statements to a marriage officer in regard to race could subject one to the same punishment as perjury in court.[26] The act was aimed mostly at unions between Europeans and coloreds. The latter already posed a problem for apartheid because some—being fair complected—were able to pass for white.

The Immorality Act of 1927 prohibited extramarital sex relationships between Europeans and Africans. Later amendments confirmed the act's original purpose, but also included coloreds and Asians. The penalty for enticing or for attempting to commit an "immoral or indecent" act—as defined by the Immorality Act— could be up to seven years in prison. While the coded penalty was stiff, the actual penalty was usually light: Suspended sentences were generally the case. The accompanying social disgrace, however, was the greater personal cost. Those prosecuted under the Immorality Act were usually white men and black women. For example, from July 1972 to June 1973, 161 white men and 135 black women were convicted for immorality. This is contrasted to 5 white women and 3 black men over the same period.[27]

The Group Areas Act of 1950

When the National Party came to power in 1948, their vow was to stem the flow of Africans into urban areas, and their first major legislation was the Group Areas Act of 1950. This act has won the dubious distinction of being the "kernel of the apartheid policy" (Dr. Malan) and the "cornerstone of positive apartheid" (Dr. T. E. Donges, South Africa's first President-elect).[28]

The Group Areas Act of 1950, as amended in 1957, was written to replace and consolidate a hodgepodge of residential and business segregation laws. Its original intention was to segregate urban areas especially, into sections for whites, coloreds, Indians, and blacks. The act designates which people are qualified in which areas to purchase, rent, or lease property. In 1957, the Group Areas Act was amended to prevent nonwhites from using sports facilities like clubhouses and from attending theaters, nightclubs, and other public facilities.

The act has also been used for slum clearance, forcing local authorities to build nonwhite housing on a scale that they otherwise would not have chosen to do. It has caused mass relocation of Indians in Durban and Johannesburg, Coloureds in the Cape and Johannesburg, and blacks all over the country. The act also applied to whites living in nonwhite areas, but the number of whites compulsorily moved was a tiny fraction compared to nonwhites.[29]

There are few apartheid laws that have caused greater resentment and agony than the Group Areas Act. When the legislation was being passed, Parliament gave assurances that it would be equitably applied and that no group would suffer special hardships. Indians and coloreds were especially hard hit, however, because they were the most likely to be the middle class and upwardly mobile among nonwhites—and hence, more likely to have businesses and residences in those areas reclassified as all white. By 1980, 115,000 coloreds and Indians had been forced to relocate, often having to sell their homes and businesses at depressed prices.[30]

The Group Areas Act provides that the state president may proclaim an area for occupation by a certain racial group. Such an area must be vacated by nonqualified persons within a year. Failure to move is a criminal offense.

The Black Urban Areas Consolidation Act of 1945

The Black Urban Areas Consolidation Act requires that local authorities set aside land for the blacks who are legally within their boundaries. It provides for compulsory residence of blacks within these designated areas only, and gives local authorities the power to expropriate land and borrow money in order to carry out their responsibilities in this regard. In addition, the act says that all enterprises in the designated areas must be owned solely by blacks, except by special consent of the governor-general. The Natives Resettlement Act of 1954 was passed as an adjunct to the Black Urban Areas Consolidation Act. It created the Natives Resettlement Board, which was given the power to remove blacks from certain areas and build townships for them in other areas.

The Black Urban Areas Consolidation Act and the Natives Laws Amendment Act (1952) are together popularly known as the "pass law" or "influx control." They set conditions for blacks when traveling to or remaining in white areas. The legal conditions for a black to remain in a white area for more than 72 hours are: (1) continuous lawful residence in that area for 15 years; or (2) continuous lawful employment for a single employer in that area for ten years; or (3) birth in that area; or (4) special government permission; or (5) being the wife or child of a black so qualified.

Even if an African has legal residence in a designated white area, his or her movement may be restricted through curfew laws. Policemen can search homes without warrants, looking for pass law violators. Moreover, under Section 29 of the Black Urban Areas Consolidation Act, a policeman can arrest any African in a white designated area—even if he is in full compliance with the pass laws—if the officer believes the African to be undesirable. Habitual unemployment, agitation, vagrancy, breach of contract and political activity may qualify a black as undesirable and "detrimental to the maintenance of peace." Such a finding by the Bantu Affairs Board can lead to the banishment—without appeal—of such a person to his ethnic homeland, even if that person has never lived in the homeland and has always resided in the white designated area.

The South African government's justification for influx control goes like this:

There are many sound socioeconomic and political reasons for such a system. Large-scale migration from rural to urban areas is a problem faced by all Third World countries where hundreds of thousands of people eke out a miserable existence in appalling squatter settlements.... There are limits to the capacity of any town or city to absorb people and provide them with essential facilities. If the South African Government were to do away with all controls... the result would be untold misery for countless Blacks.[31]

The government also adds:

It is an incontrovertible fact that most Blacks who hold steady jobs in urban areas and receive on-the-job training, good pay and considerable fringe benefits and gradually advance to more skilled occupations are themselves firmly opposed to an unregulated inflow of unskilled work-seekers from the national states... They know only too well that their ever-rising living standards will be eroded by the sheer weight of numbers... Many South African blacks also realize that the system [influx control] serves to protect them in the job and housing markets against undue competition from foreign blacks.[32]

The Black Urban Areas Consolidation Act of 1945 and its amendments were complemented by the Black Abolition of Passes and Coordination of Documents Act of 1952 and the Black Labor Act of 1964, in an effort to regulate the entry and activity of blacks in white designated areas. While these measures have caused untold human suffering through separation of families as well as loss of education and employment opportunities, the measures have nowhere been nearly as effective as the government would have liked. Despite the fact that pass law violations constitute 25 percent of all arrests, there are hundreds of thousands—perhaps millions—of blacks illegally residing and working in white areas. This is a matter that we will consider in Chapter 5.

The Reservation of Separate Amenities Act of 1953

Legal race discrimination in the area of social amenities is mandated by the Reservation of Separate Amenities Act. It empowers the jurisdictions in the nation's provinces to reserve public premises to the exclusive use of members of different races. It provides for racial segregation in libraries, museums, public transportation, hospitals, parks, beaches, and other public accommodations such as hotels, nightclubs, and restaurants. The Reservation of Separate Amenities Act represents another triumph of the South African Parliament over its courts.

In a 1910 case called *R. v. Plaatjies*, the court held that a municipality could not racially segregate a swimming stream. In 1915—in *Williams and Adendorf v. Johannesburg Municipality*—the court struck down a city law providing for segregated trams. In the 1934 case *Minister of Posts and Telegraphs v. Rasool*, the court struck down segregated postal facilities—saying that discriminatory laws are invalid if they impose greater duties, or confer greater rights, on one section of the community than on another.[33]

In later cases of discrimination, the Appellate Court chose to challenge apartheid law in dramatic ways. *R. v. Abduraham* (1950 (3) SA 136 A) concerns a case where the defendant was charged with inciting others to disregard the "Europeans Only" signs in the suburban railroad station and on the trains in Cape Town. The court said that the authorities, acting under the Railways and Harbors Control Regulation and Management Act of 1916, had made an error. They had provided facilities in which Europeans could get away from the unwanted company of blacks, but had not provided facilities so blacks could get away from the unwanted company of whites. Therefore, the discrimination was unequal and hence unlawful. In acquitting the defendant, the court held that, while the act had specific provisions for discrimination by the Railway Administration, Parliament gave it no power to discriminate unequally.[34]

This principle was applied with vigor in many other cases dealing with public accommodation. The courts were saying that authorities had to provide equal facilities or else not discriminate. Justice Albert Centlivres said, "It is the duty of the courts to hold the scales evenly between the different classes of the community and to declare invalid any practice, which, in the absence of the authority of an Act of Parliament, results in partial and unequal treatment to a substantial degree."[35] This position was again tested in *R. v. Lusu* (1953), a case involving waiting rooms in a Cape Town train station where the non-European waiting rooms were substantially inferior to the European. The Appellate Court once again held that the Railway Administration did not have the authority to apply discriminatory regulations in a way resulting in partial or unequal treatment between the different races.

Again, in the provision of public accommodation services, the courts expressed similar opinions about legal versus illegal discrimination. One such case was *Tayah v. Ermelo Local Transportation Board* (1950 (3) SA 136 A.D. 440), which involved an Indian taxi owner who was refused the reissue of a license to continue his "first class" (carrying whites) taxi business. Delivering the opinion for the court, Chief Justice Centiveres declared it unfair discrimination to require non-Europeans to carry only non-Europeans.[36]

In more recent times, the South African court chose to challenge one of the mainstays of apartheid in *Komani NO v. Bantu Affairs Administration Board, Peninsula Area* (1980 (4) SA 448 A). This case involved the plaintiff's right to live with her husband in an urban area even if she did not have a permit. The court ruled in favor of Komani, though it had to twist the spirit—if not the letter—of the regulations promulgated under the Black Urban Areas Consolidation Act of 1945.[37]

In another notable case, *Oos-randse Administrasieraad en 'n Ander v. Rikhoto*, the court again challenged the Black Urban Areas Consolidation Act. The defendant had been employed on a year-to-year basis. At the end of each year, he would go to his homeland for vacation. Afterward, he would apply for a new work permit to resume working for the same employer and living in an urban area. The Labor Bureau, which issues the permit, held that Rikhoto did not have continuous employment for the ten years necessary to qualify for Section 10 (b) covering urban residency rights. The court found for Rikhoto, saying that the government could not use labor regulations to deny a person the right to live legally in urban areas.[38]

Absent a specific act of Parliament applicable to the case, South African court tradition has maintained a rebuttable common-law presumption of equality between the races. The Reservation of Separate Amenities Act of 1953 had as its aim the elimination of this common-law presumption of the courts. The act declared that, when a separate amenity had been provided for one race, it was unnecessary to provide a substantially similar one—or any at all—for other races. For the first time, it gave to owners of hotels, restaurants, theaters, and other public places the statutory authority to exclude by race. Much more importantly, the Reservation of Separate Amenities Act expressly prohibited the courts from pronouncing on the validity of discriminatory arrangements in the provision of public accommodations.

RACIAL LABOR LAWS

It is South Africa's racially discriminatory labor laws and practices that will interest us most in this study. Their beginnings date to the nineteenth century. In 1856, the colonial Parliament passed the Master and Servants Act, "To Amend the Laws regarding the relative Rights and Duties of Masters, Servants and Apprentices." The Master and Servants Act made servants liable to prosecution for breaches of contract such as desertion, disobedience, willful dereliction of duty, and absence without leave; and on the part of the master, failure to pay wages and to supply food. The Masters and Servants Act must not have worked to the satisfaction of employers and employees, given all the amendments to it; but at least it did not discriminate between races. Indeed, a considerable thrust of the law was to enforce contracts with European employees who had been brought to South Africa at considerable expense to their employers.

One of the earliest forms of racially discriminatory labor legislation was aimed at the Chinese. The Transvaal Legislative Council passed the Transvaal Importation of Labour Ordinance No. 7 of 1904, "To regulate the introduction into the Transvaal of unskilled non-European Labourers." This ordinance permitted the employment of Chinese in the Transvaal, but sought to prevent them from competing with Europeans for the higher skilled and higher paid jobs. According to the ordinance, they were only to be employed on "such labor as is usually performed in mines in the Witwatersrand and district by persons belonging to the aboriginal races or tribes of South Africa south of the Equator."[39] It was illegal for the Chinese to perform the following scheduled trades and professions: amalgamator, assayer, banksman, blacksmith, boilermaker, brass finisher, brass molder, bricklayer, bricklayer overseer, carpenter, clerk, coppersmith, cyanide shiftsman, drill sharpener, driver of air or steam winch, driver of mechanical or electrical machinery, electrician, engine driver, engineer, fireman overseer, fitter, ganger, ironmolder, joiner, machine rock driller, machine sawyer, machinist, mason wine overseer, mechanic, miller, millwright, mine carpenter, mine storeman, onsetter, overseer in any capacity other than the management and control of laborers, painter, patternmaker, pipeman, plasterer, platelayer, plumber, quarrymen overseer, rigger, sampler, signaler, skipman, stonecutter, timberman, timekeeper, tinsmith, turner, wire splicer, woodworking machinist.[40]

Another way of discriminating against the non-European worker was the use of licensing laws or certificates of competency. The Boilers and Machinery Law—Transvaal Law No. 12, Section 104—of 1898 provided "that every person having charge of a winding engine used for raising and lowering persons shall be the holder of an engine driver's certificate of competency. No coloured person may hold an engine driver's certificate of competency."[41]

In 1907 a violent strike occurred on the Rand mines–involving death and sabotage. The Botha and Smuts government had won office with the political support of white miners, mainly British. While the government used Afrikaners as scabs during the strike, it then sought to appease the skilled white mineworkers by giving teeth to Transvaal Ordinance No. 7—discussed above—which restricted the employment of Chinese in skilled mine jobs.[42] (See the discussion in Chapter 3 on Transvaal Ordinance No. 7 of 1907.)

The Mines and Works Act of 1911

The Mines and Works Act of 1911 can aptly be called the first of a series of South African laws known as the "colour bar." It was the result of various forces that will be only briefly described here.

Militant unionism began when branches of several British labor unions opened in South Africa. There were other labor union influences as well, such as the Knights of Labor and the Industrial Workers of the World (IWW)—both of whom had their origins in the United States.

One very important character in South Africa's union movement was an Englishman from Suffolk named William Henry Andrews, a Marxist and the first person to serve as secretary of the South African Communist party. Andrews led a succession of violent strikes: one year, at the Kimberly diamond mines; another, in the workshops of the Natal government railway system; and still another, in Johannesburg among tramwaymen–an action that brought on allegations of attempted dynamiting.[43]

The government's response to labor unrest was to concede privileges to the socialists and labor unions. The government felt that, unless it excluded black Africans from certain kinds of jobs through legislation, white mineworker unions would resort to intermittent violence to accomplish the same. Therefore, the Smuts/Botha government sought measures to promote "industrial peace." The Mines and Works Act of 1911 was that measure.

The Mines and Works Act gave to the government arbitrary powers to write regulations, ostensibly in the interest of health and safety. Part of its provisions called for the issuance of certificates of competency. By law, certificates of competency could not be issued to non-Europeans in the Transvaal or the Orange Free State. Moreover, certificates of competency held by Coloureds in the Natal and Cape provinces were invalid in the northern provinces.

The Mines and Works Act also gave to the Department of Labor the power to specify the ratio between the number of foremen (whites) and mining laborers (blacks) that could be hired in the performance of any particular activity. The regulations called for 10.5 blacks to 1 white. However, white mining unions felt that this left them with less than optimal white employment, and demanded a 3.5:1 ratio.[44]

The Mines and Works Act of 1926

In 1923, the Appellate Court struck down the racially discriminatory provisions of the Mines and Works Act of 1911—declaring them to be ultra vires. The court's action caused considerable animosity among white mineworkers toward the government in power at that time. Fulfilling its campaign promise, a new government passed an amended version of the Mines and Works Act of 1911.

The amended Mines and Works Act contained specific provisions—which could not be challenged by the court—wherein Asians and blacks were prevented by statute from acquiring certificates of competency.

Civilized Labor Policy

The years following the 1924 elections mark the beginning of South Africa's "civilised labour policy." This policy was the fruit of a marriage between the socialistically oriented National party—representing Afrikaners who demanded white supremacy—and the British Socialist Labour party. It formed what was to become known as the "Nationalist–Labour Pact." The Pact and succeeding governments enacted legislation that had as its objective the deliberate dismissal of blacks from government jobs in order to make room for whites, the establishment of closed union shops to reinforce discrimination against blacks, the encouragement of businesses that discriminated against blacks, and the mandating of wage compensation levels that priced blacks out of the job market. All this in order to promote South Africa's civilized labor policy, which is officially defined as:

the labour rendered by persons whose standard of living conforms to the standard of living generally recognized as tolerable from the usual European standpoint. Uncivilised labour is to be regarded as the labour rendered by persons whose aim is restricted to the bare requirements of the necessities of life as understood among barbarous and undeveloped peoples.[45]

By no means was there a single mind among white (Afrikaner and British) South Africans about implementation of the civilized labor policy. In regard to the reservation of jobs to one race or another, Prime Minister Jan Smuts said, "It would cause blacks to hate whites." Mining magnate Sir Ernest Oppenheimer—in the 1925 House of Assembly debates—prophetically said, "It is an evil to impose class legislation and the curse of such an evil is that one must continue to do evil. It is only by efficiency and application to work that the Europeans can maintain the position we now occupy in South Africa."[46]

The Industrial Conciliation Act of 1924

The Industrial Conciliation Act (ICA) of 1924 along with its subsequent amendments, provided for industrial councils made up of employer associations and labor unions. Together, labor and management negotiate wage, fringe benefits, and working conditions over the life of the agreement. Any agreement reached is almost automatically approved by the minister of labor, and is then binding on all employers and employees in the same and related industries—whether or not the parties were signatories to the particular document.

The amendments to the Industrial Conciliation Act—specifically, those in 1956—gave to the labor minister broad powers to reserve specific classes of employment for specified races in order to "safeguard against interracial competition." And although the act created collective bargaining between employers and employees, black South Africans were to be excluded from the collective bargaining agreements. In effect, the ICA defined blacks out of the process because, for purposes of the act, an employee was "any person (other than a Bantu) employed." While coloreds and Asians (or unions comprised of whites, coloreds, and Asians) were not excluded from participation under the ICA, they had to establish separate union branches.[47] The labor minister was empowered to reserve defined types of work for particular races—which has affected about 2.3 percent of all the jobs in South Africa.[48] In 1964, the jobs legally reserved for whites only were: elevator operating, ambulance driving, fire fighting, bartending, traffic policing (in some cities), parts of the transport industry, engineering, stone masonry, marble masonry, joinery, woodworking machinery, electrical wiring, letter cutting, stone decorating, and shop, office, and bank fitting. See Appendix 2.A for the text of a 1975 determination of jobs in the building industry.

Job reservation is both a matter of law and custom. As a matter of custom, there is a tradition based on collective bargaining agreements that says blacks are not to be placed in supervisory positions over whites. If firms violate this tradition, they face the wrath not only of white union members, but of government as well. However, in recent years—under pressure from employers—both aspects of the practice of job reservation have been on the decline.[49]

The Wage Act of 1925

The Wage Act was passed as a complement to the Industrial Conciliation Act in the government's effort to promote its civilized labor policy. The Wage Act made provisions for wage regulation and work conditions in industries where employers and employees were not organized into trade associations, and hence not covered by the ICA. It excluded such regulation from agriculture and domestic service, where blacks did not compete with whites for jobs.

The act set up a Wage Board that would make recommendations to the minister of labor, who—in turn—would then make wage determinations. The Wage Act of 1925, as amended, permits the minister of labor to set minimum wages for different occupations and to designate the fringe benefits and other conditions of employment. Unlike minimum wage legislation in the United States, the Wage Board recommends minimum wages on a district-by-district basis in order to reflect what it sees as the economic conditions in each area.

At one time, employers could apply for special permission to pay wages below "civilised standards," but a 1937 revision of the Wage Act stated that the board had no power to "differentiate or discriminate on the basis of race or colour."

The Environmental Planning and Utilization of Resources Act of 1967

The Environmental Planning and Utilization of Resources Act of 1967 enabled the minister of planning to declare "controlled areas" within which "no person without the prior written approval of the Minister can establish or extend a factory." In terms of the act, "extension" to a factory means hiring more blacks.

The stated purpose of this legislation was to promote industrial decentralization in the hope that companies would move to areas near the African homeland and reduce the influx of blacks to industrial centers. The act aimed to encourage: (1) the more efficient utilization of existing labor resources, (2) greater mechanization, (3) the increased employment of other racial groups such as the Coloureds, and (4) industrial expansion in the border areas to the homelands and the homelands themselves.[50] According to the provisions of Section 3, extension of factories would be permitted for industries that were "locality bound" or had a white/African labor ratio of 1:2.5 or less.

The Environmental Planning and Utilization of Resources Act was to be one of Prime Minister Verwoerd's building blocks to "separate development," which failed to produce its desired results. The government attacked the business sector for not locating in the prescribed areas—saying that the "big names were absent." In fact, the Section 3 requirements were met with reservation on the part of not only business, but the white unions were concerned lest the plan become successful and "little Hong Kongs" sprout up—competing with and undercutting the union wage scale.

Section 3 regulations led to factory closings and loss of employment. Constant complaints from the business community prompted the passage of amendments to the act in 1977. The government-sponsored Reikert White Paper Report urged the scrapping of Section 3 in 1979.[51] And in a 1980 speech to businessmen at Good Hope (published by the Department of Foreign Affairs in 1981), Prime Minister Pieter Botha promised to abolish the offensive section as soon as it could be replaced by other incentives for decentralization and other disincentives for employing black labor in white areas.

SUMMARY

South Africa's common law system is unambiguously Roman–Dutch. As such, it embodies principles similar to English common law in what all "reasonable men" think is just or unjust under the same or similar conditions, and therefore prohibits the basic violations of personal liberty such as theft, murder, fraud, arson, and assault. In South Africa, the common law is generally applicable to all persons, regardless of race, unless it is prohibited from doing so through administrative or constitutional law and—it might be added—where tribal laws and customs apply.

The greatest legal disadvantage for black South Africans lies in the area of statutory law—that is, constitutional and administrative law—which gives to the authorities great discretionary power. Moreover, since South Africa has a parliamentary system of government—and hence, "parliamentary supremacy"—courts have only a limited ability to judge on the constitutionality of laws passed by Parliament. The job of the courts is seen as carrying out the will of Parliament.

Despite these limitations and the political power held by the central government, the South African judiciary has shown a remarkable amount of independence and willingness to make judgments against the state, as shown in cases like *Tayah*, *Komani*, and *Rikhoto*. Indeed, the strongest antigovernment opponents would agree that South Africa's judiciary is probably the most reasonable and fairest branch of its government.

This chapter has given a brief overview of South Africa's legal structure. In the following chapters, the evolution of labor laws will be connected to economic events, showing how the legal system was captured so as to confer privileges and benefits for whites that were unattainable through market forces.

APPENDIX 2.A: ICA JOB Reservation

DEPARTMENT OF LABOUR
No. R. 149   24 January 1975
INDUSTRIAL CONCILIATION ACT, 1956
DETERMINATION 28 IN TERMS OF SECTION 77.—BUILDING INDUSTRY, REPUBLIC OF SOUTH AFRICA

I, Marais Viljoen, Minister of Labour, do hereby, in terms of section 77(7) (a) of the Industrial Conciliation Act, 1956, make a Determination in accordance with the Schedule hereto and, in terms of section 77(7) (b) of the said Act, fix the first Monday following the expiration of six months after the date of publication of this notice as the date on which the said Determination shall become binding.

M. VILJOEN, Minister of Labour

SCHEDULE
1. SCOPE AND APPLICATION OF THE DETERMINATION

In the Building Industry, in—
(a) all the areas mentioned in paragraph (b), no employer shall replace any White person employed by him on any work in the said Industry by an employee who is not a White person;
(b) the urban areas falling within—
(i) the Magisterial Districts of The Cape, Wynberg, Simonstown, Bellville, Goodwood, Paarl, Wellington, Stellenbosch, Kuils River, Somerset West, Strand and Worcester, the work of general foreman, foreman and leading hand, as well as electrical installation, is hereby reserved for White persons;
(ii) the Magisterial Districts of Port Elizabeth, Uitenhage and East London, the work of general foreman, foreman and leading hand, as well as electrical installation, joinery, plumbing, shop, office and bank fitting and woodwork, is hereby reserved for White persons;
(iii) the Magisterial Districts of Durban, Pinetown, Inanda, Pietermaritzburg, Richmond (Natal), New Hanover, Camperdown, Lions River, Vryheid, Dundee, Klip River, Estcourt, Dannhauser, Newcastle, Glencoe and Utrecht, the work of general foreman,

Source: *Government Gazette*, January 24, 1975, pp. 1–7.

foreman and leading hand, as well as bricklaying, electrical installation, joinery, plastering, plumbing, shop, office and bank fitting and woodworking machining in workshops, is hereby reserved for White persons;

(iv) the area of Richard's Bay, the work of general foreman, foreman and leading hand, is hereby reserved for White persons;

(v) the Magisterial Districts of Alberton, Balfour, Benoni, Boksburg, Brakpan, Delmas, Germiston, Heidelberg (Transvaal), Johannesburg, Kempton Park, Nigel, Pietersburg, Rustenburg and Springs, and the areas within radii of 48 kilometres of General Post Office, Krugersdorp; 32 kilometres of General Post Office, Vereeniging; 32 kilometres of General Post Office, Pretoria; 16 kilometres of General Post Office, Klerksdorp; 16 kilometres of General Post Office Potchefstroom; 16 kilometres of General Post Office, Wibank; and 16 kilometres of General Post Office, Middleburg (Transvaal), the work of general foreman, foreman and leading hand, as well as bricklaying, electrical installation, joinery, metalwork, painting, plastering, plumbing, shop, office and bank fitting and woodwork, is hereby reserved for White persons; and

(vi) the area within a radious of 24 kilometres of General Post Office, Bloemfontein, and the Magisterial District of Kroonstad, the work of general foreman, foreman and leading hand, as well as bricklaying, electrical installation, joinery, metalwork, painting, plastering, plumbing, shop, office and bank fitting and woodwork, is hereby reserved for White persons; and no employee who is not a White person shall perform such work: Provided that such work may nevertheless, subject to the provisions of paragraph (a) be performed by an employee who is not a White person, providing such employee—

(aa) is a Coloured person, and

(bb) is a skilled artisan—

(i) in the specified class of work assigned to him; or

(ii) in any of the classes of work in respect of which he acts in a supervisory capacity in the case of a general foreman, foreman or leading hand; or is deemed to be a skilled artisan by an Industrial Council for the Building Industry in terms of any Act or under any training scheme, arrangement or test programme of any such Council of a registered employers' organisation or federation of such organisations instituted with a view to according artisan status to employees in the Building Industry, and is in possession of written proof thereof in the form of a certificate issued to him by any such Council; or is, in terms of any Act, or any aforesaid training scheme or arrangement, or at an educational establishment, undergoing training with a view to obtaining artisan status in the said Industry and is in possession of written proof thereof in the form of a certificate issued to him by the Industrial Council under whose jurisdiction he is employed or by the body providing such training; and

(cc) is not at any stage and in respect of any work appointed, or permitted, to act in a supervisory capacity over a White employee.

[The Act continues with a set of elaborate definitions of skills that are omitted here.]

NOTES

1. John Dugard, *Human Rights and the South African Legal Order* (Princeton, N.J.: Princeton University Press, 1978), p. 28.

2. Ibid., pp. 26–27.

3. Leonard Thompson, "The Compromise of Union," in the *Oxford History of South*

Africa, vol. 2, edited by Monica Wilson and Leonard Thompson (New York: Oxford University Press, 1971), p. 357.

4. Ibid., p. 358.

5. Dugard, *Human Rights*, p. 29.

6. 1934 A.D. 11 at 37.

7. See A. V. Dicey, *Introduction to the Study of the Law of the Constitution*, 10th ed. (London: Macmillan, 1959), especially pp. 202–3.

8. Dugard, *Human Rights*, p. 39.

9. Cited in John Cope, *South Africa* (New York: Frederick A. Praeger, 1967), p. 34.

10. H. J. Simons, "The Law and Its Administration," in *Handbook on Race Relations in South Africa*, edited by Ellen Hellman (New York: Octagon Books, 1975), pp. 41–108.

11. Leon Louw and Frances Kendall, *South Africa: The Solution* (Bisho, Ciskei: Amagi Publications, 1986), p. 189.

12. Simons, "Law and Its Administration," p. 46. The exceptions are mostly concessions to tribal laws and customs that are well advanced and bear a close resemblance to the archaic laws of Anglo-Saxon, Germanic, and Frankish peoples prior to the rise of feudal society. See Simons, p. 47ff.

13. Dugard, *Human Rights*, p. 71.

14. Ibid., p. 72.

15. Ibid., p. 108.

16. See *Mpanza v. Minister of Native Affairs* (1946 W.L.D. 225 at 229); and more recently, *Wood et al v. Ondangwa Tribal Authority* (1975 (2) SA 294 A.D.)

17. Dugard, *Human Rights*, p. 109.

18. Habeas corpus is basically a procedure for obtaining a judicial determination of an individual's custody. It provides that the individual has a right to be brought before a court to determine the legality of his or her confinement. See Steven H. Gifis, *Law Dictionary* (New York: Barron's Educational Series, 1975), pp. 93–94.

19. See *Stanton v. Minister of Justice* (1960 (3) SA 355). Cited in Dugard, *Human Rights*, p. 111.

20. Dugard, *Human Rights*, p. 327.

21. In 1977, Winnie Mandela, wife of the imprisoned black leader Nelson Mandela, was banished from Johannesburg—under Internal Security Act provisions—to Brandfort, a small village in the Orange Free State.

22. Dugard, *Human Rights*, p. 356.

23. Ibid., p. 61.

24. Henry John May, *The South African Constitution* (Westport, Conn.: Greenwood Press, 1970), pp. 439–40.

25. René de Villiers, "Afrikaner Nationalism," in the *Oxford History of South Africa*, vol. 2, edited by Monica Wilson and Leonard Thompson (New York: Oxford University Press, 1971), p. 409.

26. May, *South African Constitution*, p. 435.

27. Dugard, Human Rights, p. 71.

28. de Villiers, "Afrikaner Nationalism," p. 410.

29. Ibid.

30. Merle Lipton, *Capitalism and Apartheid: South Africa, 1910–84* (Totowa, N.J.: Rowman and Allanheld, 1985), pp. 23–24 and 239–40. See also Christopher Saunders, *Historical Dictionary of South Africa* (Metuchen, N.J.: Scarecrow Press, 1983), p. 76.

This source cites that, by 1979, there were 374,990 coloreds, 172,156 Indians, and 8,299 whites who had been required to move.

31. South African *1983 Official Year Book of the Republic of South Africa* (Johannesburg: Department of Foreign Affairs and Information, Chris van Rensburg Publications, 1983), p. 215.

32. Ibid.

33. May, *South African Constitution*, p. 424.

34. See Dugard, *Human Rights*, ch. 10, for a discussion of these cases. See also May, *South African Constitution*, chs. 19 and 20.

35. May, *South African Constitution*, p. 450.

36. See S. Kavalsky, "Validity of Municipal Bye-laws," *South African Journal of Law* 53 (1936): 170–85, 287–301, and 446–57, for the Appellate Court's criteria regarding unfair discrimination.

37. Christopher Forsyth, "The Judges and Judicial Choice: Some Thoughts on the Appellate Division of the Supreme Court of South Africa Since 1950," *Journal of African Studies* 12, no. 1, (October, 1985): pp. 110–11.

38. Ibid., pp. 111–12.

39. Sheila T. van der Horst, *Native Labour in South Africa* (London: Frank Cass, 1971), p. 171.

40. Ibid.

41. Frederick A. Johnstone, *Class, Race, and Gold: A Study of Class Relations and Racial Discrimination in South Africa* (London: Routledge and Kegan Paul, 1976), p. 66.

42. William H. Hutt, *The Economics of the Colour Bar* (London: Andre Deutsch, 1964), p. 61.

43. Ibid., pp. 61–62.

44. Ibid., p. 68.

45. Bureau of Information, on behalf of the Department of Foreign Affairs. *Official Year Book of the Union of South Africa, and of Basutaland, Bechuanaland Protectorate and Swaziland, 1926–27* (Pretoria: Government Printer, 1926): p. 203.

46. B. J. Liebenberg, "Hertzog in Power," in *Five Hundred Years: A History of South Africa*, edited by C. F. J. Muller (Johannesburg: Academia Press, 1981), p. 417.

47. Dugard, *Human Rights*, p. 88.

48. Hutt, *Economics of the Colour Bar*, p. 118.

49. Dugard, *Human Rights*, p. 86.

50. W. F. J. Steenkamp, "Labour Problems and Policies of Half a Century," *South African Journal of Economics* 51, 1 (December 1983): 70.

51. South African Department of Labour, *Report of the Commission of Inquiry into Legislation Affecting the Utilization of Manpower* (Pretoria: Government Printer, 1979).

3
The Drive for Racial Labor Laws

The broad question that this book considers is: What are some of the forces behind South Africa's history of almost complete racial regulation? The focal point of this chapter is less ambitious: We will examine the forces that led to regulation of race in the labor market. Tempting though it may be to follow popular opinion and conclude that pure and simple racism is the controlling factor—and all reasonable people agree that apartheid laws are indeed racist—characterization alone does not provide much of an understanding.

The reason why pure and simple racism cannot provide an adequate explanation becomes apparent when we consider South Africa's legal history of racial regulation over the labor market—including laws like the Motor Transportation Amendment Act (1959) and the Industrial Conciliation Act (1956), both of which mandate that certain jobs be held by whites only. Then we recognize that businesses controlled by these laws (such as mines, factories, and building contractors) and government facilities controlled by these laws (like the railroads and public works) are white owned or managed. In view of the fact of white ownership and/or management over the bulk of economic activity, we might then ask: Why are racially restrictive employment laws necessary?

If racism were the complete answer, racial laws would be unnecessary because white business owners and government agencies simply *would not* hire blacks for jobs desirable to whites. The mere existence of laws restricting certain jobs to whites only—such as bus drivers in white areas, elevator operators, engine drivers, and dynamite blasters—suggests that, were it not for these laws, white business owners *would* hire blacks. Otherwise, it is hard to explain why racially discriminatory laws were thought to be necessary.

THE DEVELOPMENT OF DISCRIMINATORY LABOR LAWS

Early in the economic development of South Africa, non-European labor and skilled European labor could be considered as complementary, in the sense that an increase in the supply of one would increase the wages and productivity of the other. At the turn of the twentieth century, conflicts of interest in the labor market arose between European and non-European employees, on the one hand, and between European employers and employees, on the other. The conflict developed for at least two reasons: (1) Non-European workers were gaining greater skills, particularly in mining; and (2) Europeans who had worked the land as farmers were losing this as a means of support.[1]

Both of these factors meant that Europeans and non-Europeans were increasingly in competition to some degree for skilled work and to a larger degree for unskilled work. Non-Europeans were building skills through informal apprenticeship, and mineowners were prepared to give them jobs commensurate with their skills. At the request of the Transvaal Engine Drivers Association, the Transvaal government introduced laws in 1896, 1897, and 1898 mandating that engine drivers (who hauled workers) be white and in possession of certificates of competence.[2] In 1903, the Transvaal Mine, Works, and Machine Regulations restricted the jobs of banksmen (underground laborers) and onsetters (managers of underground mining operations) to whites only. This was after the mining houses had defeated an 1896 version of the same law in 1897.[3]

Thus, in response to increasing competition, European workers and employers established more mechanisms for restricting that competition. One mechanism was collusive hiring arrangements. The Witwatersrand Native Labour Association (WNLA) was formed in 1896. Among its provisions was the declaration that:

No Company, whilst a member of the Witwatersrand Native Labour Association, will be allowed under any circumstances to engage any but white labour, except through the agency of the Association. This will apply: (1) to all natives who, from having previously worked on your mine, or who from any cause may come forward and seek such work voluntarily; (2) to those who have been recruited within or without the Transvaal—in fact to all natives or coloured men employed either above or below ground on your property.[4]

The WNLA was seeking to establish a labor-purchasing cartel (in effect, a monopsony). Like other cartels, it was only partially successful because of cheating by its members. The high demand for mine labor led individual mining houses to bid up black wages and encourage blacks to breach labor contracts with competitor mines.

In 1900, the government gave to the association the exclusive right to recruit workers in Mozambique for South African mines. Even though this represented a welcome addition to the domestic labor force, as another attempt to win monopsonistic gains it met with limited success due to competition from Rhodesian employers.[5]

In 1911, the government passed the Native Labour Regulation Act, which licensed recruiters and banned the familiar mining-company practice of getting blacks to break labor contracts with competitor mines by offering higher wages. Through the Native Labour Regulation Act, the Native Recruiting Corporation was formed; this setup amounted to a collusive hiring arrangement, which made for lower mine labor costs.[6]

A U.S. Digression

The attempts to set up hiring collusions, with its attendant problems, is not unique to South Africa. During the Reconstruction period in the United States many landowners resented the increased bargaining power of blacks. Often, these landowners formed cartels in order to restrict the terms of sharecropping contracts. Before the Joint Committee on Reconstruction in 1866, General George E. Spencer told of a planter's association in Tuscaloosa County, Alabama. The planters had agreed among themselves to give no more than one-eighth of the net proceeds of the crop to black tenants. One landowner violated the agreement and contracted to give his tenants one-sixth.

Newspapers and journals carried numerous appeals for landowner cooperation and organization. In 1865, a contributor to the *Southern Cultivator* urged that planters stand together in enforcing contracts; with landlords acting as one, he continued, the freeman "must consent or starve." Four years later, in the *DeBow's Review*, a planter lamented that "there is no concert of action on the part of the planters to oppose these ever increasing exactions [of the freeman]." The same lament was heard in the *Southern Cultivator* of 1889: "If they desire success let the farmers, as a body, cooperate together, and work by rule, order and system; attend to their own labor, and let other's labor alone."[7]

An official of the Freedman's Bureau correctly saw why planter collusions had failed: "Such was the demand for negro laborers . . . that any combination to abridge their freedom in seeking and changing homes, or to control the price of labor, failed utterly."[8] General Wager Swayne said, "The planters made a strong combination to hire no negro away from home. The freedmen stood it out until the planters gave way, and they finally hired at random, at a little higher wages than were generally paid elsewhere."[9] General Gregory referred to "a competition for labor which in many localities [in Texas], has become a scramble."[10]

There are numerous examples of how planter associations failed to organize an effective collusion against black labor. This is precisely what economic theory would predict: The advantages of a cartel and the actual achievement of those advantages are two entirely different things. This failure was also seen in the early years of South Africa's Witwatersrand Native Labour Association, with miners cheating on the agreement. The key advantage that the South African miners had—accounting for their partial success—but that the Southern planters in the United States did not have, was government backing for their cartel—thus, an enforcement technique bearing on the actions of the cartel members. In other words, in the South African case, cheating—that is, enticing blacks through higher wages—had become no longer a violation of a gentleman's agreement; it was a violation of law.

Anti-Chinese Sentiment

Initially, white miners in South Africa did not fear blacks as competitors—believing that they did not have "the brains enough" to go beyond a certain efficiency. The miners did, however, fear competition from the Chinese in skilled employment.[11] Agitators said, "We are ruined by Chinese cheap labour! To hell with the heathen Chinese."[12]

In fact—to pursue our U.S. digression for a moment—a similar disdain for Chinese workers was prevalent in the United States. To a question from the chairman of the U.S. Senate Committee on Education and Labor in August 1883, labor union leader Samuel Gompers answered thus:

Q. Had there been no strike we would have not complained?

A. No sir; I have no objection to the people of any country coming to America, Chinese excepted (I'm not so sentimental as all that), provided they come here of their own free will, and not influenced by deception.

Q. On that point, do you think there is any feeling among American laborers or workmen adverse to free and open competition with foreign laborers from European countries when they come here?

A. No sir; I believe they have no objection. They do wish, however, to put a stop to the introduction of the Chinese into this country, at least for a period, so as to give the American workman a breathing spell. Our people had hardly recovered from the Panic and they were not to be trodden down by the Chinese undermining them.

Q. But a European laborer will work more cheaply than the American laborer, will he not?

A. He becomes easily acclimated and soon harmonizes with the American people.

Q. And he soon wants as much wages as anybody?

A. Yes, sir; and, as a certain senator said, "It is a question whether the working men of America shall eat rats, rice, or beefsteak." I choose beefsteak. I will vote for that everytime. I do not want it understood that my vote can be purchased for a beefsteak but I will vote always for measures that will improve the condition of the working men.

Q. You speak of this opposition to the Chinese being designed to give the working men a breathing spell after the Panic. Do I understand you to mean that the opposition to Chinese immigration is temporary?

A. No, sir.

Q. Then, there is a permanent opposition, you think, to that immigration?

A. Decidedly.[13]

Union Actions

In South Africa, white miners' tolerance of black workers because they did not have brains enough was not to last. As blacks began to develop skills, white miners came to fear black (as well as Coloured) competition as they feared the Chinese. The leader of the Mine Workers Union said, "What we are up against is the unfair economic condition we have to contend against. We realize that if we have to compete with the native at the native's standard it will be hopeless."[14]

Craft unionists wanted a policy to segregate blacks in reserves and to totally exclude them from industrial work. Until this wish could be realized, the unions wanted the color bar extended so that blacks could not run machines. Despite the color bar laws, employment for whites decreased as Africans learned skills. In 1907, the Chamber of Mines members employed 2,234 whites to supervise 1,890 machines. In 1913, they were only 2,207 whites supervising 4,781 rock drills handled by Africans, with white gangers (supervisors) being replaced by African "bossboys." On the Randfontein mines from 1911 to 1913, the number of white stationary engine drivers fell from "forty to seventeen or eighteen."[15]

In 1913, the Transvaal Federation of Trade Unions presented their grievances to business and government in a document called the "Workers Charter." After a general strike that same year, the government sympathized with some of the union's grievances, which included trade union recognition; demands for an eight-hour day, overtime, and holidays; attention to the health problems in the mines (phthisis); and, above all, relief from interracial competition.

THE POOR-WHITE PROBLEM

Compounding white fears was the severe depression from 1904 to 1909, which brought greater attention to what was becoming known as the "poor white problem." Development of the mining industry was creating a rapid transition from subsistence agriculture to a more complex economic system. Cattle disease (rinderpest) had impoverished many white farmers, and the inability of others to adjust to changing agricultural markets sent many into the towns and villages seeking other alternatives.[16] In addition to these factors, the British scorched-earth policy during the Boer War had destroyed farm homes, buildings, and stock—leaving many whites landless and destitute.

The poor-white problem and the proposed solutions to it caused considerable controversy. Poor white shantytowns sprang up outside cities, with residents living in tents. Government officials granted plots of land to these homeless newcomers, but this policy was disputed by other government officials who wanted them resettled in rural areas. One indigency commission referred to the poor whites as "undesirable influx" in its recommendation that they be resettled to the countryside.[17]

Despite the "back to the land" movement supported by some government officials and the Dutch Reformed Church, many poor whites stayed in urban areas. Many of these whites—virtually all of them Afrikaners—were dependent on public and private welfare for sustenance. Aggravating the problem was their attitude toward work. The Transvaal Indigency Commission reported in 1908:

We have been impressed with the frequency with which it has been stated in evidence that unskilled labour was "Kaffir's work" and as such not the kind of work which a white man should perform. [The poor white's] inefficiency as an unskilled labourer and the higher wage he requires, have had the natural result that coloured labour, inefficient though it is, is cheaper to the employer for unskilled work than white labour.... It is essential to realize the importance of the practical monopoly of the unskilled labour market possessed by the native.[18]

The "practical monopoly" of unskilled labor by blacks was reinforced when Transvaal Province decided to repatriate Chinese laborers after their current contracts had expired and to permit no further importation. Mineowners were then forced to replace Chinese labor either with those black workers who were reliable and trainable or with unskilled white workers. The mineowners chose to hire the blacks. One mine official testifying before the Mining Industry Commission said:

A. We have some of the Kaffirs who are better machine men than some of the white men. I have boys who have been working on the mine from twelve to fifteen years, and they are better than many on the Rand nowadays.

Q. Can they place holes?

A. Yes, they can place the holes, fix up the machine and so everything a white man can do, but, of course, we are not allowed to let them blast.

Q. If the law was not what it is, do you think they could blast with safety?

A. I do not think; I feel sure about it. I have had experience with natives since 1879, and I know what a native can do.[19]

During the early 1900s, there was political pressure for reserving certain jobs for whites but there was considerable resistance against the imposition of this policy. The Transvaal Indigency Commission condemned it—saying, "To protect the white man from native competition at this stage is simply to bolster up the aristocratic tradition for a few years longer without doing anything to qualify the white man for the ultimate but inevitable struggle for economic surperiority with the native."[20] Similarly, the Mining Commission of 1908, the Economic Commission of 1913, the Native Grievance Commission of 1913–1914, and the Relief and Grants-in-aid Commission of 1916 found no justification for job reservation.[21]

As the poor-white problem continued, the Dutch Reformed Church started in 1916 to throw its weight behind the back-to-the-land movement. Official government policy encouraged rural retention and resettlement of Afrikaners. Government assistance took several forms: aid for farmers, welfare grants, educational facilities, and protection against nonwhite competition in rural areas.

Relocation alone offered little opportunity for poor whites; they found considerable competition from rural blacks. Prime Minister Louis Botha and his minister of native affairs, Gen. J. B. M. Hertzog, traveled throughout the countryside urging white farmers to fire their black workers and replace them with poor whites. This admonishment fell on deaf ears because farmers had little incentive to do so. First of all, black workers were cheaper and more reliable; and second, many poor whites were unwilling to do *kaffirwerk* (the American translation would be "nigger work").

MILITANT UNIONISM AND THE COLOR BAR

Fear of competition, poverty among whites, and erosion of the color bar laws of the Transvaal Ordinances gave rise to militant unionism, particularly on the Rand. The earliest union on the scene was the (mostly British) South African Mine Workers Union (MWU), formerly the Transvaal Miners Association. In May 1907, a violent strike, which in one month included 20 percent of the white miners, hit the Rand mines—inflicting murder, property destruction, and sabotage. The strike was caused by the substitution of blacks for white workers. The Smuts/Botha government seized the opportunity to use 1,250 Afrikaners as trainees in the mines. These men were viewed as "scabs" by the predominantly British members of the Mine Workers Union.

The use of scabs, the arrival of imperial troops to maintain order, a change in mine regulations so that unqualified men could do certificated work, and a lockout by the mines finally broke the strike.[22] Afterward—in a gesture of peace to the skilled miners—the government introduced Transvaal Ordinance No. 7 of 1907 as a measure to protect whites against skilled competition from the Chinese. But even while the Mine Workers Union was calling for the repatriation of Chinese, the Chamber of Mines was using the considerable influence of its most prestigious mineowner-member, Lord Nathaniel Rothschild, to try to delay Chinese repatriation from the Transvaal.

Whether there is any connection is anybody's guess, but during the same period in the United States there was similar union anti-Chinese sentiment (as there had been in the 1880s; see earlier in the chapter). In 1906, Samuel Gompers—by that time, leader of the American Federation of Labor—was calling for immigration restrictions against Orientals because he believed that "the maintenance of the nation depended upon the maintenance of racial purity and strength."[23]

Back in South Africa, Jan Smuts rejected much of the call for a "white labour policy." Seeing that state revenues and foreign investment depended on a profitable mining industry, Smuts felt that, if there absolutely had to be a white labor policy, it would be best achieved through government employment.[24] Siding with the Chamber of Mines, Smuts said, "The Chamber of Mines told me at the . . . interview that white labour was impossible; too expensive, too inefficient (in fact much worse than Kaffir labour) and too intermittent and too discontinuous. . . . The question is no doubt very difficult, as there is a sound sub-stratum of fact in the contention of the Chamber of Mines."[25] Despite the apparent contradiction involved in doing so, Smuts then called for the substitution of Afrikaner miners for those British unionists whom he felt had been corrupted by outside influences. Smuts thought that poor Afrikaners should replace foreign-born white miners, and he urged them "to go down the mines and oust the British workers."[26] His advice appears to have been taken. After the 1907 strike, the number of Afrikaner miners increased from 17 percent to nearly 25 percent. As a result of this conflict and their employment loss, the British trade unionists—led by Frederick Creswell—formed their own South African Labour party in 1909.

Labor unrest continued. In 1908, a long bitter strike took place at the Kimberly diamond mines, followed the next year by a strike in Natal protesting piecework rates at the government railway system. In 1911, a violent strike occurred among the Johannesburg tramwaymen and probably involved an attempted dynamiting.[27]

During the unrest in 1911, labor unionist William Henry Andrews called for the government "to protect against the encroachment of coloured labour in the skilled trades of South Africa," and added, that "the Government was guilty of a crime not only against the white people, but against the 'nigger' himself in forcing him to go to the mines and work for the benefit of the capitalist class."[28]

Introduction of the Color Bar

Fear of violence and unrest led the Smuts/Botha government to give legislative sanction to union demands for monopoly power. It was against the background of strikes and political agitation that the South African Parliament passed the Mines and Works Act of 1911—the first color-bar law. While ostensibly aimed at safety, the Mines and Works Act allowed the color bar to creep in through regulation. Certificates of competency were required for many kinds of work. In the northern provinces of the Orange Free State and the Transvaal, certificates of competency were not to be given to natives; and the few certificates issued to natives in the Cape and Natal provinces were invalid for use in the north. By 1920, there were 32 mining occupations—covering 7,057 employees—that were restricted to whites only. Union influence extended the color bar to 19 other occupations, covering 4,020 jobs.[29]

The color bar provisions of the Mines and Works Act of 1911 did not produce the desired results. Labor unrest continued. In 1914, some 19,000 white miners in the Rand mines—led by W. H. Andrews—went out on strike. White miners descended on the mine compounds and threatened black workers "to down their tools or be dynamited."[30] The attitude toward nonstrikers was expressed by George Mason, leader of the carpenters: "There is no scab for which there is not a pond large enough to drown him or a rope long enough to hang his carcass."³¹ By the time the strike ended, there were 21 civilians and six police and military personnel killed, and widespread property destruction.

World War I saw a large number of South African white miners enlisting for active duty. Non-European miners were used as replacements in some semiskilled and skilled previously "white" jobs, such as drill sharpening in the mines. During the summer of 1918, the South African Industrial Federation—on behalf of five unions—issued several demands to the Transvaal Chamber of Mines. One demand was that "Coloured drill sharpeners on the Witwatersrand be dismissed." The chamber said that there were only 74 drill sharpeners, and it refused to dismiss them.³²

The 1918 Status Quo Agreement

During World War I, about 25 percent of white labor force on the gold mines left their jobs for military service. This brought about two major changes in the labor force composition on the mines. First, there was a rise in employment of the relatively unskilled Afrikaners who were new to the urban industrialized areas. At the beginning of the war, these workers comprised 40 percent of the white mine work force; and by the war's end, they formed about 75 percent. Second, as a result of years of experience, many blacks were able to replace skilled British workers who had joined the military. It is estimated that between 5 and 10 percent of the black labor force had come to acquire certain mining skills.³³

Frequently, blacks taught whites skilled jobs, as suggested in this testimony to the Low Grade Mines Commission:

You may say that in many cases, the native teaches the white man his work underground?—Yes, in many cases I might say.

But how does that come about?—Well, a man comes from the backveldt and goes down the mine for six months. Sometimes he learns and he finally gets a couple of machines to work himself. He is not able to do it, and if he were not there the natives could do it. They are skilled machine men some of these natives....

And you maintain that the men from the backveldt know so little that the boys are teaching them?—It is quite clear that it is so. I can take you down and show you, any mine any time.³⁴

The employment of nonwhites in semiskilled and skilled jobs caused considerable tension and many strikes among white miners who feared displacement. White skilled miners demanded that, if black skilled and semiskilled workers were to be employed, *they should be paid the same wage as white workers.*³⁵ Less skilled—mostly Afrikaner—workers were against black employment in higher skilled jobs altogether.

In February 1917, the Mine Workers Union submitted a list of demands to the Chamber of Mines; included on the list was a call for the exclusion of nonwhite workers from semiskilled jobs. The Chamber of Mines rejected the demand by saying:

The question of the "colour bar," and the general economic and industrial relationship between the European and coloured population, is one of the most difficult of South African problems. The European population is naturally desirous of maintaining its position and retaining for itself the field of employment which it has held in the past. The coloured population, on the other hand, claims the right to work and to progress.[36]

The chamber argued that to deprive nonwhite semiskilled workers of their employment was immoral. Industrial leaders agreed—such as Lionel Phillips, who said, "the colour bar... should be abolished because it is irrational and immoral."[37] Repeatedly, the white miner unions demanded that blacks be dismissed from skilled and semiskilled work. And just as repeatedly, the Chamber of Mines rejected the union demands; the chamber would concede only to maintain the present ratio of black to white workers. Finally, in September 1918 the Mine Workers Union accepted this offer, which became known as the "Status Quo Agreement":

That the status quo as existing on each mine with regard to the relative scope of employment of European and coloured employees should be maintained, that is to say, that no billets which are held by European workmen should be given to coloured workmen and vice versa.[38]

The Mine Workers Union was not satisfied with the Status Quo Agreement, but it was part of a package deal favored by other unions that were also negotiating with the chamber. The other unions too, were not satisfied with the inroads made by nonwhites, but they saw the Status Quo Agreement as a temporary expedient to "prevent the complete flooding of the white workers' position until the nation can be aroused to the dangers of the present labour policy of the mines."[39]

The color bar provisions of the Mines and Works Act of 1911 already protected the skilled among the white miners against displacement by nonwhites. Therefore, the skilled were not so concerned with the problems faced by semiskilled and low-skilled white miners. The fears of the latter were expressed in testimony before the Low Grade Mines Commission. The Mine Workers Union said:

The existing colour bar, whether it is justifiable on general grounds or not... has always been looked upon by the European worker of these fields as a protection set up by law against the tendency of the system of indentured native labour to encroach upon his sphere of livelihood.[40]

The union added, "The native is cheaper and he is employed for that reason throughout the country.... One man gets 3s., and the employer says that he is doing as good for 3s. as the white man for 20s. He will obviously take the 3s. man."[41]

THE PRECIPITATION OF A CRISIS

During 1921, a sharp fall in the price of gold—from 130s. per ounce in February 1920 to 95s. per ounce by December 1921—helped to precipitate one of South Africa's most serious crises. The Chamber of Mines, which already opposed the color bars of the Transvaal Ordinances and the Mines and Works Act, was under pressure to accommodate rising costs and falling gold prices. The cost pressures had been present earlier, but premium prices for gold had postponed them.

The Chamber of Mines felt that, to prevent half of its member mining companies from going under, their profitability had to be restored. The mines sought to reduce production costs, but were facing limited means to do so. The pay of black miners was already low; therefore, a reduction in their pay did not appear to be a viable option. The other alternatives were to reduce the costs of employing white workers or to work both black and white workers harder. To do this, the Chamber of Mines was obliged to attack the gains that whites had won in working conditions, and to storm the color bar as well.

The Chamber of Mines chose two methods to reduce labor costs. First, it reduced white wages and laid off some white workers. Second, it began to substitute cheaper black workers—whose wages averaged one-tenth that of the whites—for white workers in semiskilled jobs. White workers complained about erosion of the Status Quo Agreement, particularly in occupations such as drill sharpening, winch and locomotive driving, timbering, and waste packing. The Chamber of Mines responded to the complaints with: "[A] certain proportion of natives . . . , by reason of their long mining experience character and ability, could be more usefully employed than they are at present."[42] What stood in the way of a more productive employment of these natives were the color bar laws. The Chamber of Mines representative on the 1920 Low Grade Mines Commission recommended complete abolition of the color bar.[43]

Mining regulations prohibited blacks from doing certain kinds of work without the supervision of a white. Often black workers were ready and available to work, but they had to remain idle because a white supervisor was not present. In other cases, the supervisory responsibilities of white workers were not consistent with the needs of the black workers. The Chamber of Mines thought that whites could supervise many more black workers than the law allowed. All attempts at reducing costs by more effective utilization of labor were thwarted or hampered by the color bar. As one mining official put it:

Is the colour bar the greatest stumbling block to the mines being worked profitably?— No, it is not the greatest stumbling block, but it is the only thing over which we have control which will enable the mines to continue working. The greatest stumbling block is the poverty of the ore.[44]

Slumping gold prices kept the pressure on the mining companies to cut costs wherever they could. Retrenching white workers with replacement by blacks and demanding more work responsibilities from both was a constant source of unrest, strikes, hearings, and conflict.

During the post–World War I period, South Africa saw a rapid increase in the cost of living. Between 1917 and 1920, consumer prices rose 50 percent. White unions were able to secure higher wages for their members, but black workers were not so lucky. Between 1916 and 1921, black wages fell 13 percent in real terms.

Industry leaders tried to persuade Prime Minister Smuts that fixed gold prices and the rising wages of white miners spelled disaster for the mines and for South African industry in general. The industry thought that the color bar should be lifted because blacks were just as good as white workers.[45]

After repeated failures at negotiation between the Chamber of Mines and the South African Industrial Federation (representing the miners)—and despite a warning from Prime Minister Smuts that the color bar must be treated as sacrosanct—the chamber announced that it would withdraw the Status Quo Agreement and would increase the number of blacks that it hired (10.5 blacks : 1 white), in an effort to cut wage costs. This move set into motion forces that were ultimately to defeat the Smuts/Botha South African party and lay the groundwork for the ultimate rise and supremacy of the Afrikaner National Party.

The Red Revolt

Before the turn of the century, there had been a socialist and communist influence during the spawning of South Africa's labor movement. The white labor movement remained in its embryonic stages during World War I, but continued to lay ground for the elimination of black competition. H. W. Sampson, the major architect of the Labour party's "native policy," said that South Africa should be divided into black and white states because black and white people are separate by nature and unfitted for social relationship and intercourse with each other. Sampson held that intermingling was not conducive to the moral or economic interests of either race. To Sampson, "intermingling" meant exploitation of whites by blacks who offered cheaper labor.[46]

Playing on the same sympathies in a speech to the Oranje Unie Conference on June 1911, General Hertzog—who later became prime minister through an alliance with the Labour party—said,

White men would sink to the level of the native—(applause)—and he would no longer be a white man.... In the nature of things the fittest would survive, but the fittest was not the European. The fittest was the native, who could live more cheaply.... Parliament would have to take steps to stop the kind of economic forces which was against the European and meant death of the white man.

Hertzog continued,

I am strongly in favor of the Native receiving full justice and every consideration apart from political equality and social fraternity.[47]

Increasing attention to the poverty situation among whites, along with the economic slowdown, unemployment, and the conflict between the Chamber of Mines and the mineworkers, gave to South Africa's communists and socialists the ammunition that they needed to organize and make their presence felt. In 1921, the Communist Party of South Africa (CPSA) was formed by a combination of preexisting organizations such as the International Socialist League, the Social Democratic Federation of Cape Town, the Communist Party of Cape Town, the Jewish Socialist Society (Poalei Zion) of Johannesburg, and the Marxian Club of Durban.

In addition to the unrest among whites, there was black labor unrest as well. In a 1920 action, 71,000 black miners struck for higher wages and to protest the color bar laws. The demonstration was put down with the aid of the South African Mounted Rifles and the use of strikebreakers. There was a peaceful return to work, but no increase in black wages. By the strike's end, three people had been killed, and 50 wounded; a dozen of the wounded were government men.[48] But the labor unrest was not over.

Early in 1922, communist and socialist white miners called for a general strike on the Rand. This turned out to be the most violent strike in South Africa's history; it became known as the Red Revolt or the Rand Rebellion. The 20,000 white miners on strike were fighting against two forces: black miners who were willing to work for lower wages *and* mineowners who were only too willing to substitute black miners for whites. Moreover, mineowners wanted to retrench 2,000 of the white workers. Led by communists and socialists, the white miners marched and protested through the streets of Johannesburg. They waved red flags and chanted, "Workers of the World Fight and Unite for a White South Africa"; they sang, "Red Flag."[49]

Led by W. H. "Comrade Bill" Andrews (who in 1910 had organized the Amalgamated Society of Engineers, was now secretary of the white miners' Council of Action, and would later be the first CPSA secretary), white miners and communists called for an overthrow of the government as they roamed the streets committing robbery and arson.[50] In part, this action was a Marxist revolution organized by white workers to prevent the Chamber of Mines from hiring black semiskilled workers. A manifesto issued by the Communist party at the time of the revolt declared that, "without necessarily identifying itself in every slogan heard in this strike, the Communist Party of South Africa gladly offers its assistance to the Strike Committee, convinced that essentially this is a fight against the rule of the capitalist class."[51]

During the unrest, strikers wandered through Johannesburg and the surrounding district making unprovoked attacks on blacks and coloreds[52]—an action that the Industrial Federation and the Council for Action blamed on agents provocateurs.[53] The strikers made these attacks despite having been warned by Andrews earlier that racial hate was not to be flouted, lest it allow the capitalist to compensate the coloreds with employment.[54]

In contrast, Sidney Bunting—an influential leader in the South Africa Communist party—appealed to whites to combine with blacks and make a unified labor effort against capitalists, but his call meant nothing to privileged white workers. Moreover, there was little sympathy for Bunting's appeal even among his comrades. One communist writer said:

Although the cry for a "White South Africa," which became the chief slogan in the dispute, appears reactionary on the surface, it was nevertheless founded on a sound working class instinct. The "White South Africa" slogan embodied a defence against capitalist aggression and was a challenge against the capitalist class. That the White workers saw no identity of interest with the Black workers and were not prepared to cooperate with them was a concrete reality of the time and had to find its expression.[55]

Edward Roux tells of his father—who was a South African socialist during the Rand Rebellion— boasting, "After the revolution they [blacks] will be segregated in their own territories where they will grow food under expert guidance."[56]

In March 1922, the Industrial Federation held a meeting of the mineworkers to decide whether to end the strike or not. Not only was there a no vote, but it was also decided to call on other workers to strike in sympathy. The deadlock with the Chamber of Mines, along with the strong show of government police force, provoked strikers into attacking police stations. In fact, the strikers held control of most of the Witwatersrand for several days. Martial law was proclaimed. Government troops moved in, and there was open warfare between 7,000 government troops and the striking miners. The South African government used massive force, which included aerial bombing and an artillery barrage of union headquarters. When the Red Revolt was finally quelled, between 200 and 250 people—200 of whom were whites—were dead, and hundreds more wounded.

White feelings ran high against the Smuts government, which was criticized for brutally suppressing the rebellion. Government leaders were seen as "sellouts" to the capitalist mineowner's interests. Communists and Afrikaners alike labeled Smuts as a "puppet of Goldbugs." After the 1922 rebellion, the communists and Afrikaner miners threw their political support to General Hertzog and Daniel F. Malan.

Victory for the Mining Companies

After the Rand Rebellion was put down, the Chamber of Mines—in open defiance of the 1918 Status Quo Agreement—began a campaign to substitute black labor for the more expensive white labor. Moreover, on the advice of its counsel, the Chamber of Mines decided to challenge the color bar provisions of

Table 3.1
Selected Mine Employees by Race

	1921 (Dec.) White	African	1924 (Sept.) White	African
Drill-sharpening	397	1,583	297	2,526
Winch driving	99	382	32	547
Locomotive driving	90	361	67	523
Timbering	1,253	12,253	864	14,439
Waste-packing	312	3,276	67	4,791
Pipe fitting & plate-laying	695	5,210	461	6,346

Source: Frederick A. Johnstone, *Class, Race and Gold* (London: Routledge & Kegan Paul, 1976), p. 139.

the Mines and Works Act of 1911.[57] In August 1923, a manager of the Crown Mine—named Hildick-Smith—was charged in the magistrate's court of contravening the color bar by permitting a black worker to operate an underground electric locomotive. The magistrate acquitted Hildick-Smith on the grounds that the regulation in question was ultra vires because it was racially discriminatory and because, while the Mines and Works Act permitted the government to make regulations, it did not sanction racially discriminatory regulations.[58] The attorney general who was representing the government appealed to the Supreme Court. Ruling in favor of the magistrate's verdict, Justice Frederick E. T. Krause said:

But, here, Regulation 179 does not discriminate between persons so employed and entitled to be so employed because of their skill or want of skill or other personal disqualifications; it absolutely prohibits a large section of the population from being so employed at all, because the colour of their skin does not happen to be white.[59]

The Hildick-Smith decision dealt a powerful blow to both the union and the color bar. Mineowners began to substitute cheaper black labor for more expensive white labor—a move made even more compelling by the falling price of gold.

Mine unions complained about the decline in white employment relative to black employment. The Engine Drivers Association complained that between 1921 and 1924 the number of white hauling drivers fell from 781 to 703 while, at the same time, black hauling drivers rose from 170 to 461. The Reduction Workers Association complained that during that same period their workers experienced a fall in employment from 1,825 to 1,454 while the number of black workers employed in reduction works rose from 7,971 to 9,722.[60]

Table 3.1 shows other substitutions of black for white mineworkers during the period 1921–24. Not only were the mines substituting black for white labor, they were demanding greater responsibilities from the white workers. Where there had once been one white pipe fitter per mine level, this was now changed to one white pipe fitter per four mine levels. Where there had once been several white timbermen per mine level, by 1924 there was one timberman per two or three levels.[61] The additional work load made it more probable that white miners would select bossboys—black foremen—a process that tended to exacerbate the competitive problems of white miners in that it fostered skills acquisition among black workers. One mineworker lamented, "The coloured man is gradually encroaching on that sphere of work—Yes, he is taking it all, slowly, it is true, but he is still taking it."[62]

The Chamber of Mines had won a significant battle against the color bar, but it would lose the color bar war. The violent strike and the attack on the privileged positions of white workers became a permanent memory and was to become a permanent justification for apartheid, job reservation, and the civilized labor policy.

THE UNHOLY ALLIANCE

By 1923, the Smuts government had incurred considerable resentment along several fronts. First, there was the continuing resentment on the part of the mineworkers whose strike had been brutally suppressed the previous year. Workers were dissatisfied with the Chamber of Mines' decision to nullify the Status Quo Agreement and with the Supreme Court's finding that the color bar provisions of the Mines and Works Act were unconstitutional. Both decisions angered Afrikaners who believed in the principle of white supremacy. On top of this, a severe drought was depressing farm income, a worldwide slump had caused a fall in trade, and declining revenues forced the government to lay off workers and raise taxes.

The Smuts government—the South African party—was rapidly losing popularity and power. Between February 1921 and March 1924, the Smuts majority in the House of Assembly fell from 24 members to eight. Jan Smuts was increasingly accused of reflecting the interests and views of South Africa's British minority. Smuts regarded his country's communist movement as hostile and subversive. On the other hand, the Afrikaner National party viewed Bolshevism with pronounced sympathy at that time. General Hertzog saw Bolshevism as "The will of the people to be free." He declared that some people wanted to "oppress and kill Bolshevism" because "national freedom means death to capitalism and imperialism."[63]

Hertzog's National party was the official opposition party in the Parliament. Hertzog gave his support to the Labour party—headed by Frederick Creswell, a socialist union man who stood for white labor policy and the color bar—in its condemnation of Smuts. The National party aimed its appeal to British and Afrikaner poor whites, many of whom had formerly been supporters of Smuts's South African party.

Therefore, the Labour party (which was modeled on its British counterpart) and the National party joined in denouncing the Smuts regime and called for the formation of a Nationalist–Labour alliance to defeat the South African party in the next elections. Negotiations proceeded smoothly, and a coalition—the Nationalist–Labour Pact—was announced on April 23, 1923.

The Elections of 1924

In 1924—against the advice of his counsel—Smuts dissolved Parliament and called for a general election. It was a hard-fought, bitter election. Hertzog openly courted the communists and socialists.[64] In a gesture of political deception of the highest magnitude, his colleague Daniel Malan extolled the "true patriotism" of the "Native" whom he declared was "entitled to take his place side by side with the Nationalist in the common political arena."[65]

The campaign was characterized by vitriolic accusation and counteraccusation. According to Hertzog, Jan Smuts was "The man whose hands dripped with the blood of his own people."[66] Hertzog talked about how Smuts and the South African party planned to allow blacks to push white men out of their jobs. He accused the Cape *Times*—a leading English-language newspaper—of advocating Kaffir supremacy.[67] For his part, Smuts labeled the Pact as an "Unholy alliance between Christian Afrikaners and Bolsheviks."[68]

In the general elections of June 1924, the coalition led by Gen. James Hertzog and Col. F. H. P. Creswell won; it formed what came to be known as the "Pact" government.

The Pact Government Labor Laws

In 1923, the Smuts government commissioned the Industrial Board to study the 1922 disturbances and make legislative proposals for protecting white workers. The Industrial Conciliation Act of 1924 was an outgrowth of the board's work. It was introduced as a bill in the House of Assembly in 1923 while Smuts was still in power, and became legislation in April 1924—several months before the dissolution of the Smuts/Botha government in June 1924.

Therefore, the ICA of 1924—though frequently associated with the Pact government—had its origins with Smuts/Botha and was only implemented by the Pact government. The purpose of the ICA was "To make provision for the prevention and settlement of disputes between employers and employees by conciliation; for the registration and regulation of trade unions and private registry offices and for other incidental purposes." The ICA made the registration of white trade unions a requirement. It excluded blacks from the definition of "employee"; therefore, blacks were barred from registration and, hence, from participation in collective bargaining. Other than the exclusion of blacks from the definition of employee, the ICA had no other explicitly racial barriers. Nonetheless, it was powerful in its racial effects.

The mineworkers demanded that the new government change the Mines and Works Act so that "It *shall be* lawful to frame Regulations discriminating between white and coloured workers."[69] They wanted regulations changed to prevent the mines from demanding more work from white workers and to prevent replacement by blacks. Moreover, the Mine Workers Union demanded the establishment of a minimum wage law (a "rate for the job" law), and—should that be not possible—as an alternative, they wanted racially discriminatory job laws codified. In the words of the Mine Workers Union:

The real point on that is that whites have been ousted by coloured labour. It is not because a man is white or coloured, but owing to the fact that the latter is cheap. It is now a question of cheap labour versus what is called "dear labour," and we consider we will have to ask the commission to use the word "colour" in the absence of a minimum wage, but when that [minimum wage] is introduced we believe that most of the difficulties in regard to the coloured question will automatically drop out.[70]

The urban working-class whites of the Labour party and the agrarian interests of the National party found it easy to agree on the Pact's civilized labor policy. However, disagreements arose with regard to racial legislation. The socialists in the Labour party accepted the color bar legislation as a necessary device to protect wage standards. They did not want what they saw as greedy, profit-driven mineowners throwing whites out of their jobs and replacing them with low-paid blacks. On the other hand, the Nationalists saw the legislation as having another purpose: "to keep the kaffir in his place." They thought that blacks' only purpose was to serve whites and that all measures must have as their primary focus the furtherance of white interests and survival. These differences in their purposes led to great divisions between the Labourites and the Nationalists later on.

However, this was not before the Pact government managed to introduce the second "Colour Bar Act." Despite the Chamber of Mines' heavily financed campaign against the new legislation—and its own stance *against* the color bar—the Parliament passed the Pact amendments to the Mines and Works Act in 1926.

This was no easy task. While the second Colour Bar Act passed the South African House of Assembly twice with large majorities, it was rejected by the Senate on both occasions. The South African party—the now opposition party led by Smuts—had considerable power in the Senate. Smuts and his party were not concerned about the ends—white supremacy—so much as they were about the means. Smuts argued,

Make no mistake, my whole political effort and public life in this country has been to establish and render firm and secure white civilisation in this country. But there are ways of doing it and the question is whether this Bill and the statutory enactment of this colour bar . . . is the way to establish the white position in South Africa. I am very doubtful about it.[71]

The South African party opposed statutory discrimination for several reasons: (1) It would embarrass South Africa in the eyes of the world; (2) it would earn whites the hatred of all the other communities; and (3) it was redundant since racial domination—the party felt—had already been achieved de facto. Some members of Parliament also advanced practical arguments against statutory provisions for discrimination. They said that: (1) the bill would create hate and agitation among the black population, and (2) this artificial protection to poor whites would lead to failure since the only real job protection was in efficiency and hard work.

Those in the South African party who argued against statutory discrimination but were also white supremacists saw it as a flimsy protection for whites in the face of economic realities that would lead to its widespread contravention. They felt that, after a while, the new Wage Act (see below) would make legalized racial discrimination unnecessary since it would mandate wages exceeding black productivity, and hence the incentive for hiring blacks in those jobs would be reduced.

None of these arguments won the debate. The new Mines and Works Act of 1926 was enacted into law. Its effect was to reverse the earlier victory of the mining establishment in the Hildick-Smith decision against the color bar—where the court held that the 1911 Mines and Works Act provisions did not sanction racially discriminatory regulations.

In other areas, the color bar protection for whites was reinforced—in effect—by the Wage Act. Under the provisions of the 1925 Wage Act, in industries where whites were not unionized, rate for the job (minimum wages) could be instituted by determinations of the Wage Board. The Wage Act was explicit in excluding discrimination on the grounds of race or color. The sponsors made it clear that their purpose was to eliminate what they called "competition between higher civilization and lower civilization." But in application, the act was clearly racist. The Wage Board concentrated its wage determinations only on those areas of industry where nonwhites were in competition with whites, and made no wage determinations in areas where there was no such competition. Despite the nondiscriminatory language of the Wage Act, it became one of the most effective weapons in the hands of South Africa's racists, as will be discussed in Chapter 4.

Outside mines, blacks had dominated several important industries. The color bar and wage legislations sought to give whites a competitive advantage. In 1920, out of a total manufacturing work force of 103,985, black employment was 70,582 while white employment was 33,403—a black to white ratio of 2.1:1. By 1940, the total work force *rose* to 239,412, with black employment at 151,735 and white at 87,667; but the black/white ratio *fell* to 1.73:1.[72] In 1911, the South African Board of Railways work force was 93 percent black workers. By 1916, black employment fell to 81 percent; and by 1936, it had fallen to 73 percent of the work force.[73]

SUMMARY

A considerable amount of popular opinion concludes that apartheid is the South African government's way of providing its powerful industrialists with a source of cheap labor. While this may be true with respect to the Land Act of 1911, it cannot explain why the government enacted laws—such as the Wage Act—that would certainly *raise* the cost of black labor. Moreover, the theory that government caved in to the industrialists does not explain the political demise of Prime Minister Smuts and the South African party, who were staunch supporters of powerful industrialist interests in both the financial and political arenas. Even today, financial giants like Harry Oppenheimer, backer of the Progressive party, are all but impotent in shaping South Africa's political forces. Furthermore, as will be more fully documented in the next two chapters, the view that legalized discrimination was implemented to serve South African industrialists cannot explain why legalized discrimination encountered so much resistance, contravention, and evasion by English—and ultimately Afrikaner—businessmen throughout the country and why white supremacist workers saw the payment of *low* wages to blacks as exploitation of the whites.

NOTES

1. Sheila T. van der Horst, *Native Labour in South Africa* (London: Frank Cass, 1971), p. 157.
2. Elaine Katz, "White Workers' Grievances and the Industrial Colour Bar," *South African Journal of Economics* 42, 2 (June 1974): 146.
3. Ibid., p. 147.
4. van der Horst, *Native Labour*, p. 163.
5. Roger Leys, "South African Gold Mining in 1974: The Gold of Migrant Labour," *African Affairs* 74, 295 (April 1975): 207.
6. See Mats Lundahl and Eskil Wadensjo, *Unequal Treatment: A Study in the Neoclassical Theory of Discrimination* (New York: New York University Press, 1984), pp. 215–16.
7. Cited in Robert Higgs, *Competition and Coercion: Blacks in the American Economy 1865–1914* (London: Cambridge University Press, 1977), p. 48.
8. Ibid.
9. Ibid.
10. Ibid.
11. Katz, "Workers' Grievances," p. 147.
12. Edward Roux, *Time Longer than Rope: A History of the Black Man's Struggle for Freedom in South Africa* (Madison: University of Wisconsin Press, 1964), p. 124.
13. *Samuel Gompers' Papers*, vol. 1: *The Making of a Union Leader, 1850–86*, edited by Stewart B. Kaufman (Chicago: University of Illinois Press, 1986), pp. 300–301.
14. Frederick A. Johnstone, *Class, Race, and Gold: A Study of Class Relations and Racial Discrimination in South Africa* (London: Routledge and Kegan Paul, 1976), p. 72.
15. Ibid., p. 152.
16. van der Horst, *Native Labour*, p. 173; also Francis Wilson, "Farming, 1866–1966," in the *Oxford History of South Africa*, vol. 2, edited by Monica Wilson and Leonard Thompson (New York: Oxford University Press, 1971), pp. 116 and 127.
17. David Welsh, "The Growth of Towns," in the *Oxford History of South Africa*,

vol. 2, edited by Monica Wilson and Leonard Thompson (New York: Oxford University Press, 1971), p. 182.

18. van der Horst, *Native Labour*, p. 174.

19. Ibid., p. 175.

20. Cited in W. F. J. Steenkamp, "Labour Problems and Policies of Half a Century," *South African Journal of Economics* 51, 1 (December 1983): 74.

21. Ibid.

22. David Yudelman, "Lord Rothschild, Afrikaner Scabs, and the 1907 Strike," *African Affairs* 81, 323 (April 1982): p. 257.

23. See Walter E. Williams, *The State against Blacks* (New York: McGraw-Hill, 1982), p. 108.

24. Yudelman, "Lord Rothschild," p. 261.

25. Ibid.

26. Ibid., p. 265.

27. Hutt, *Economics of the Colour Bar*, pp. 61–62.

28. Roux, *Time Longer than Rope*, p. 124.

29. van der Horst, *Native Labour*, p. 179.

30. Nathaniel Weyl, *Traitor's End: The Rise and Fall of the Communist Movement in Southern Africa* (New York: Arlington House, 1970), p. 60.

31. Ibid.

32. Alex Hepple, *South Africa: A Political and Economic History* (New York: Frederick A. Praeger, 1966), pp. 228–29.

33. Johnstone, *Class, Race, and Gold*, p. 106.

34. Ibid., p. 106.

35. Ibid., p. 107.

36. Ibid., p. 108.

37. David Yudelman, "Industrialization, Race Relations, and Change in South Africa," *African Affairs*, 74, 294 (January 1975): 87.

38. Johnstone, *Class, Race, and Gold*, p. 109.

39. Ibid., p. 110.

40. Ibid., p. 73.

41. Ibid., p. 72.

42. Ibid., p. 121.

43. Merle Lipton, *Capitalism and Apartheid: South Africa, 1910–84* (Totowa, N.J.: Rowman and Allanheld, 1985), p. 113.

44. Johnstone, *Class, Race, and Gold*, p. 125.

45. Yudelman, "Industrialization, Race, and Change," p. 87.

46. Martin Legassick and Duncan Innes, "Capital Restructuring and Apartheid: A Critique of Constructive Engagement," *African Affairs* 76, 305 (October 1977): p. 466.

47. Ibid., p. 467.

48. Francis Wilson, *Labour in the South African Gold Mines 1911–1969* (London: Cambridge University Press, 1972), pp. 9–10.

49. Roux, *Time Longer than Rope*, p. 148.

50. Leon Louw and Frances Kendall, *South Africa: The Solution* (Bisho, Ciskei: Amagi Publications, 1986), p. 37.

51. John Cope, *South Africa* (New York: Frederick A. Praeger, 1967), p. 157.

52. Peter Dreyer, *Martyrs and Fanatics: South Africa and Human Destiny* (New York: Simon and Schuster, 1980), p. 136.

53. Hepple, *South Africa: History*, p. 231.
54. Roux, *Time Longer than Rope*, p. 127.
55. Dreyer, *Martyrs and Fanatics*, p. 137.
56. Ibid., p. 136.
57. Katz, "Workers' Grievances," p. 147.
58. I. Abedian and B. Standish, "Poor Whites and the Role of the State: The Evidence," *South African Journal of Economics* 52, 2 (June 1985): 146.
59. Ibid.
60. Johnstone, *Class, Race, and Gold*, p. 139.
61. Ibid., p. 141.
62. Ibid., p. 146.
63. Weyl, *Traitor's End*, p. 73.
64. Dreyer, *Martyrs and Fanatics*, p. 137.
65. Ibid.
66. B. J. Liebenberg, "Hertzog in Power," in *Five Hundred Years: A History of South Africa*, edited by C. F. J. Muller (Johannesburg: Academia Press, 1981), p. 411.
67. Cope, *South Africa*, p. 103.
68. Liebenberg, "Hertzog," p. 415.
69. Johnstone, *Class, Race, and Gold*, p. 148. Emphasis added.
70. Ibid., p. 158.
71. Ibid., p. 164.
72. Abedian and Standish, "Poor Whites and Role of the State," p. 145.
73. Ibid., p. 148.

4
Market Manipulation to Support Apartheid

To help us understand some of the forces behind South Africa's apartheid labor policy, this chapter briefly reviews the standard economic treatment of labor laws and policies such as minimum wages, closed shops, and apprenticeship practices, as well as government regulation and taxation of business. Having done so, our attention will turn to how these government policies can reinforce racial discrimination and white privilege in South Africa.

MARKET INTERVENTION AND RACIAL DISCRIMINATION

Most legal intervention into the free market consists of restrictions on prices, wages, and profits, and on who may enter the market. These categories of legal intervention include minimum wages, occupational and business license requirements, union membership and apprenticeship laws, and regulation of profits in public utilities through regulatory commissions and in private industry through taxation.

Legal intervention in the market tends to interfere with individual wealth-maximizing incentives being used as a means to modify behavior and tends to focus more attention on personal attributes. Because legal intervention into the market causes people to place greater emphasis on personal attributes, it constitutes an effective means to subsidize racial discrimination.

Legislation that regulates wages is an effective tool in a racist's arsenal. Wage regulation is effective because it enjoys the benefit of at least four powerful forces: (1) It evokes voluntary cooperation with the racist goals; (2) it gives the appearance of being racially neutral; (3) it is relatively cheap to enforce; and (4) it sometimes enjoys the political support of the people whom it is intended to victimize, as well as their benefactors.

Typically, wage regulation sets a minimum hourly compensation for employment. Wage regulation can also be in the form of equal-pay-for-equal-work laws; collective bargaining agreements between management and unions fall into the category of wage regulation, too. Regardless of the particular mechanism chosen, the imposition of a wage below which transactions cannot occur will produce predictable effects—among them, discrimination against the labor services of some people. Legislated wage minima have the same economic effect as tariffs imposed on foreign products. Tariffs impose a minimum price under which no foreign goods may be legally sold. There is little economic difference between the efforts of tariffs and minimum wages; the primary difference is the rhetoric used to gain political support.

A tariff is fully recognized as a political tool of protectionism that seeks to raise the sales—and hence, income—of one group of sellers (domestic) relative to another (foreign). Tariff supporters are often explicit in the statement of this end. Typically, no such motivation is attributed to legislation calling for wage minima. The typical justification for wage minima is that of helping the "disadvantaged" seller of labor services.

No such plea is made when advancing the case for tariffs (minimum prices) on Japanese automobiles being sold in the United States, for instance. That is, none of the tariff promoters argue that they support higher prices for Japanese cars so that the Japanese autoworkers and managers can achieve a higher standard of living. The thrust of their argument is just the opposite: Protect one class of sellers (Americans) from competition by another class of sellers (Japanese).

However, the economics literature abounds with hundreds of academic studies and reports on the actual effects of legislated wage minima. Virtually all scholarly studies conclude that minimum wage laws discriminate against employment of the less preferred worker.[1] This conclusion is given added support by the professional consensus seen through a cursory examination of elementary economics textbooks. Indeed, when one is looking for areas of broad professional consensus in almost any subject, one should examine the elementary textbooks in the field. In the economics profession, most elementary economics textbooks containing any discussion about minimum wage laws conclude that their burden is borne by young, unskilled, and minority workers, that is, the less preferred sellers of labor services.[2]

A Race-neutral Example

A less preferred object of desire—whether it be a painting, a car, food, clothing, or a unit of labor—competes with a more preferred in open markets by offering what economists call a "compensating difference." Compensating differences simply refer to the age-old practice whereby sellers charge a lower price to offset what buyers perceive as a handicap.

Some people consider chuck steak less preferable than filet mignon. That puts chuck steak at a competitive disadvantage with filet mignon. The way that chuck steak offsets its disadvantage is by "compensating" the buyer. The chuck may sell for $2 a pound while the filet mignon sells for $5. The compensation that chuck steak makes to the purchaser is $3 a pound (the difference in price).

Therefore, if one chooses to indulge one's preference for filet mignon, there is a price to pay.

Suppose there were legislation mandating a minimum steak price: Economic theory could easily predict the outcome. Consider first an extreme case where the law called for both chuck steak and filet mignon to sell at the same price—say, $5—when market forces would otherwise have produced the prices of $2 and $5, respectively. In that case, chuck steak would be unable to offer a compensating difference for its less preferred status. Predictably, the buyer would have a reduced incentive to purchase the less preferred chuck steak. After all, if one can have filet mignon for the same price as chuck steak, there is little inducement to select the latter. Economic theory predicts that the chuck steak would become "unemployed," in the sense that customers would always discriminate against it and favor the filet mignon.

In our example, the reason for the discrimination is quite simple. Given the buyer's decision to purchase steak, discrimination costs nothing when $5 a pound will yield either filet mignon or chuck steak. Untroubled by economic considerations, the buyer selects what is most pleasing to him.

The above is a scenario where the cost of preference indulgence is zero. We might also consider variations on the cost. Again, imagine that free market forces would yield a $2-a-pound price for chuck steak and $5 for filet mignon. But the law specifies, say, a $3 minimum steak price. In that case, the cost to discriminate against chuck steak would be $2. If the law mandated a $4 minimum price, the cost of discrimination would be $1. The higher the legislated minimum price, the lower the cost of discriminating against the less preferred chuck steak.

The predicted effect of legislated price minima is a direct implication of the law of demand, which holds that, the lower the cost of something, the greater the quantity taken—and the higher its cost, the smaller the quantity taken. In our example, we can expect a certain amount of discrimination when it cost $3 a pound to discriminate, more when it is $2, still more when it is $1, and the most discrimination when the cost is zero. Regardless of the object of desire in question, there are no known exceptions to the law of demand.

The principle of compensating differences relative to minimum prices applies not only to nonhuman goods such as steak, cars, and paintings—but also to human services such as carpenters, lawyers, and mineworkers. Some people may object to the comparison by saying, "People are not cuts of steak and should not be analyzed as such!" Such a claim is without foundation, for the law of demand is generally applicable and applies to human services just as it does to goods. In this respect, the law of demand has the broad applicability of the law of gravity, which holds that the independent influence of gravity on the acceleration of a steel ball—say—is approximately 32 feet per second per second. The law of gravity is not invalidated by the cry, "People are not steel balls and should not be analyzed as such!"

Another possible objection to applying the principle of compensating differences to human beings may have to do with our notions of justice. Some people might ask, "Is it fair that some individuals, through no fault of their own, have to work for a lower wage in order to become employed?" Answers and agreement on normative questions like fairness and justice are beyond the special competence of economists qua economist. On the other hand, economic theory is competent to predict the effects of *not* allowing some people to work for a lower wage—that is, by destroying the opportunity to gain from compensating differences. Moreover, our ability to predict the outcome of policy may give us an important tool for untangling the thorny fairness question.

Wage Minima as a Labor Collusion

Most people think of minimum wage policy as a means to improve the market opportunities of disadvantaged workers. The following analysis will help us decide whether it can have other motivations, as well.

Assume that 100 yards of identical fence per day can be produced by either a black worker or a white worker. The black worker offers his or her services for $10 per day while the white worker demands $15. The fence-building firm that is seeking to maximize profits—even if its executives prefer white people to black—will find that their profits are higher if they choose the black worker. If the employer discriminates against the equally productive black worker, it will cost the firm an additional $5 per day in labor costs. Discrimination exposes this employer to competitive market pressures from employers who have chosen not to indulge their racial preferences and who are only too anxious to undercut their rivals.[3]

Under open market competition, demanding $15 per day would price the white worker out of the market. One strategy for the white worker is to seek legislation that mandates a minimum wage of $15 per day in the fencing industry. After the law's enactment, the firm's cost in discriminating against the equally productive black worker is zero. The law of demand predicts that the employer will then have greater incentive to act out his racial preferences and to discriminate against the black worker.

South Africa's Wage Regulation

Under market allocation of resources, price is the major determinant to resource usage—which is not to say that racial discrimination is absent. It is recognized that market allocation tends to exact a penalty from those who engage in racial discrimination. As such, the free market is no respecter of race, ethnicity, religion, sex, or nationality. By contrast, politics does respect these personal attributes. The privileges that politics can confer on certain people may explain some of the generalized hostility to markets.

A hostility toward market allocation of resources constitutes much of the history of South Africa. Time after time, other South African whites have complained about a behavior of the white industrialists that—in actuality—is precisely what one would expect in a market setting: little ethnic solidarity.

In 1925, the Mining Regulations Commission examined white employment in the mines and said that it had been reduced by a company policy of "maximising profitability through making the most profitable possible utilisation of ultra-cheap forced labour at the expense of white labor."[4] The commission concluded that it was necessary "to rescue the European miner from the economic fetters which at present render him the easy victim of advancing native competition" and that the white worker needed the protections of job reservation and other forms of race laws for the purpose of "counteracting the force of the economic advantage at present enjoyed by the native."[5] The economic advantage seen by whites was the native's willingness to offer compensating differences— to work at a lower wage. As a long-term solution, the commission's report proposed a minimum-wage-per-job system as a means to stem the competitive advantage of the black South African.[6]

It is interesting how, in pursuit of economic interests, men can triumph over irrational ideology. Apartheid is no exception to this process. In the face of cost-cutting moves by the Chamber of Mines—J. Seddon, the Mine Workers Union's first secretary, said, "If any wages had to be reduced, let the wages of black labour be cut down."[7] But by 1909, Wilfred Wybergh—a white supremacist and hence a staunch proponent of the civilized labor policy—was advocating that blacks be covered by the same industrial labor laws as whites.

To the naive, Wybergh's call might be seen as a longed-for change of heart— an improvement in South African white attitudes toward blacks. But the fact of the matter is that his stance reflected just the opposite. Economic theory could have predicted Wybergh's advocacy by inference; but in South Africa, inferences are unnecessary: We have explicit statements. Wilfred Wybergh was pressing for the extension of the Industrial Disputes Prevention Act to blacks, "because they were being made humble slaves [who were] therefore easier to be dealt with and more satisfactory to employers than white people."[8] He recognized that higher wages won by white unions placed them at a competitive disadvantage, thereby increasing the attractiveness of cheaper black workers.

Whites came to realize that the nonwage component of their earnings was also beginning to put them at a competitive disadvantage. Therefore it should not be surprising to find that, in 1912, the Labour party urged Parliament to extend compulsory employer compensation to blacks when they were injured on the job or suffered from miners' phthisis. The reason is obvious. The fact that the mine companies were not required by law to compensate blacks for industrial injuries made blacks cheaper to hire, thus providing additional incentive to substitute black workers for white workers. This is a variation of minimum wages: minimum nonwages. A fear of white "debasement" was shared among white workers and showed itself in legislation to entrench "civilised standards" through minimum wage policies.[9] White unionists "argued that in absence of statutory minimum wages, employers found it profitable to supplant highly trained (and usually highly paid) Europeans by less efficient but cheaper non-whites."[10]

The powerful market forces aligning themselves against the privileges of white supremacy were seen over and over again. In the *Anatomy of African Misery*, Lord Sidney H. Olivier lamented,

The imported European Mine Worker found himself in a community whose traditional first principle was and is that the white man is an aristocrat, admitting the black no equality in Church or State, and doing no manual labour; that the black is an inferior species of animal and must be kept so. He taught the black to stope, to work machine drills and sharpen tools, and all the jobs of the mine, and took contracts for work which the black man did under his direction—at Kafir wages.... The mine manager, however, does not see white men and black men, he sees only grades of labor—and it is the technique of his training, from which he could not depart, to try to reduce his labor costs by the most economical blending of dear grades and cheap. He had the impiety to attempt to take the Kafir out of his traditional South African place and use him to backleg the white man. Why not? He is not a sociologist or politician, he is a capitalist organizer of industry. South African racial tradition and trade union principles, therefore, invariably coalesce in demanding that the Kafir shall not be given such opportunity to improve his status. A conventional colour bar is established by collective bargaining in the mines, and it is demanded that it shall be made stable by the sanction of law.[11]

F. H. Creswell, leader of the Labour party, was convinced that white labor could be protected from the competition of black labor through a strict application of minimum wages, and rate-for-the-job legislation. Writing on the subject, G. V. Doxey concludes that "Of the legislation introduced by the Pact Government the Industrial Conciliation Act and the Wage Act can be regarded as a *disguised* application of these ideas [racial discrimination], but the Mines and Works Amendment Act must be looked upon as *undisguisedly* racially prejudiced in content."[12]

In fact, "equal pay for equal work" became the rallying slogan of the white labor movement. Edward Roux writes that Keir Hardie—a British labor leader—was greeted with rotten eggs during his visit to South Africa in 1907 because he advocated equality between whites and Indians. "He was afterwards allowed to speak, however, when the workers found that he believed in 'equal pay for equal work' regardless of colour or creed."[13]

When Creswell became minister of labor, he introduced the Wage Bill of 1925 with these words: "If our civilisation is going to subsist we look upon it as necessary that our industries should be guided so that they afford any men desiring to live according to the European standards greater opportunities of doing so, and we must set our face against the encouragement of employment merely because it is cheap and the wage unit is low."[14]

The Economic and Wage Commission of 1925 responded to the Wage Bill thus:

While definite exclusion of the Natives from the more remunerative fields of employment by law has not been urged upon us, the same result would follow a certain use of the powers of the Wage Board under the Wage Act of 1925, or of other wage-fixing legislation. The method would be to fix a minimum rate for an occupation or craft so high that no Native would be likely to be employed. Even the exceptional Native whose efficiency would justify his employment at the high rate, would be excluded by the pressure of public opinion, which makes it difficult to retain a Native in an employment mainly reserved for Europeans.[15]

Sheila T. van der Horst's findings tend to support the commission's conclusions: "Neither the Industrial Conciliation Act nor the Wage Act permits differential rates to be laid down on the ground of race. Consequently, where Non-Europeans, in practice principally the Cape Coloured, are employed as artisans they are subject to the same statutory minimum rates as Europeans. Wage legislation of the type has tended to restrict the openings for the less capable workmen and particularly for Non-Europeans as they are prevented from offsetting lack of skill by accepting lower wage rates."[16]

In the 1930s, white workers approved of the Wage Board's efforts to extend statutory minimum wages to nonwhites. Dr. T. H. Boydell, the Labour party minister for posts and telegraphs, explained that whites were being ousted from jobs by "unfair competition," particularly from the Indians in Natal. Boydell urged that employers be forced to pay to Indians the same wages that they were paying to whites.[17]

More recent South African history has seen an erosion of apartheid labor law—the result of which has been a renewed concern over black wages. Professional associations such as the South African Nursing Association have begun to demand the reinstitution of rate-for-the-job regulations. They condemn the low wages received by black nurses as "unfair" and as adversely affecting "the status and integrity of the nursing profession." Some branches of the nursing association—fearing that they will be priced out of the market—have gone so far as stating that their members (white nurses) *would not accept a wage increase until the wages of black nurses are raised.*[18]

With similar motives—and convinced that scrapping job reservation would mean a greater employment of black workers at the expense of white workers—Ben Nicholson of the Confederation of Metal and Building Unions has called for higher minimum wages as a test of employer sincerity.[19] Not to be outdone in the modern "concern" over low wages for blacks, the Railway Staff Association and the Surface and Underground Officials Association on the mines say that they would agree to relaxations in job reservation laws only if blacks promoted as mine officials were receiving the same wages and benefit package as white mine officials.

To the naive and gullible, these calls for more equal wages between blacks and whites appear as gestures of goodwill. Such a motivation is suspicious in South Africa. People are taken in by legislated wage minima—and that is no exaggeration. An organization no less prestigious than the International Labor Organization (ILO) gave its blessings to the Wage Act of 1925 because there was no mention in the act of "race or colour of the persons to whom it applies." The ILO publication went on to add:

From the standpoint of the dominant social purpose of the Act there are two outstanding dangers to be averted: (1) the undermining of civilised standards by the competition of low-paid low standard uncivilised labour; (2) the impoverishment of the country as a whole by the encouragement of a low level of productive efficiency.[20]

What is even more naive about the ILO's acceptance of South Africa's Wage Act as a racially neutral law designed to raise workers' standard of living is that the same article contains a brief acknowledgment of how the Industrial Conciliation Act of 1924 arose as a result of white fears that the "oncoming Kafirs" would replace white workers in the mines.[21] It seems the height of innocence to believe that the same white supremacists who one year were calling for the protections of job reservation would the next year call for racially neutral minimum wage legislation—now having also the interests of blacks in mind.

A U.S. Digression

In the United States, too, some of the whites who face competition from black workers have employed tactics similar to their South African counterparts. One of the most remarkable stories involves the extensive employment of blacks on U.S. railroads at the turn of the century. On some railroads—most notably in the South—blacks were 85–90 percent of the firemen, 27 percent of the brakemen, and 12 percent of the switchmen.

While the Brotherhood of Locomotive Firemen could prevent blacks from becoming members of the union, it had difficulty preventing them from being employed by the railroads. The high rate of black employment on the railroads had nothing to do with feelings of benevolence on the part of railroad owners and managers. Their reason for employing blacks is revealed by the following complaint of white firemen, "Everytime the firemen ask for an increase in wages or overtime due them, they are told by the superintendent, 'Why, I can get a Negro in your place for one dollar, while I'm paying you $1.50 per day.' "[22]

In 1909, the Brotherhood of Locomotive Firemen called a strike against the Georgia Railroad. One of their demands called for the complete elimination of blacks from the employment rolls. Instead of eliminating blacks, however, the arbitration board decided that black firemen, hostlers, and hostlers' helpers should be paid wages equal to the wages of white men doing the same job. The white unionists were delighted with the decision; they said, "If this course of action is followed by the company and the incentive for employing the Negro thus removed, the strike will not have been in vain."[23]

The power of wage regulation to promote racially discriminatory ends is seen in the famous "Washington Agreement" between the Brotherhood of Railway Trainmen and the Southern Railroad Association signed in Washington, D.C., in January 1910.

No larger percentage of Negro firemen or yardmen will be employed in any division or in any yard than was employed on January 1, 1910. If on any roads this percentage is now larger than on January 1, 1910, this agreement does not contemplate the discharge of any Negroes to be replaced by whites; but as vacancies are filled or new men are employed, whites are to be taken until the percentage of January first is again reached.[24]

This part of the Washington Agreement has all the characteristics of the Chamber of Mines Status Quo Agreement of 1918, when the South African Mine Workers Union was able to place a limit on the number of blacks employed in the mines. The slightly earlier Washington Agreement continued thus:

Negroes are not to be employed as baggagemen, flagmen or yard foremen, but in any case in which they are now so employed, they are not to be discharged to make places for whites, but when the positions they occupy become vacant, whites shall be employed in their places.[25]

This is the counterpart to the South African job reservation section of the agreement. The Brotherhood of Railway Trainmen—like their brothers in South Africa—recognized that "Where no difference in the rates of pay between white and colored exists, the restrictions as to the percentage of Negroes to be employed does not apply."[26] This section of the Washington agreement comes to the same conclusion reached in 1919 by the South African Mine Workers Union, which said,

The real point on that is that whites have been ousted by coloured labour. . . . It is now a question of cheap labour versus what is called "dear labour," and *we consider we will have to ask the commission to use the word "colour" in the absence of a minimum wage, but when that [minimum wage] is introduced we believe that most of the facilities in regard to the coloured question will automatically drop out.*[27]

Both the U.S. Brotherhood of Railway Trainmen and the South African Mine Workers Union recognized the power of wage regulation as a means to accomplishing racist goals. They both saw that setting a floor on wages could be more effective and politically cheaper than the imposition of quotas and color bars, in part because a legislated minimum wage is seldom seen as racially discriminatory and is hence more politically acceptable among decent people (even those victimized by it) and less subject to constitutional challenge.

Minimum wage legislation has a life beyond its first, racially discriminatory purpose. For example, at least some of the original motivations underlying today's Davis–Bacon Act, which was written in 1931, were racist in the same way as South Africa's Mines and Works Act of 1924 and its Wage Act of 1925—

namely, a desire to protect white workers from the competition of black workers. This is expressed in testimony by Congressman Miles C. Allgood before the U.S. Congress at the time: "That contractor has cheap colored labor that he transports, and he puts them in cabins, and it is labor of that sort that is in competition with white labor throughout the country."[28] Congressman Allgood was testifying in favor of the Davis–Bacon Act and its provisions, which mandated the payment of "prevailing" wages (minimum wages) for the various construction trades in all federally financed or assisted construction contracts.

UNION COLLUSION

There are a variety of techniques that unions use to restrict worker competition as a means to higher income for their members. Wage legislation is just one of these techniques, which fall broadly under two main categories. First, there is collusion with rivals, where unions seek to control all the workers in a particular industry. Second, there is statutory legal closings of markets, where the union is able to have laws written whereby every worker in a particular occupation must be a member of the union. Regardless of any other stated purpose, these tactics reduce the number of substitute workers available to the employer—which, in turn, raises the wages of union members to a level higher than that possible without the restrictions.

Higher than market wages create an incentive for other workers to enter the industry in order to enjoy the benefits. However, if these workers were permitted entry, the higher than market wage could not be sustained; it would be bidded down through worker competition. Therefore, every union must devise some technique to limit entry. Since union membership is not sold, membership criteria must—at least in part—be based on a worker's nonmarket or personal characteristics. There are many nonmarket criteria for including or excluding workers: nepotism rules, residency, skill, education, sex, religion, race, nationality, apprenticeship, and so on.

Unions face conflict not only with workers attracted to the occupation because of higher wages—who would bid the wages down—but they also face conflict with employers who would be only too happy to hire the cheaper nonunion workers. Therefore, in order for their collusion to be successful, unions must be able to forestall the hiring of their cheaper competitors. It is commonly believed that to accomplish their goals, unions employ the threat of strike. But the strike by itself is not the union's major weapon in its struggle for higher wages for its members. The major strength of labor unions lies in their ability to prevent employers from hiring other workers in their place. If the unions could not accomplish this, a strike would have the same significance to the employer as a mass registration: The employer would simply hire other workers. Unions must either acquire labor laws or else use violence and intimidation to deny employers the option of labor substitution.

The Industrial Conciliation Act of 1924

In South Africa, the central statute in the field of labor relations is the Industrial Conciliation Act of 1924 (amended in 1956). Under the ICA, industrial councils are established, made up of employer associations and union representatives. Industrial councils negotiate wage rates, hours of employment, and fringe benefits. Any agreement that receives the approval of the minister of labor has the force of law. Most of the time an employer/union agreement is automatically approved. At the discretion of the minister of labor, the provisions of any agreement reached by the industrial councils may apply to employers and employees in related industries who have not been a party to the agreement.[29] During the period of any labor union/management agreement, all lockouts, strikes, and other labor actions are illegal. The ICA also establishes a system of collective bargaining on all other matters of labor dispute.

Popular opinion in South Africa sees the ICA as reducing the power of unions. However, this is a misconception. The ICA gives the force of law to agreements reached between one segment of employees and their employers. Certain South African businessmen find their interests served by industrial council agreements, because all other firms in the industry are bound. Hence, through the ICA, companies maintaining a "civilised labour policy" enjoy a reduced competitive threat of being underpriced by other firms who can and would be willing to take advantage of cheaper labor.

Job Reservation

As W. F. J. Steenkamp has written, "The wage bar introduced into the secondary and tertiary sectors by means of the ICA and the Wage Act presently proved too flexible to exclude non-white competition from jobs that had come to be regarded as white preserves."[30] Therefore, the South African government was pressured to do something to restrict contravention of the spirit of the civilized labor policy.

In 1956, the color bar was rescued by the Section 77 amendment to the 1924 Industrial Conciliation Act. Section 77 empowered the minister of labor to reserve specific classes of work for specific races. The new Section 77 amendment was defined as a "safeguard against inter-racial competition." It stated that, should the minister deem it advisable, he may order the Industrial Tribunal (a body of five government appointees) to investigate "any undertaking, industry, trade or occupation or class of work" and make recommendations as to whether a color bar should be applied, and in what form.

The minister may then issue an official determination, which may: (1) prohibit the replacement of one race by persons of another race; (2) compel employers to maintain a fixed quota of a particular race; (3) reserve a class of jobs for members of a particular race; or (4) fix minimum and maximum racial quotas of persons to be employed in any factor, industry, or other place of employment.

(See Appendix 2.A for an example of a Section 77 determination in the building industry.)

The very first industry to be investigated by the Industrial Tribunal was South Africa's clothing industry. On the tribunal's recommendation, the minister of labor decreed that, from October 1957 onward, four categories of work were to be reserved for whites only. At the time of the decree, the jobs in question were held by 3,500 whites and 35,000 nonwhites. Given the shortage of white labor, it would have been impossible for the industry to replace the 35,000 blacks with whites.[31] Strict enforcement would have destroyed the clothing industry, but destruction was not the government's design.

After issuing its Section 77 determination in the clothing industry, the government granted mass exemptions that permitted businesses to continue employing nonwhites in white jobs; but in order to do so, each firm had to apply for a permit. Firms would be granted exemptions if they are on good terms with the government. Despite a legal quota of 25-percent black permitted in the four whites-only jobs, in 1970 whites were only 9 percent (10,577) of 115,000 workers in the clothing industry.[32]

Since the first job reservations in the clothing industry, Section 77 determinations have been made in 26 industries, including bartending (in Durban, Pietermaritzburg, East London, and the Western Cape), the building industry, the footwear industry, liquor and catering (the Cape and Natal), motor assembly, motor vehicle driving (Durban, the Orange Free State, and the Transvaal), passenger lift attendance (Johannesburg, Bloemfontein, and Pretoria), road passenger transport (the Cape), traffic police, ambulance, and fire services (Cape Town), and the abattoir section of the wholesale meat trade.

Section 77 does much more than discriminate against nonwhites. Economic reality says that job reservation can never be completely realized; there simply are not enough whites for all the positions that have been reserved for them. Alex Hepple argues that Section 77 is a system for government intimidation and control:

The Minister has the power to apply the colour bar to employment and then to grant and withdraw exemptions. In this way the government has given itself arbitrary power to direct labour at will and to compel employers to seek the Minister's favours to overcome labour shortages created by his orders.... Exemptions are in the gift of the Minister, and it is not surprising that applicants are careful not to ruin their chances by showing themselves to be opposed to apartheid or the government.[33]

Hepple points out that, just in the two years 1969 and 1970, the labor minister granted exemptions to 1,631 coloreds, 779 Africans, and 263 Indians—making them "temporary whites."

Job reservation never applied to more than 3 percent of the South African labor force. "The real power of job reservation"—claimed Robert Kraft, assistant general secretary of the Trade Union Council of South Africa (TUSCA)—

"is that it hangs over most employers as a threat.... The authority of this legal instrument far outweighs the very limited number of actual reservations."[34] Former Minister of Transportation Ben Schoeman has echoed the same sentiment and has referred to job reservation as a "sword above an employer's head."[35]

The protections of job reservation were extended also to the colored population. In the Western Cape—where there is a large concentration of Coloreds—the minister of Bantu administration and development says that Coloreds must be protected after white needs are met. In 1971, he warned employers against the illegal hiring of Africans; in an official document, the minister wrote, "No Bantu worker is to be placed in employment unless the employer has in his possession a certificate from the Department of Labour to the effect that Coloured labourers are not available."[36]

Two Section 77 determinations made in 1963 in the engineering industry were rescinded in 1968 when industry employers and its ten registered trade unions entered an agreement whereby "no employee shall be employed on work classified in this agreement at Rates A, AA, AB, C, or D unless he is eligible for membership of any trade union parties to this agreement."[37] Since—at the time—Africans were barred from belonging to any registered union, in effect the agreement excluded blacks from employment. The minister of labor hailed this as a "voluntary application of the principle of job reservation," and said that it had resulted from the "watchdog" Section 77.

Not everybody lived up to the agreement. In December 1970, the industrial council consisting of union and management—acting as watchdogs indeed—instituted prosecution for violation of the agreement against the Germiston engineering firm, for employing three Africans on molding machines. The director of the firm pleaded that he had advertised extensively for white workers to fill the positions but that all he could find were those who were unreliable and shiftless. When the white workers failed to show up for work, the director had allowed African assistants to run the machines. The firm was convicted and fined.[38]

One of the predictable effects of job reservation—and this was confirmed by Hepple—has been a massive turnover in white employment of 120–150 percent. Under the circumstances of an apartheid-driven demand, skilled white workers are being lured from job to job by offers of higher pay.

The Apprenticeship Act of 1944

Another method by which unions control entry is through apprenticeship requirements, which can be stipulated in the form of law, custom, or collective bargaining agreements. While these requirements may not be racially discriminatory in explicit terms, union control over apprenticeship can be—and has been—effectively used against racial groups.

There are several apprenticeship conditions frequently set by unions everywhere: age, sex, and citizenship requirements; length of apprenticeship; educational qualifications for eligibility; competency tests at the end of apprenticeship; nepotism rules on member sponsorship requirements; and an assortment of other provisions.

It takes little imagination to see how aprenticeship qualifications can be used in ways that exclude a particular racial group. The stated demand for apprenticeship laws in South Africa was to preserve skilled vocations for whites as "the inheritance of white men."[39]

The Apprenticeship Act (No. 37) of 1944—originally enacted in 1922—allowed white apprenticeship committees to seek and use a variety of techniques to block black entry into apprenticeship programs. The demand was even made that, in order for blacks to be eligible, they should be subject to a call-up for military training—to which blacks were ineligible.[40]

Though the act made no reference to race, it permitted the use of conditions that ruled out all but a few non-Europeans. When the act was passed, it carried a minimum educational requirement of Standard VI level (high school freshman) for indenturement—which automatically ruled out most non-Europeans. The few non-Europeans who did reach Standard VI had professional aspirations and were not interested in union apprenticeship.

Where there were closed-shop union agreements, blacks were also automatically ruled out. In order to be an apprentice, union membership was required; and until quite recently, it was illegal for blacks to belong to registered trade unions.

Moreover, custom and informal agreements between employers and employees called for only white youths to receive apprenticeship training. If an employer were to break the convention, the skilled white workers would not train the nonwhites.[41]

Other Union Tactics

Indians posed a considerable competitive threat to whites, particularly in Natal. White ingenuity in thwarting that competition knew no bounds. In 1955 Tom Rutherford, secretary of the South Africa Typographical Union (SATU), called for Indian membership in the all-white union after Indians had been refused—under the Industrial Conciliation Act—permission to have their own union. Again, the naive might see this as a goodwill gesture—a lessening of tensions and discrimination. Tom Rutherford, however, had his own vision behind Indian admission:

Up until 1927 we refused to have Indians in the Typographical Union. They then commenced negotiating separately and eventually practically eliminated the European printer from Natal. We took them into our union in order to stop that. The result is that I suppose you could count the number of skilled Indian printers in Natal on the fingers of your hand. They have almost been eliminated. That happened because we took them into the union. But when they were separate, they practically eliminated us.[42]

Bringing Indians into the union made them subject to the union-negotiated wage and work provisions, and therefore not able to undercut the wages of white printers as a means of making themselves attractive to employers. And yet even when coloreds and Indians were in the white unions, they were denied the full benefits of membership.[43]

Shades of the Color Bar

Statutory minimum wages do not always successfully exclude blacks from jobs considered to be that of the white preserve. Therefore, it was necessary to find other forms of exclusion. The Nationalist party chose numerous such measures, which were implemented with mixed success.

The Native Building Workers Act (1951) prohibited blacks from doing skilled construction in white urban areas. They were permitted by law to build only in black townships and reserves. Apprenticeship programs were permitted, and blacks could get certificates of competency if they passed the required tests. The statutory minimum wage for black artisans was about one-third that of white or colored artisans.

The fact of increasing black construction skills, along with the significant pay differential between black and white construction workers, made for forces that came to destabilize the statutory prohibitions against blacks doing skilled construction in white areas. In 1970, almost 40 percent of all building construction jobs were reserved for whites only. The Native Building Workers Act of 1951 was still effectively excluding blacks from working in white areas as skilled artisans or apprentices. By 1977, however, only 29 percent of building jobs were protected through job reservation laws. Job reservations had fallen victim to large-scale government exemptions that permitted building contractors in white urban areas to hire blacks.

Besides the wage differential between blacks and whites being a strong inducement for employing blacks (and their increasing skills), there also happened to be a great deal of public resistance to the rising price of housing. Moreover, there was an important split between the two major trade unions—which reduced the possibility for a strong united stance against black competition. The Amalgamated Union of Building Trade Workers supported rate for the job, while the Blanke Bouwerkersbond (White Building Workers Union) supported strict job reservation. Despite protests from the secretary of the White Building Workers Union, George Beetge, the government continued to grant exemptions to many building contractors—thus permitting them to hire blacks.

In addition to all the exemptions, there was a massive evasion and contravention of the job reservation laws. In 1974, the Industrial Tribunal reported that it found "alarming malpractices" on visits to building sites, with blacks "openly engaged" in nearly all classes of skilled construction.[44] During this period, hundreds of building contractors were prosecuted for contravention of the law but even more managed to escape. After a while, however, the minister of labour became more and more reluctant to prosecute job reservation violations, despite union accusations that there had been a "cold-blooded sellout" of white workers.[45]

The failure of job reservation to protect white workers from competition with blacks led Beetge of the Building Workers Union to plead that "There is no job reservation left in the building industry, and in the circumstances I support the rate for the job [paying whites and blacks the same wage] as the second best way of protecting our White artisans."[46] It is also interesting to note that coloured and Asian members of the Amalgamated Union of Building Trade Workers were "also seriously worried at the breakdown of job reservation."[47] Tom Murray of the Boilermakers Union—another prominent union leader—argued the merits of rate for the job (equal pay for equal work): "Job reservation is a dead duck, therefore the only protection is a policy of paying the rate for the job."[48]

PROPERTY RIGHTS, PROFIT, AND APARTHEID

Everybody has distinct preferences when it comes to the noneconomic factors of the workplace. People may prefer such amenities as stately offices, expense accounts, or long vacations. Similarly, employers have preferences when it comes to the noneconomic characteristics of employees—such as congeniality, religion, political party, sex, or race. Moreover, decisions regarding noneconomic worker characteristics—such as race in South Africa—can be imposed on the employer by the government.

Economic scarcity implies that indulging one's preference for a noneconomic work amenity will entail a cost. When a firm's owner or manager chooses stately offices, the sacrifice (cost) is lower money profits. Similarly, if the manager hires a "more congenial" white worker when an equally productive black worker is available at a lower cost, the sacrifice is again lower money profits. These costs are borne independent of the factors behind the selection. That is, if the employer voluntarily selects a higher cost white worker over a lower cost black worker, the employer foregoes higher profits; when government forces the employer to make this selection, the employer foregoes higher profits just the same.

Just how much racial preference will influence decisions—and subsequently, profits—partly depends on the property rights structure. To show how this structure can influence discrimination, we will briefly consider some alternative forms of property rights.

Property rights has to do with who can decide to acquire, keep, use, and dispose of property. When these rights are held by individual persons—deemed as owners—we say that property rights are privately held. Private property rights are never absolute; they are socially defined. When people are said to have private property rights, this means they can make decisions about their property in nonprohibited uses that do not interfere with the same rights held by others.

Some societies prohibit prostitution (of that most basic private property: the body itself), while others prohibit speculative commodity sales. Therefore, we should think in terms of the *degree* of private property rights, and how restrictions on it influence choice.

Profit Restrictions

There are several ways that private property rights to money profits can be restricted. One way is an outright ban on the earning of profits, such as in the case of government organizations; or a strict regulation of profits, as in the case of public utilities. Another way that private property rights to profits are restricted is through profit taxes. If there is a 50-percent tax on profits, then the private property rights to profits are reduced by 50 percent. This simply means the firm does not have property rights to that percentage of its profits. Restricted property rights to profits have predictable effects.

Consider a simple example. There is a transcribing firm whose inputs are one typist and the entrepreneur. The firm can hire a black typist for $50.00 per week or a white typist at $75.00 per week. Both typists are equally productive (typing, say, 60 words per minute).[49] We may even assume that the entrepreneur prefers white typists but will not indulge this preference at any cost.

In the first instance, we assume that the firm seeks to maximize money profits. Its balance sheet is given in Table 4.1.

Table 4.1
Profit Maximization without Taxes

Total Sales	Total Cost
$150.00	$ 50.00 wages
	$100.00 profit
$150.00	$150.00

Under the assumption that the firm seeks to maximize money profits, it will hire the black typist. Since they are equally productive, the cost to discriminate against the black typist would have been $25 in foregone money profits.

Now assume that all else remains the same but that the government imposes a 50-percent profit tax. If the firm continued to maximize money profits, its balance sheet would look like Table 4.2. The profit tax has reduced part of the firm's property rights to money profits by $50.00.

Table 4.2
Profit Maximization with Taxes

Total Sales	Total Cost
$150.00	$ 50.00 wages
	$ 50.00 tax
	$ 50.00 after tax profits
$150.00	$150.00

People always seek to minimize taxes. In an effort to increase their level of satisfaction, they will seek measures to reduce, avoid, or evade taxes. One legal method to avoid part of the profits tax is to shift one's choices toward nonmoney—and hence, nontaxable—forms of income. Both money and nonmoney income are forms of compensation, and hence can be substituted for each other. There are many examples of how people do this. When income taxes increase, more employees prefer to have more of their compensation in the form of nonwage benefits that are not taxed. Similarly, business owners facing higher profit taxes will prefer income in the form of nonprofit benefits.

Economics can make this prediction because a tax raises the cost of taking compensation in money form and thus lowers the cost of taking compensation in a nonmoney form. In our example of the transcribing firm, the 50-percent profit tax may give the firm an inducement to adjust its input selection.

Table 4.3
Optimization with Profit Tax

Total Sales	Total Cost
$150.00	$ 75.00
	$ 37.50 profit tax
	$ 37.50 profit after tax
$150.00	$150.00

Table 4.3 shows the firm indulging its discriminatory preferences by hiring the costlier white typist over the equally productive black typist. The firm optimizes by taking more income in a nonmoney form—that is, hiring what the owner sees as the more preferable worker.

Prior to the profit tax, to discriminate in favor of the costlier white typist meant that the firm would have to sacrifice $25 in foregone earnings—the white/black wage difference. After the profit tax, race discrimination only costs the firm $12.50 in foregone earnings. In other words, if the employer did not discriminate, the firm's money profits would be only $12.50 higher, as compared to $25.00 higher in the absence of a profit tax. With a lower cost attached to discrimination, we can expect to see more of it.

Taxes weaken property rights, and hence lower the cost of taking income in untaxed nonmoney forms. Other ways to take income in nonmoney forms include expense accounts for executives, ornate offices, and company-paid memberships to country clubs—besides hiring more pleasing and more costly employees rather than equally productive less pleasing and less costly ones.

The effects of restricted property rights to profit applies to organizations whose profits are regulated, such as public utilities; to nonprofit organizations, such as universities; and to government agencies, where the profit motivation is altogether absent. We can expect discrimination of all forms to be more prevalent in regulated and not-for-profit organizations.

The ability of discriminated-against people to modify the hiring behavior of a regulated company through lower wage offers is reduced, because the company's rewards (profits) for hiring them are constrained. Even more damaging to the discriminated-against person is that regulated companies can fund the higher cost of hiring a more preferred employee by going to the regulatory commission and demanding higher product or service prices to cover the higher costs. In government, this process can be carried to the extreme because there are no profits at all and the high cost of an employment policy can be shifted to taxpayers.

This suggests that—contrary to popular wisdom—constrained profit motives do not serve the interests of less preferred groups.[50] This conclusion requires no judgment on or even an acknowledgment of the personality traits of managers in for-profit organizations versus those in not-for-profit organizations. It requires only the acknowledgment that people's decisions are influenced by costs.

Moreover, this analysis applies not only to instances where profits are restrained but also where entry is restricted through licensing or franchise laws. When market entry is restricted—and hence, there are fewer competitive pressures—the hiring decision maker is under less pressure to make efficient input choices, and discrimination is cheaper. Also, when market entry is limited and regulated by the state, "Their [regulated businesses'] cardinal sin is to be too profitable."[51] Therefore, open market firms—with greater private property rights to profit—will place a greater emphasis on using resources at their most highly valued level because the market puts a price tag on selecting irrelevant criteria—such as race—a determinant of resource usage.

Apartheid Friends and Foes

Sheila T. van der Horst reports, "In Government employment, where cost is not the deciding factor, and the substitution of European for Native labourers has consequently taken place to a considerable extent, the 'civilized labour policy' has had the result of restricting the demand for Native labour."[52] There is some evidence that between 1924 and 1933 the number of European laborers hired by the Railways and Harbours Administration, which controls the government railways, rose from 9.5 to 39.3 percent (from 4,760 to 17,783). The number of Africans employed during the same period fell from 75 to 48.9 percent (from 37,564 to 22,008).

Other government departments experienced similar changes in their labor force. As van der Horst writes, "In 1937, they [government agencies] employed some ten thousand Europeans on types of work previously done by Natives, while employment was found on subsidized works for approximately the same number. The Public Works Department employed the policy of hiring only Europeans in the Orange Free State, Natal and the Transvaal as far as unskilled work for the central government is concerned."[53]

Private industry has been another matter: "Private employers, for whom cost is the fundamental consideration, have not shown the same readiness to follow the 'civilized labour policy,' and various official expedients have been adopted to induce and compel them to follow the lead set by the Government."[54] Since the incentive to discriminate is reduced in private industry, the government must use carrots and sticks in order to get firms to follow its civilized labor policy. Some of the methods that the South African government has used to induce compliance came in the form of subsidies and government manipulation of tariffs and customs, whereby firms received either favors or else penalties and government control of wages and other work conditions.

As discussed earlier, one way that the government forced firms to discriminate racially was through the Wage Act of 1925, which was passed as supplement to the Industrial Conciliation Act. The Wage Board fully understood that statutory wages would affect the racial composition of the labor employed. In its report of 1935, the Industrial Legislation Commission said, "It is, of course, plain that wage levels, though fixed without discrimination, do affect the race composition of employees."[55]

Statutory wages set by the industrial councils and the Wage Board had the effect of excluding those workers whose value to the employer was less than the wage rate. As the Industrial Legislation Commission explained,

In an unregulated market, the available supplies or the numbers determine the wage, but, under regulated conditions, wages determine the numbers and set in motion a selective process in which all who are not worth the determined wages must make room for those who justify the payment of that wage.[56]

Though there are not many statistics available, we do know that the wage determinations achieved some of their intended effects. According to van der Horst, in 1932 there were approximately 73,000 natives affected by wage determinations. Five years later, their number in such jobs had fallen to 69,000.

As one might predict, once statutory minimum wages had been imposed in one industry or region, there were calls for its extension to others. Employers forced to pay statutory minimum wages would complain of unfair competition from those paying lower wages.[57] The Wage Board once instituted an investigation into the depression of the textile industry in white areas. It found that textile factories near black reserves paid wages only 50 percent of those paid in white areas. The board concluded that the wages paid by these "unfair competitors should be raised."[58]

Employers who were forced to pay "civilised wages" also faced foreign competition from exporters who could sell their goods in South Africa at a lower price. This aspect of civilized wages was seen as early as 1911 when the Commission on Trade and Industries recommended that South African agriculture and industrial undertakings should be protected, on the condition that a "fair proportion of white labor" be employed. In 1925, in its report on revision of the customs tariff, the Board of Trade and Industries said that

the board has also had in view the use of the tariff as a means of encouraging the employment of civilized labour, tariff assistance in industries being partly conditional on good labour conditions and on the understanding that, whenever possible, a larger proportion of civilized labour be employed.[59]

Tariffs were used as a way of encouraging the development of secondary industry in order to provide employment for low-skilled whites.[60] In 1933, a divisional inspector of the Labour Department—seeing the benefits of tariff protections—advised thus:

It is the Minister's wish that the departmental officers should now do everything in their power to insure that industries maintain a fair ratio as between civilized and non-civilized labour, particularly those industries that have benefited as a result of protectionist policy of the Government.[61]

There was a marked contrast between the government's willingness to discriminate in hiring and that of private industry. No doubt there were white supremacists in private industry, but their sense of loyalty to white workers was not sufficient enough to withstand the voluntary forces of the marketplace. The reason for the different behavior and interests of white government managers and those in private industry is inferred from our discussion (above) of property rights. There is no wealth loss to the government official who hires a more costly white over a cheaper—and sometimes more efficient—black. The official gets the same pay, and the cost of discrimination is borne by the taxpayers. When the owner of a private firm does the same thing, there is a cost in lower profits and a reduction in the owner's private wealth. The evidence that private industry had less incentives to discriminate—compared to government—is seen in all the laws and bureaucratic machinery aimed at forcing private industry to acknowledge and promote white privilege. If voluntary discrimination could have supported white privilege, then it is difficult to explain the necessity for the costly apartheid apparatus.

PRODUCER COLLUSION

The Native Land Act of 1913 was another attempt to subvert nondiscriminatory market forces. The last decade of the nineteenth century saw a rapid increase in gold and diamond production. This provided a stimulus to the agricultural sector that was reflected in the rising prices of agricultural products. In order for farmers to cash in on the favorable economic climate, they required more black laborers. However, the very forces making for the boom in the agricultural sector (diamonds, gold, and railroad building) were also providing more attractive employment opportunities for black workers in the nonagricultural sector.

Farmers complained about the increased competition for native workers, who were leaving the Transkei, the Cape, the Orange Free State, and Natal to work for "exorbitant" wages on the mines, railways, and other public works. A typical complaint is made in the 1897 report of the magistrate of Weenen, who said:

The sole cause of the trouble continues to be the constant exodus of Natives to Johannesburg, where, attracted by the high wages paid them there, they persist in going, despite damages sued for by their landlords under their contracts and prosecution and punishment under the Masters and Servants (Native) Act on their return.[62]

This echoed the remarks of the Select Committee on Labour, which in 1890 had said that

the conditions of pay and other privileges offered to such labourers by those in charge of such works [railways and harbors] does materially and seriously affect the labour market to the detriment of both corn and wine farmers, especially at certain seasons of the year, such as pruning, winemaking, ploughing and reaping.[63]

Through the South African Agricultural Union (SAAU), farmers sought the tightening of pass laws as a means of restricting the mobility of blacks who were going to urban areas in search of higher wages in primary and secondary industries. The 1948 Nationalist government victory at the polls was due largely to rural support. The Nationalists paid off that support with tightened pass laws, and the "farm labour force swelled by the addition of convict labourers, largely resulting from pass law violations."[64]

The complaints of the farmers continued. Some were against the repeal of the Masters and Servants Act; others were against the mines recruiting labor from the rural areas. But by the 1970s, farmers had lost much of their political clout, and their complaints fell on deaf ears in Parliament. In 1976, the minister of Bantu affairs said, "It would be totally wrong to pass laws binding black workers to industries like agriculture and mining.... This outdated system was now totally unacceptable. It affected the basic freedoms and rights of individuals."[65]

White farmers not only saw competition for labor from other sectors of the South African economy, but they also saw direct competition from blacks as farmers. Van der Horst reports that, in 1874, natives serving major cities in the Cape Colony produced wool, hides, horns, tobacco, and cattle valued at three-quarters of a million pounds. The Basuto supplied 300,000 bushels of grain to the Orange Free State. The Pondo and Gcaleka produced and exchanged "considerable quantitites" of leaf tobacco. The natives were so prosperous that the magistrate in the area of Pietermaritzburg complained that the supply of native labor "has year by year become more inadequate, as the Natives become richer, and yearly cultivate a larger acreage with the plough, besides engaging in transport-riding on their own account."[66] At the turn of the century, Lesotho was known as the granary of the Orange Free State.

In 1835, the Mfengu, who had been displaced by the rise of the Zulu Kingdom, were invited into the Cape Colony by Governor Benjamin D'Urban, who—according to Louw and Kendall—said that

The "Fingo community" would supply military support against Mintza, the Xhosa paramount chief; the colony would gain the labour of "sober, industrious people, well skilled in the tasks of herding and agriculture"; the land in the Peddie district to which they were moved was "worse than useless" but, he confidently expected, would be turned into a "flourishing garden" by the newcomers.[67]

By 1858—just over 20 years later—508 blacks had purchased 16,200 acres of grain land, and another 6,000 acres were rented by 106 blacks. The success of the black farmers was noted in testimony before the 1865 Commission on Native Affairs: "Even this year (after the drought) I think their exhibition far surpassed that of the Europeans. It was a universal remark in the district that the Fingo exhibition far excelled that of the Europeans both as to number and quality of articles exhibited."[68] A Cape statistician noted, "Taking everything into consideration, the native district of Peddie surpasses the European district of Albany in its productive powers."[69]

Black competition threatened the market interest of white farmers. The Cape Assembly passed the Location Acts as a means to reduce the number of black squatters (tenant farmers) on white-owned land, in order to force more blacks to become wage laborers. These laws were widely evaded; and in 1893, the Cape Labour Commission looked into the labor shortage problem. They were told: "The natives are independent. They have land and they grow what they choose, and their wants are extremely small."[70]

Mineowners also complained about blacks' access to land. In 1911, the Chamber of Mines president said,

"He (the black) cares nothing if industries pine for want of labour when his crops and home-brewed drink are plentiful." He called for a policy to force the blacks into the labour force and urged the government to "do everything to encourage the native to be a wage earner by extending the policy of splitting into family holdings land now held in the native reserves under tribal tenure."[71]

In 1894, the Glen–Grey Act—proposed by Cecil Rhodes—which set a ten-acre limit on land ownership in the black reserves, became law. The effect of the law was to deny self-sufficiency to blacks, because the land was of such poor quality that ten acres could not support a family. In order to survive, the owner had to enter the work force. This tactic successfully reduced black farmers' ability to compete with white farmers. Charles Pamla, an influential black spokesman of the time, said, "No man is allowed to occupy more than *one* lot. This shuts out all improvements and industry of some individuals who may work and buy. . . . Surely Mr. Rhodes can't expect that all natives will be equal. He himself is richer than others; even trees differ in height."[72]

In 1899, an antisquatting Act 30 was passed, requiring white farmers to buy a £36-per-annum license before they could lease land to blacks. This act gave more clout to an earlier version of the Squatter's Law, which had prohibited (except by special permit) more than five African families on a farm. The law's purpose was to distribute the available black labor more evenly across farms. Under the Squatter's Law, the Native Commission could relocate blacks from one farm to the next. In answer to a request that the government drive blacks onto white farms as laborers, John X. Merriman—head of the South African party—said, "I would not drive them, but they will drive themselves when they get congested in land held under individual tenure."[73]

As Merle Lipton puts it, "The Land Act of 1913 destroyed a class of African tenant farmers in the 'white areas' and led to increasing population pressure in the homelands which, combined with taxes, converted many African farmers into labourers, migrating to white areas to work."[74] White farmers were subsidized and, in addition, had easy access to subsidized Land Bank loans; black farmers were not, and did not. Despite these and other advantages, white farmers continued to see themselves threatened by the existence of blacks in agriculture.

In 1938, the secretary of the Livestock and Meat Industries Control Board complained,

In practically all secondary industries and mining, the labour of the white man is protected against the cheaper labour of the Native. But in agriculture, particularly in the livestock industry, the White man competes with the Native on difficult terms . . . The Native . . . has free communal lands, and virtually no direct cost of production. It should be quite obvious that this White agriculturalist is up against one of the most serious problems that faces a White standard of civilization.[75]

In 1936—well aware of the dissatisfaction of white farmers with what they saw as dumping practices by the native, leading to lower farm prices—J. G. Strijdom (later to become prime minister) objected to a proposed purchase of tractors and ploughs for the black reserves, on the grounds that "If the Government went on this way, natives would soon cease to be labourers and become farmers, with disastrous effects on white farming, where the problem of markets was already serious."[76] In 1952, H. F. Verwoerd sided with the white farmers in a discussion on the extension of irrigation projects in the homelands; he acknowledged the continuing opposition of white farmers to "unfair competition" from Africans.[77]

Mineowners supported the Land Act because, by driving blacks from agricultural opportunities, it helped to ensure a cheap, readily available supply of unskilled labor. The president of the Chamber of Mines spoke in seemingly altruistic terms: "The surplus of young men, instead of squatting on the land in idleness . . . earn their living by working for a wage."[78] Mineowners rewarded tribal chiefs for persuading their subjects to go to the mines where they would earn cash to pay taxes, and traders encouraged blacks to buy on credit and pay their debt by going to the mines.[79]

As the mining activity in South Africa increased, mineowners continued to face labor shortages that brought them into conflict with farmers. Political confrontation between the two interests was avoided—or postponed—through the development of an elaborate migrant labor system, which actually enhanced the monopoly hiring power of the mining houses.

SUMMARY

To realize apartheid ideology requires inefficient resource allocation. Some producers and consumers are forced to choose costlier patterns of production and consumption. The fact that people seek wealth maximization implies a tendency toward least-cost behaviors. This suggests that even among people who generally consider themselves to be white supremacists, apartheid laws are bound to encounter strong market-force resistance.

White South African workers had to enlist the coercive powers of the government through minimum wage, rate for the job, and job reservation laws. These laws were meant to silence white worker complaints that they were being exploited by blacks willing to work for lower wages. As powerful a force for racial discrimination as wage and workplace regulation are, they were not powerful enough. Government had to implement many other measures—such as tariffs, licensing, and vendor regulations—in an effort to force businesses to acknowledge white privilege.

In agriculture, blacks had to be driven from the land to promote privilege for white farmers; and in mining and other industries, labor markets had to be manipulated with government backing to promote privilege for white industrialists.

Chapter 5 will continue where this one left off, showing us just how frustrating it has been to achieve apartheid goals—even among people who express general support for its aims.

NOTES

1. See, for example, J. Peterson and C. Stewart, *Employment Effects of Minimum Wages* (Washington, D.C.: American Enterprise Institute, 1969); J. Mincer, "Unem-

ployment Effects of Minimum Wages," *Journal of Political Economy* 84, 4, pt. 2 (August 1976): 87 ff.; J. Ragan, "Minimum Wages and Youth Labor Markets," *Review of Economics and Statistics* 59, 2 (May 1977): 129 ff.; E. M. Gramlich, *Impact of Minimum Wages on Other Wages and Family Income*, Brookings Papers on Economic Activity, No. 2 (Washington, D.C.: Brookings Institution, 1976), pp. 409 ff.; F. Welch and J. Cunningham, "Effects of Minimum Wages on the Level and Age Composition of Youth Employment," *Review of Economics and Statistics* 60, 1 (February 1978): 140 ff.; M. Kosters and F. Welch, "The Effects of Minimum Wages on the Distribution of Changes in Aggregate Employment," *American Economic Review* 62, 3 (June 1972): 323 ff.; J. P. Matilla, "The Impact of Minimum Wages on Teenage Schooling and on the Part-time/Full-time Employment of Youths," in *The Economics of Legal Minimum Wages*, edited by S. Rottenberg (Washington, D.C.: American Enterprise Institute for Public Policy Research, 1981), pp. 61–87; P. Linneman, "The Economic Impacts of Minimum Wage Laws: A New Look at an Old Question," mimeographed, Center for the Study of the Economy and the State, University of Chicago, April 1980; T. G. Moore, "The Effect of Minimum Wages on Teenage Unemployment Rates," *Journal of Political Economy* 79 (July/August 1976): 897 ff.; J. F. Boschen and H. I. Grossman, "The Federal Minimum Wage, Employment, and Inflation," in *Report*, by U.S. Minimum Wage Study Commission (Washington, D.C.: Government Printing Office, 1981), vol. 6, p. 19; J. S. Pettengill, "The Long-run Impact of a Minimum Wage on Employment and on the Wage Structure," in ibid., p. 64; J. C. Cox and R. L. Oaxaca, "Effects of Minimum Wage Policy on Inflation and on Output, Prices, Employment, and Real Wages by Industry," in ibid., p. 195; C. Brown, C. Gilroy, and A. Kohen, "Effects of the Minimum Wage on Youth Employment and Unemployment," in ibid., vol. 5, p. 2; J. Heckman and S. Sediacek, "The Impact of the Minimum Wage on the Employment and Earnings of Workers in South Carolina," in ibid., p. 253; D. Hammermesh, "Employment Demand: The Minimum Wage and Labor Costs," in ibid., p. 27; B. M. Fleisher, "Comments," in ibid., p. 85; R. H. Meyer and D. A. Wise, "Discontinuous Distributions and Missing Persons: The Minimum Wage and Unemployed Youth," in ibid., p. 198; J. R. Behrman, P. Taubman, and R. Sickles, "The Short- and Long-run Effects of Minimum Wages on the Distribution of Income," in ibid., vol. 7, pp. 105–6; W. R. Johnson and E. K. Browning, "Minimum Wages and the Distribution of Income," in ibid., pp. 31–32; L. P. Datcher and G. C. Loury, "The Effect of Minimum Wage Legislation on the Distribution of Family Earnings among Blacks and Whites," in ibid., pp. 125–26 and 149; David E. Kaun, "Minimum Wages, Factor Substitution, and the Marginal Producer," *Quarterly Journal of Economics* (August 1965): 478–86; Yale Brozen, "The Effect of Statutory Minimum Wages on Teenage Unemployment," *Journal of Law and Economics* (April 1969): 109–22; William G. Bowen and T. Aldrich Finegan, *The Economics of Labor Force Participation* (Princeton, N.J.: Princeton University Press, 1969); Edmund S. Phelps, *Inflationary Policy and Unemployment Theory* (New York: W. W. Norton, 1972); Arthur F. Burns, *The Management of Prosperity* (New York: Columbia University Press, 1966); Martin Feldstein, "The Economics of the New Unemployment," *Public Interest* (Fall 1973); and Andrew Brimmer, *Minimum Wage Proposals, Labor Costs, and Employment Opportunities in the Nation's Capital* (Washington, D.C.: Brimmer, 1978), which demonstrates the adverse employment and business migration effects of the minimum wage law as studied in Washington, D.C.

2. See, for example, G. L. Bach, *Economics*, 10th ed. (Englewood Cliffs, N.J.: Prentice-Hall, 1980), p. 526; P. Samuelson, *Economics*, 11th ed. (New York: McGraw-

Hill, 1980), pp. 369–70; R. G. Lipsey, *An Introduction to Positive Economics* (London: Weidenfeld and Niconson, 1963), pp. 308–9; A. A. Alchian and W. R. Allen, *University Economics* (Belmont, Calif.: Wadsworth, 1964), pp. 485–86; R. Attiyeh et al., *Basic Economics* (Englewood Cliffs, N.J.: Prentice-Hall, 1973), pp. 87–88; F. Benham, *Economics: A General Introduction* (London: Sir Isaac Pitman and Sons, 1960), p. 318; R. T. Bye, *Principles of Economics*, 5th ed. (New York: Appleton Century-Crofts, 1956), p. 489; S. T. Call and W. L. Holahan, *Microeconomics* (Belmont, Calif.: Wadsworth, 1980), pp. 420 and 433; R. Campbell, *People and Markets, An Introduction to Economics* (Menlo Park, Calif.: Benjamin-Cummings, 1978), pp. 268–71; R. Chisholm and M. McCarty, *Principles of Economics* (Glenview, Ill.: Scott, Foresman, 1978), p. 340; C. E. Ferguson and J. P. Gould, *Microeconomic Theory*, 4th ed. (Homewood, Ill.: Richard D. Irwin, 1975), pp. 470–72; J. E. Hibdon, *Price and Welfare Theory* (New York: McGraw-Hill, 1969), pp. 378–80; R. G. Lipsey and P. O. Steiner, *Economics*, 4th ed. (New York: Harper and Row, 1975), pp. 108–10; E. Mansfield, *Microeconomics, Theory and Applications*, 3rd ed. (New York: W. W. Norton, 1979), p. 383; and W. Nicholson, *Intermediate Microeconomics and Its Applications*, 2nd ed. (Hinsdale, Ill.: Dryden Press, 1979), pp. 380–83.

3. Some may object to this line of reasoning by alleging that these competitive forces are only applicable under the special assumption of a perfectly competitive market. In fact, our example only requires the existence of competition and private property rights. The particular market structure—whether perfect competition, monopolistic competition, oligopoly, duopoly, or monopoly—only influences the *degree* of the outcomes postulated.

4. Frederick A. Johnstone, *Class, Race, and Gold: A Study of Class Relations and Racial Discrimination in South Africa* (London: Routledge and Kegan Paul, 1976), p. 160.

5. Ibid., p. 161.

6. Ibid., p. 248, fn. 42.

7. Merle Lipton, *Capitalism and Apartheid: South Africa, 1910–84* (Totowa, N.J.: Rowman and Allanheld, 1985), p. 188.

8. Ibid., p. 189.

9. G. V. Doxey, *The Industrial Colour Bar in South Africa* (London: Oxford University Press, 1961), p. 111.

10. Ibid., p. 112.

11. Cited in Edward Roux, *Time Longer than Rope: A History of the Black Man's Struggle for Freedom in South Africa* (Madison: University of Wisconsin Press, 1964), p. 144.

12. Doxey, *Industrial Colour Bar*, pp. 126–27. Emphasis added.

13. Roux, *Time Longer than Rope*, p. 125.

14. Doxey, *Industrial Color Bar*, p. 155.

15. Ibid., p. 156.

16. Sheila T. van der Horst, "Labour," in *Handbook on Race Relations in South Africa*, edited by Ellen Hellman (New York: Octagon Books, 1975), pp. 133–34.

17. Lipton, *Capitalism and Apartheid*, p. 189.

18. Ibid., p. 199.

19. Ibid.

20. Anonymous correspondent of the International Labor Organization, "The New Wage Act in South Africa," *International Labour Review* 13, 3 (March 1926), p. 329.

21. Ibid., p. 334.

22. *Locomotive Firemen's Magazine* (August 1899): 203.

23. Sterling D. Spero and Abram Harris, *The Black Worker* (New York: Kennikat Press, 1931), p. 291.
24. Ibid.
25. Ibid.
26. Ibid.
27. Johnstone, *Class, Race, and Gold*, p. 158. Emphasis added.
28. *Congressional Record*, 71st Cong., House, 3rd sess., 1931: 6513.
29. William H. Hutt, *The Economics of the Colour Bar* (London: Andre Deutsch, 1964), pp. 76–87.
30. W. F. J. Steenkamp, "Labor Policies for Growth during the Seventies: In the Established Industrial Areas," *South African Journal of Economics* 39, 2 (June 1971): 107.
31. Alex Hepple, *South Africa: Workers under Apartheid*, 2nd ed. (London: International Defence and Aid Fund, July 1971), p. 37.
32. Ibid., p. 39.
33. Ibid., p. 41.
34. Lawrence Schlemmer, *Employment Opportunities and Race in South Africa* (Denver, Colo.: University of Denver, 1973), p. 24.
35. Ibid.
36. Hepple, *South Africa*, p. 40.
37. Ibid., p. 41.
38. Ibid.
39. Elaine Katz, "White Workers' Grievances and the Industrial Colour Bar," *South African Journal of Economics* 42, 2 (June 1974): 153. See also Lipton, *Capitalism and Apartheid*, pp. 19 and 185–86.
40. Lipton, *Capitalism and Apartheid*, pp. 207–9.
41. Hepple, *South Africa*, pp. 210–11.
42. South Africa Department of Labour, *Report of the Select Committee on the Industrial Conciliation Bill* (Pretoria: Government Printer, 1955), pp. 208–9.
43. Schlemmer, *Employment and Race*, p. 27.
44. Lipton, *Capitalism and Apartheid*, p. 209.
45. Ibid.
46. G. M. E. Leistner and W. J. Breytenback, *The Black Worker of South Africa* (Pretoria: Africa Institute of South Africa, 1975), p. 28.
47. Ibid.
48. Ibid., p. 39.
49. Here we assume equal worker productivity for the sake of expository simplicity. The analysis does not change if we allow for unequal productivity between workers. We could define our measure according to output per dollar's worth of input expenditure.
50. See Armen A. Alchian and Reuben A. Kessel, *Competition, Monopoly, and the Pursuit of Money* (Princeton, N.J.: Princeton University Press, 1962), pp. 157–75. See also Gary S. Becker, *The Economics of Discrimination*, 2nd ed. (Chicago: University of Chicago Press, 1971), especially ch. 3; and Harold Demsetz, "Minorities in the Market Place," *North Carolina Law Review* 43, 2 (February 1965): 271–97.
51. Alchian and Kessell, *Competition*, p. 169.
52. Sheila T. van der Horst, *Native Labour in South Africa* (London: Frank Cass, 1971), p. 251.
53. Ibid.

54. Ibid., p. 252.
55. Ibid., p. 256.
56. Ibid., p. 257.
57. Ibid., p. 258.
58. Paul Giniewski, *The Two Faces of Apartheid* (Chicago: Henry Regnery, 1965), p. 187.
59. van der Horst, *Native Labour*, p. 265.
60. I. Abedian and B. Standish, "Market Imperfections and Employment: A Model of the South African Labour Market 1900–1940," *South African Journal of Economics* 54, 4 (December 1986): 415.
61. van der Horst, *Native Labour*, p. 265.
62. Ibid., p. 145.
63. Cited in van der Horst, *Native Labour*, p. 146.
64. Lipton, *Capitalism and Apartheid*, p. 92.
65. Ibid., p. 94.
66. van der Horst, *Native Labour*, pp. 104–5.
67. Leon Louw and Frances Kendall, *South Africa: The Solution* (Bisho, Ciskei: Amagi Publications, 1986), p. 7.
68. Ibid., pp. 9–10.
69. Ibid., p. 10 ff., for other evidence of early black successes in agriculture.
70. Ibid., p. 12.
71. Ibid., p. 13.
72. Cited in ibid., pp. 13–14. Emphasis in original.
73. Cited in ibid., p. 14.
74. Lipton, *Capitalism and Apartheid*, p. 104.
75. Ibid., pp. 105–6.
76. Ibid., p. 106.
77. Ibid.
78. Ibid., p. 120.
79. Ibid.

5

Apartheid: Rhetoric versus Reality

> There are people who for a century have made it their point of departure that simply everything—even the survival of white civilisation—must be made subordinate to their so-called economic laws.... It is fortunate that under a Nationalist government these worshippers of economic laws have never had their way but that a higher and nobler goal has been strived after—the maintenance of white civilisation.
>
> *Die Transvaler*, October 11, 1958

Beginning in 1940—with downturns here and there—South Africa has experienced a high rate of growth. Before World War II, steel production was 344,700 tons; by 1945, it had risen to 520,000 tons. During the same period, South Africa's value of clothing output almost trebled from £8,160,000 ($23,000,000) to £22,530,000 ($63,000,000). Similar advances were recorded in other branches of primary and secondary industry.[1]

South Africa's wartime expansion continued after the war. From 1946 to 1956, its real national income increased at an annual rate of 4.8 percent. This included the agricultural sector; from a base index of 106 in 1938, output rose to 176 by 1957. During the mid–1960s, South Africa's growth rate exceeded that of all the Western countries—including the United States—as indicated in Table 5.1.

Rapid expansion added to the already present antiapartheid economic forces, particularly those bearing on the South African labor market. In 1956, the Commission of Inquiry (Viljoen Commission) estimated that the shortage of European artisans was 7.4 percent; the shortage of apprentices was 11.5 percent, and the shortage of male and female clericals was 5.5 and 4.1 percent, respectively. The Viljoen Commission's policy prescription for the skilled labor shortages was that government should "adopt a positive and effective immigration policy with the appropriate financial assistance of the State," in order to attract 25,000 Europeans each year.[2]

Table 5.1
A Comparison between South Africa and Other Industrial Countries[a] in Annual Percent Growth of Gross Domestic Product (by volume) at Market Prices, 1964–74

	1964	1965	1966	1967	1968	1969	1970	1971	1972	1973	1974
Europe (Six)	5.9	5.0	3.7	3.1	5.9	7.0	5.8	3.6	4.2	5.4	2.4
Europe (Nine)	5.9	4.4	3.3	3.1	5.3	5.8	5.0	3.4	3.9	5.3	2.1
Germany	6.6	5.5	2.8	-0.4	6.7	7.8	6.0	3.1	3.5	4.8	0.4
France	6.3	5.9	4.0	4.8	4.7	7.0	5.9	5.4	5.6	5.6	3.9
U.K.	5.8	2.2	1.9	2.5	3.4	1.1	2.2	2.5	2.6	5.5	0.8
Italy	2.6	3.2	5.8	7.0	6.3	5.7	5.0	1.6	3.1	6.3	3.4
U.S.A.	5.3	6.3	6.6	2.7	4.2	2.6	0.5	3.2	6.1	5.6	-1.9
Japan	13.3	5.1	9.8	12.9	13.5	10.8	10.9	7.3	8.5	10.2	-1.8
South Africa	9.5	9.7	8.5	10.8	7.4	11.3	8.9	10.9	12.2	22.1	19.5[b]

Source: Howard Brotz, *The Politics of South Africa: Democracy and Racial Diversity* (London: Oxford University Press, 1977), p.76.

Notes: (a) South Africa's improvement in economic growth rate during 1972 is in strong contrast to most other industrial countries in the Western World. (b) At constant (1963) prices this still represents a 7.2% increase over the previous year.

South Africa's immigration program was ineffective, and bore little fruit. In 1954, net immigration was 5,080; in 1955, 3,684; and in 1956, 2,038. The failure of the government to launch an aggressive campaign to lure immigrants, along with improving economic conditions at home, reduced the incentive for Europeans to pull up stakes and move to South Africa.

In the face of a weak flow of desirable immigrants, South Africa's apartheid labor restrictions, and the growing economy, the supply of white workers could not keep up with the demand for labor. These factors had the effect of creating enormous windfalls for the white workers who were there. In 1944–45, the average annual wage of a white worker in private manufacturing was £389 ($1,089). By 1953–54, it had risen to £706 ($1,977) per annum. In 1944–45, the average annual colored and Indian wage was £168 ($470); by 1953–54, it was £264 ($739). African wages in 1944–45 were £92 ($258) per annum; by 1953–54, they had risen to £139 ($389). Despite the increases all around, there were nonetheless considerable differences between white, black, colored, and Indian wages in 1953–54. Colored and Indian wages were 37 percent of white wages, while black wages were only 24 percent of whites. Moreover, these wage disparities existed even when blacks were performing the same jobs as white.

In 1956, white artisans in the building trades averaged a wage of 7s. ($3.92) an hour, while black artisans doing the same work in black townships and rural reserves (under the restrictions of the Native Building Workers Act) were receiving 2s. ($1.08) per hour—only 29 percent the wages of whites. In the mining industry, similar wage differences existed—with the average white wage being £1,000 ($2,800) a year in 1956, compared to £70 ($196) for blacks. Put another way, white workers constituted only 12 percent of the labor force in the gold mines, but received 71 percent of the wages paid. Nonwhites were 88 percent of the work force, but received only 29 percent of the total wage bill.[3]

The skilled and semiskilled labor scarcity—coupled with the significant wage differences—laid the groundwork for natural economic forces to start attacking apartheid and repealing it by stealth. Moreover, the postwar era had seen some qualitative changes in the labor situation: Nonwhites now possessed skills that they did not hold earlier. These factors combined to make contravention of apartheid a more tempting proposition to employers.

Apartheid distorts resource allocation simply because race—rather than economic criteria, such as worker productivity—decides who should work in what job, where a business should be located, and where people should live. Inefficient resource allocation clearly reduces South Africa's overall material wealth from what it might otherwise be. However, not very many people—anywhere—base their private decisions on a concern for the nation's material wealth. Individuals are more concerned with their own wealth, and their private decisions reflect that interest.

As we have seen, much of the motivation behind South Africa's apartheid system is that group interests seek to use the coercive powers of the state to steer more wealth in their direction than would be indicated by market forces. Efforts to subvert market forces can meet with varying degrees of success. Moreover there can be additional, unintended consequences of those efforts—as well as unanticipated beneficiaries and victims—where government intervenes to steer benefits from one group to another. Apartheid is no exception to the rule. It is difficult—not to mention costly—to subvert completely the operation of market forces. Therefore, economic reality has a tendency to bring people to their senses, allowing rationality to win some skirmishes against ideology.

The forces that produce these particular gains for rationality stem from the fact that all people are imbued with self-love and a powerful desire to have more for themselves. This results—as Adam Smith said in the *Wealth of Nations*—in "a certain propensity in human nature . . . to truck, barter and exchange one thing for another." Supporters of apartheid—that is, of irrational racial discrimination—are not immune to this propensity. Just like anything else, ideology requires sacrifices: It costs something. The costs of apartheid—which is in a class with other collusions such as price ceilings, regulation, cartels, and embargoes—produce strong private incentives for contravention, violation, and connivance.

Popular opinion holds that big businesses in general benefit from and are the architects of South African apartheid. According to this argument, the business interest in apartheid is that it provides employers with a plentiful supply of cheap and docile labor.[4] Such an assertion should be examined. Among the questions we might ask are: How much political support did business actually give to the government measures that instituted and implemented apartheid policy? Or did business have to be "paid" to accept apartheid? To what extent have businesses been seeking to exempt themselves from apartheid laws, through legal action or outright contravention? Finally, were there any apartheid laws that did benefit business?

In examining these questions, we need not place moral interpretations on the behavior of businessmen. If businessmen come out against a particular apartheid law or custom (such as the Mines and Works Act of 1911, as discussed in Chapter 3), it need not be assumed that the action is indicative of righteousness and a caring attitude toward blacks. The protest for or against apartheid labor law can be evaluated solely in terms of economic interests.

BUSINESS PROTEST AND CONTRAVENTION OF APARTHEID

The Federal Chamber of Industries (FCI)—established in 1917, and comprising 70 percent of South African firms by 1970—and the Associated Chambers of Commerce (Assocom), representing 17,000 businesses in 1970—have always opposed the government's color bar. In 1925, *Industrial South Africa* represented the views of FCI and Assocom as such:

The natives today are more widely educated than in the past.... Many thousands have grown up in the towns, many having been born in the cities or brought there in the early youth.... It is therefore no easy matter to bring into operation compulsory laws which will have the effect of throwing natives on the streets, where, unemployed, they will become a menace to the community.... The Native must be given every opportunity to progress in the directions for which he is most fitted.[5]

From a business point of view, the "civilised labour policy" has restricted the supply of skilled labor and raised its cost. The ban on occupational advancement for blacks restricted their educational training and hence discouraged their motivation and productivity. During World War II, businessmen had initial success in convincing government about the high costs of white worker protection. The Industrial and Agricultural Requirements Commission accepted businesses' argument that apartheid policy raised their costs, limited their domestic markets, and made them uncompetitive relative to their international trading partners; the commission urged reform.[6] The pressures for reform were assisted by the wartime booming economy and its associated skills shortage. Black job restrictions were informally relaxed.

The fact that job restrictions were relaxed and the fact that blacks were able to take advantage of skills training in some cases led to their being increasingly preferred to white labor. Greater numbers of blacks became hired as semiskilled and skilled operatives. These wartime occupational gains were accompanied by a small reduction in the wage differential between blacks and whites. In 1940, the ratio of white to black wages was 5.3:1; by 1945, it had fallen to 4.2:1. It is likely that these trends would have continued, but the 1948 elections brought the National party to power, and reversals in black gains.

The protection of white workers from open market competition with blacks was a costly proposition. The wage differentials due to the civilized labor policy gave businesses considerable inducement to find ways to substitute black for white labor. Private manufacturing, services, and commerce were not covered under the statutory provisions of the job bar. The protection of white workers was secured, in part, through special government privileges to business. The 1925 Customs Tariff and Excise Duties Act made eligibility for trade protections conditional on a satisfactory employment policy. A "satisfactory" employment policy consisted of hiring a reasonable percentage of white workers at civilized wages, maintaining segregated worker facilities, and not permitting whites to be supervised by blacks. The act required the labor minister to publish the names of companies that failed to maintain a civilized labor policy. Section 4(2) of the act said, "The duty applicable could be cut down in the failure of the industry to introduce satisfactory labour conditions."[7]

The Tender and Supplies Board makes acquisitions for government supplies from the private sector. Businesses not maintaining a civilized labor policy have been excluded from the list of approved government suppliers.

The Industrial Conciliation Act of 1924 provided for the recognition and registration of trade unions. Under its provisions, self-governing industrial councils jointly controlled by unions and business employers were set up. Unions now had the power to control entry and apprenticeship conditions through closed shop agreements, in such a way that they could easily exclude blacks from skilled and semiskilled jobs.

The effort to protect white workers produced its own adversaries and unanticipated consequences. Tariff protections restricted competition, which in turn led to the development of large monopolistic firms. These firms had a tendency to become highly capital intensive. This had several consequences: (1) It aggravated the shortage of skilled labor, which was needed to run industry; (2) it enhanced the need for firms to find a formalized means of communication to keep track of the large and growing labor force; and (3) it highlighted the need for a larger domestic market to buy domestic production. All three of these consequences brought considerable pressures to bear on apartheid. First, they produced greater pressures to educate and train blacks; second, they gave rise to black labor unions and to the integration of some formerly all-white unions; and third, they made business aware of the potential of a large black consumer's market.

What the law mandates and what people find it in their interest to do are often two entirely different things. There is considerable evidence showing a widespread contravention of the apartheid labor laws. In 1979, the Riekert Report documented the large-scale evasion of apartheid laws by employers who were illegally hiring black workers (see Chapter 2, Note 51). According to the report, two-thirds of the clothing factories in the Pretoria, Witwatersrand, and Vereeniging (PWV) area had illegal black workers, and there was reason to believe that the situation was no different in other branches of secondary industry. In

1972, the Federated Chamber of Industries estimated that 47 percent of the industries in the PWV area hired more blacks than the legal quota of 2.5 Africans to 1 white.[8]

The Riekert Report recorded complaints from the Labor Bureau about massive violations of the influx control law. Heavy penalties and fines were imposed on hundreds of employers who were in violation of influx control. These violations were so prevalent that employers began to budget fines as just one of the costs of doing business. Labor Bureau officials responded to this by calling for imprisonment, loss of the privilege to employ black workers, and the outright closing of business for repeat offenders.[9]

In the mines, the mineowners' preference for profits repeatedly overcame any sense of solidarity with their white workers. Mineowners evaded, sought exemptions, and used every other measure at their disposal to get around the higher production costs associated with apartheid labor laws. Even the government itself utilized some of these business practices devised to avoid the spirit of the apartheid laws.

Despite apartheid rhetoric regarding the "civilised labour policy," which was to be the goal of government employment, reality prevented its full implementation. The shortage of white labor led to breaches in the usual job discrimination on the state-owned South African railways. In October 1967, the Railways Administration brought teams of Africans into the Durban yards—at night—to perform shunting (switching trains) operations. Speaking of the acute shortage of white workers, the minister of transport said,

> I can solve the problem fairly easily by employing nonwhites as firemen, driver's assistants, . . . shunters, guards and station-foremen, artisans, etc. I can easily do so. But there would be tremendous opposition from the staff. . . . I am already employing nonwhites in work previously done by whites. . . . At present there are seven or eight thousand Bantu who do the pick-and-shovel work on the permanent way which used to be done by whites. This is also the case as far as flagmen and pointmen are concerned. . . . There is tremendous opposition from the staff, and I back them up.[10]

By the end of 1970, the minister of transport revealed that 15,355 railway jobs formerly classified as white—which were temporarily being filled by nonwhites—would be reclassified as nonwhite jobs. Toward the end of 1971, the minister was again warning white railway workers to get accustomed to blacks doing work traditionally preserved for whites. By 1973, the railroad had 2,646 more blacks temporarily employed in jobs formerly held by whites only. There were 34 blacks employed as crane drivers; 87, as forklift operators. In order to hurdle some of the objections to blacks performing white jobs, the railways simply changed the name of certain jobs. For example, due to a shortage of white "shunters," the railway selected 1,468 black candidates to train as "marshallers" or "compilers."[11] Of these candidates, 85 percent completed the training successfully, and more than 80 percent were considered successful on the job.¹² Similar job name changes were made when blacks were hired in the white job of ticket collector. Blacks doing the same work were given the title of ticket takers.

South African whites are very concerned with status, and do not wish to be seen as doing kaffirwerk. When the government wanted to grant exemptions to colored building workers, J. E. Young of the white Building Workers Union in the Transvaal said, "We are proud of our status and want to keep it . . . and our standard will obviously be lowered with the employment of Coloureds as artisans."¹³ J. H. Liebenberg, President of the Railways Artisan Staff Association, echoed the same sentiments: "Most white workers believe that sharing occupation would lower their codes and that familiarity would breed . . . assimilation."¹⁴

Within two years after the National party won office in 1948 on a declared program for a civilized labor policy, 1,290 blacks had been dismissed from the state-owned Post Office. As with other government agencies, nonwhite workers were kept to a minimum and relegated to menial work. By 1968, the Post Office employed 34,788 whites and 13,671 nonwhites. The acute shortage of white workers, who had gone off to better jobs, meant that the Post Office had to hire more and more blacks as "temporary" messengers and postal carriers. By the end of 1967, there were 1,835 blacks in these so-called temporary jobs. Despite vocal opposition by white workers, by the end of 1970 the Post Office was employing 1,023 Africans, 721 coloreds, and 243 Indians as postal carriers and messengers—positions formerly occupied by whites.¹⁵

Blacks continued to make inroads at the government-owned Post Office. Of the 21,757 blacks employed by the Post Office in 1973, 43 percent were laborers, and the others were employed in the semiskilled and management jobs of telephone electrician, senior telephone worker, and chief and senior inspector.

National party politicians traditionally saw government employment as the protected sphere for "sheltered" white semiskilled and skilled workers. This was particularly so on the government-owned railways. As shown in Table 5.2, from 1926 to 1972 the number of white employees exceeded black workers. After 1972, black railway employees exceeded whites.

This was the result of at least two forces. (1) Rapid economic growth had expanded job opportunities for whites, and (2) blacks were gaining greater skills. Moreover, the economic growth required an expansion in railway services. These factors forced some of the apartheid ideology to give way to economic rationality. Howard Brotz observed,

Thus, while the Minister of Labour was in charge of a policy that sought to keep down the number of Blacks in urban industry, the former Minister of Transport, Mr. Ben Shoeman, was not only hiring non-Whites to do jobs that had formerly been done by Whites but was telling objectors, "You want White railway workers. Find me them." What is almost comical is that when the Minister of Labour was given the portfolio of Posts and Telegraphs in a cabinet reshuffle, it became apparent that he too was hiring

Table 5.2
Employment of Whites and Blacks on South African Railways and Harbors, for Selected Years, 1926–75

Year	A: Whites	B: Blacks	A as % of A B
1926	50,800	44,900	53.1
1933	49,300	28,000	63.8
1938	66,100	54,900	54.6
1948	98,100	89,600	52.3
1950	103,400	84,600	55.0
1968	114,539	93,583	55.0
1970	110,314	96,579	53.3
1972	110,854	99,815	47.4
1975	111,120	116,599	48.8

Source: Howard Brotz, *The Politics of South Africa: Democracy and Racial Diversity* (London: Oxford University Press, 1977), p. 78.

more non-Whites as postmen. He, indeed, had to do so since there were not enough Whites to run the Posts and Telegraph service. The Government often behaved, not surprisingly, like a business."[16]

Recognizing reality, in 1973 Prime Minister Vorster said, "It should be clear that in terms of government policy there is nothing to prevent employers, with the cooperation of unions, taking the necessary steps to bring about improvement in the productive use of nonwhite labour."[17]

This behavior is not wholly consistent with the popular Marxist line that capitalists benefit from apartheid. Even Afrikaner businesses, which developed much later in South African history than the more numerous English-speaking business concerns, shared the same opposition to apartheid labor policy. As early as the 1960s, the Afrikaners in the business community started becoming more vocal in their opposition to features of apartheid that reduced their flexibility in labor usage. These views were expressed in a memorandum to Prime Minister Verwoerd by the Federated Chamber of Industries, the Associated Chambers of Commerce, the Steel and Engineering Industries Federation of South Africa—representing more than 16,000 firms—and the Afrikaanse Handelsinstituut, which represents 7,500 Afrikaans-speaking business concerns. The representations of these business people brought an angry response from Verwoerd. He refused to address their gathering and denounced them as "paving the way for black domination." Indeed, Verwoerd labeled the Associated Chambers of Commerce as "traitors." For a number of years afterward, government departments refused to meet with or even reply to letters from Associated Chambers of Commerce officials.

These businesses that saw in apartheid labor laws a handicap to productivity and profitability had already begun by stealth the process of seeking exemptions and—ultimately—repeal. For example, according to Section 77 of the Industrial

Conciliation Act of 1956, a special exemption was necessary for blacks to drive trucks weighing more than 10,000 pounds unladen. Yet—according to the 1971 Manpower Survey—there were 13,927 blacks so employed, as against 7,186 whites, 3,911 coloreds, and 2,731 Asians. According to a survey by the Johannesburg *Star* (February 5, 1971), "When 53-year-old Mr. Lake began doing it 30 years ago, all his driving colleagues were White men. Today he is the only one left among all who load up at the Kaseme yards. Even 10 years ago it was different. One well known firm employed 35 White drivers. There was one non-White who had special permission. Now it is exactly the opposite way round."[18] The *Star* survey quoted the chairman of the Witwatersrand and Pretoria Coal Trade Employers Association as saying that almost 100 percent of coal truck drivers were black.

One of the first Section 77 (ICA) determinations was made in the clothing industry, which at the time—1957—employed 11,500 whites (19.6 percent of the total), 25,700 coloreds, 7,100 Asians, and 14,500 blacks. By 1973, white employment in the clothing industry had fallen to 10,100 (8 percent of the total), and black employment had risen two and a half times to 35,500. The Labour Department found that, of 3,381 cutters- and choppers-out, 908 were blacks as compared to 276 whites. There were 16,060 black female sewing-machine operators as compared to 1,083 white females. Knitting machines were run overwhelmingly by blacks, and blacks were even performing the skilled jobs of pattern maker and grader.[19]

The disparities between apartheid rhetoric and economic reality have become increasingly apparent to South African government. In 1971, the editor of the progovernment newspaper *Rapport*—after acknowledging that white workers had a right to expect job protection from the government—said,

However it becomes a different matter if suitable White labour is not available and White workers still keep resisting non-White employment. If this resistance is successful, an artificial shortage arises for which there can be no excuse whatsoever. The result is artificially high wages for this group of White workers (surely no encouragement for good and dedicated work). Further, the work needed remains undone. Add to this that the injustice is being inflicted upon non-White workers able and willing to do the work.[20]

Along these same lines, in 1973 Prime Minister Vorster told a meeting of the Motor Industries Federation that the government does not stand in the way of adaptations to traditional employment patterns, "provided that these changes come about in an orderly fashion and with the concurrence of the trade unions."[21]

The government appeared willing to allow changes in labor apartheid so long as there was a guarantee of white worker protection. It preferred to relax apartheid through collective agreements in terms of the Industrial Conciliation Act—rather than repeal of apartheid law—for several possible reasons: (1) Collective bargaining to increase black employment tended to promote "labor peace"; (2) even though the apartheid laws had been eroded in practice, they were still on the books and could be used as a fallback position for white workers; and (3) the government could retain its apartheid bargaining chip in its relations with the business community.

RATIONALITY WINS AGAIN

The *reddingsdaad* (act of rescue) movement of the 1940s and thereafter called for the South African government to play a role in promoting Afrikaner business ownership. A chief focus of the movement was the "Indian question." As petty traders, Indians were actively engaged in the part of commerce that was most readily accessible to the Afrikaner middle class.

Indians have always been competitive traders and merchants. As such, they have encountered varying degrees of hostility throughout Africa from both the indigenous black population and Europeans. Wherever Indians have settled, they have at one time or another served as political scapegoats. White South Africans and Indians collided because of the whites' fear of being numerically overwhelmed (especially in Natal, where 80 percent of the Indian population resides), racial prejudice, and the whites' concerns about economic competition.[22]

From 1870 onward, the Indians increasingly emerged from their first role as manual indentured laborers to being traders and merchants. In Natal, early white reaction to Indian competition led to appointment of the Indian Immigrants Commission in 1885 (the Wragg Commission). According to the commission report, Indians competed with white merchants in the supply of merchandise to Indians and blacks. They were able to undersell white merchants because they hired family members and thus had to pay out little in wages and they were willing to accept very small profit margins. The Wragg Commission found that Africans could purchase goods from Indians at 25–30 percent less than from whites. The commission concluded that Indian traders benefited both the general public and the colony. Even in the Transvaal, where Indians were later to encounter considerable hostility, President Kruger refused to take action against them because—he said—the Indians were useful to his people [Afrikaners].[23]

The Lange Commission (1921) concluded that the anti-Indian agitation in the Transvaal had largely been instigated by white traders, and this was also the case in Natal. The commission also found strong anti-Indian feelings among European farmers, who were disturbed by the increase in large farms owned by Indians. The farmers alleged that Indians were able to offer higher prices for land than the Europeans. The Lange Commission recommended that the authorities limit Indian rights to purchase land along coastal areas in order to reduce Indian/European competition; but no such legislation emerged.[24]

By the 1940s, Indians were entering petty businesses, as Jews had done earlier. The anti-Semitic racism of a moment before was redirected against the Indian "alien coolies." One Afrikaner business association—Volkshandel—took upon itself to monitor the issuance of trading licenses to Indians. In 1944, the Volkshandel reported with dismay that between 1940 and 1943 there had been 66,369 trading licenses issued to Indians.[25]

In 1939—responding to antagonism toward the Indian trader operating in white areas—the South African Parliament passed the Asiatic Act (No. 28) in order to restrict Indian trading in Transvaal Province. The law prohibited additional renting or selling of buildings and land to Indians and coloreds after April 1939. Indians and coloreds already trading in white areas were permitted to stay.[26] Concern over the Indian question was important enough that *Inspan* (1946) devoted an entire issue to the Indian trader. Its editorial said:

The one time pitiful peddler has become a *financially strong trader, whilst many hardworking established white businessmen have been squeezed out by the previously despised interloper*. The Indian has captured for himself a position of power—power, inter alia, over his white customer. In place of a bundle on his back, today he owns valuable premises and buildings in the European section of the city or town. His employees are in many cases whites—frequently former competitors; his customers are whites, who, particularly in this time of limited supplies, are dependent upon him for their daily necessities; his neighbors are whites whom he treats with suspicion and enmity, but with whom he also demands equality.[27]

While the Indian population is most numerous in Natal Province, their presence and competitiveness were felt in other provinces as well. In early 1947, antagonism toward this presence led to a boycott by Afrikaners who, according to *Inspan*, felt that the Indian was

an unwelcome alien in our portals, not only from a moral and religious point of view—he has enriched himself at the expense of his white clients, he has attempted to squeeze his European competitor out of the business world through illegitimate trading methods—but has, moreover, challenged and defamed the country in which he trades as a guest, in an insolent manner. To this the volk has reacted instinctively—a fact for which we ought to give thanks, because had the opposite been the case, we must necessarily have reached the conclusion that white South Africa suffers from an unbelievable lack of insight or is devoid of all self-respect and vitality.[28]

Rhetoric to the contrary, pleas to the Afrikaner *volk* to buy from their own actually fell on deaf ears. Despite all the demagoguery, the Afrikaner masses traded with the Indian rather than with the less competitive Afrikaner businesses. In the face of a failing "buy from your own" campaign, Afrikaner merchants started instigating racial incidents in an attempt to win the patronage of the cost-conscious white customer.

The rising agitation led to increased political efforts to repatriate Indians back to India. Dr. Donges (who was to become the first President-elect of South Africa in 1961) made this announcement:

The Government is prepared, as a temporary measure and for a limited period, to increase the bonus payable to Indians who wish to return to India. . . . The scheme provides for financial assistance and a free passage from any place in the Union to any place outside the Union for any adult Indian and his family under certain conditions. Emigrants are also provided with food during the journey.[29]

Restricting Indian Business

In 1941, agitation against Indians led to appointment of the Indian Penetration Commission to investigate complaints of Indian land purchases in white areas (especially Durban). The commission reported that there had been no further Indian penetration into the Natal rural areas since 1927. Its report said that this was because "many of the areas where no penetration has taken place since 1927 had already been overrun by Indians before that date."[30] The commission had searched the deeds registry and found extensive Indian land ownership, with certain areas (Verulum, Tongast, Chakaskraal, and Stanger) being predominantly Indian owned. After the report, it became apparent that Indian land ownership in urban areas was continuing at an accelerated rate.

The Indian Penetration Commission findings led to the Trading and Occupation of Land Restriction Act of 1943, in the Natal and Transvaal provinces—popularly known as the "Pegging Act." This act prohibited transfers of fixed property between Asiatics (Indians) and Europeans, but did not prohibit the transfer of property between coloreds and Asians. In 1946 the act was amended to close its loopholes. The Pegging Act was designed to peg Indian fixed property holdings to what they were on January 21, 1946, in Natal and on March 15, 1946, in the Transvaal. The Pegging Act also defined fixed property as mortgage bonds and leases.

The act prohibited Asiatic occupation of property that was not lawfully occupied by an Asiatic prior to its effective date, in non-Asiatic areas. In Natal, there were two designated areas: (1) non-Asiatic, which consisted of the whole of Natal; and (2) exempted or controlled areas, where Asiatics could occupy property. Within these exempted areas—delineated in schedules to the act—Asiatics were not restricted at all. They could purchase, lease, and expand their property ownership. Interestingly, the Pegging Act provided that, in areas scheduled for Asiatics, European occupancy was prohibited.

The Pegging Act was deeply resented by Indians. They appealed to India for help. As a result of the appeals, India withdrew its high commissioner in South Africa, trade relations between South Africa and India were suspended, and the Indian government petitioned the United Nations regarding the poor treatment of Indians.

During debates in the South African Parliament over the Asiatic Land Tenure and Indian Representation Act of 1946, both Prime Minister Smuts and Daniel Malan—leader of the opposition—accused Indians of being themselves responsible for the hate directed toward them. The statesmen referred to the fact that India was using the United Nations as a forum to accuse South Africa of abuses toward its Indian population. Reiterating Nationalist policy, Dr. Malan said,

The Government would do its best to bring about the repatriation of as many Indians as possible. Those satisfied to remain in South Africa will have to do so under restrictions because, by systematically going abroad with their grievances instead of submitting them to the South African Government through the proper channels, they have proven themselves to be a foreign element which did not belong in South Africa.[31]

This charge, however, was not quite true. Dr. Donges had refused to meet with delegations of Indians from Natal and the Transvaal who were dissatisfied with provisions of the Asiatic Land Tenure and Indian Representation Act of 1946.

Dr. E. G. Jansen, former Nationalist minister of native affairs, accused Indians of using the United Nations to accomplish their designs on not only South Africa, but the whole continent. Jansen is reported to have said that this was the reason for

a great deal of adverse, and very often untrue propaganda that is being made against us in India, in America, in Britain, on the continent and especially at the meetings of the United Nations.... It is not the Indian workers in South Africa who are causing all the agitation, said the Minister, it is the man flourishing under the white man's laws. He has been allowed to compete with him, to oust the white man and to grow fat and prosperous. They are the people who are crying about oppression overseas. They give examples of shacks where Indians are living but you can go to parts of Durban where Europeans are living under worse conditions in the back yards of Indian-owned property and you could not call that oppression. That is the result of economic conditions which we should not allow to continue.[32]

The Afrikaner was not alone in feeling antagonistic toward the Indian, as seen by the Zulu/Indian riots in Durban on January 1949. Bands of Africans stormed, looted, and burned Indian stores. By the time the carnage was over, 142 people had been killed and 1,087 were injured. In a *Commonweal* (May 6, 1949) article called "African Indians versus Natives," blacks were quoted as saying, "All we desire is that the Government provide ships and we will see the Indians on their way to India."[33]

An investigating commission blamed the riots on the Zulus. The natives mostly complained about immoral contact between Indian men and Zulu women, Indian exploitation of natives in the native areas by charging high prices and selling inferior merchandise, and special treatment that the Indians were supposedly receiving from the government. Blacks were also disturbed with the licensing of Indian traders in native areas. They thought that profits from trade should benefit their own native people. Additional hostility on the part of blacks toward Indians resulted from the latter's having a virtual monopoly on bus licenses along routes serving native areas.

Indians were not welcome among coloreds either. A colored delegation presented to the government a memorandum stating that Indians had made serious business inroads into colored areas. If the government would venture to remove the Indian, coloreds could then develop their own trade. The delegation also warned the government that its first duty was to the coloreds, not the Indians. Therefore, the government should not allow Indians to strengthen their economic hold on the colored people.[34]

The antagonism that Indians encountered may very well have been a result of their "clannish" ways and customs; but, without question, a lot of it stemmed from their superior entrepreneurship relative to Afrikaners, blacks, and coloreds. Moreover, one must remember that the Afrikaners, blacks, and coloreds who formed the clientele for the Indian traders *could* have patronized the businesses of their own races, or have done without. The fact is that they did not, because they viewed purchasing from Indians to be superior to their next best alternative. The people most grieved by the presence of the Indian merchant were not so much the Indians' customers, as their competitors.

Thus, it was an appeal to the Afrikaner business community—and to the sense of nationalism among the volk, organized by the Afrikaner business community—that the National party incorporated as a part of its 1948 election platform:

The Party holds the view that the Indians are an alien foreign element which can never be assimilated. They can never become natives of this country, and must therefore be treated as an immigrant community.[35]

According to the National party, the primary way of dealing with the Indian question would be repatriation; and in the interim, Indians would be removed to group areas and not allowed to live, own property, or trade in white areas.[36] Dr. Donges felt that complete racial segregation would eliminate racial conflict, and he added, "There is no reason why the majority of the services in particular areas should not be conducted for a certain group by members of that particular group."[37]

The free flow of market forces had "decided" that Indians could do business in white, black, and colored areas. In order to compete with the Indians, competitors would have had to produce a better product at a cheaper price. Their inability and/or unwillingness in this led them to use an age-old tool for accomplishing what cannot be accomplished through the voluntary forces of the marketplace: goverment-backed collusion.

The Asiatic Land Tenure and Indian Representation Act of 1946 did not deprive Indians of land that they already owned in white areas. It did reduce the number of farms acquired by Indians from Europeans. Continued competition from Indians led to appointment of the Asiatic (Indian) Land Tenure Laws Amendments Committee, which in 1950 stated,

There is no doubt that the best solution of the Asiatic problem is repatriation. Failing or pending repatriation of the Asiatics, however, the present situation has to be dealt with incisively if civil commotions arising from racial strife are to be avoided. We can see no way of attaining this end except to legislate for total territorial segregation of different

Table 5.3
Black Urban Population, 1936–70

Year	Total (in thousands)		Blacks as %	Index of Blacks	
	All races	Blacks	of all races	(1936=100)	(1904=100)
1936	3218	1252	38.9	100	347
1946	4482	1902	42.4	100	527
1951	5494	2391	43.5	126	662
1960	7474	3471	46.4	182	961
1970	10280	4989	48.5	262	1382

Source: Howard Brotz, *The Politics of South Africa: Democracy and Racial Diversity* (London: Oxford University Press, 1977), p. 73.

racial groups, so that in the course of time homogeneous racial group areas are brought about.[38]

The call for territorial segregation ultimately led to passage of the Group Areas Act of 1950. Its provisions allow the government to determine where different racial groups may live, own, and lease land. The government controls all interracial land transfers. The Group Areas Act was a consolidation of earlier attempts to restrict Indian traders from setting up businesses in European and African areas.

Despite government-supported collusion against the Indian merchants, they have nonetheless prospered and grown. In Natal, moderate-size Indian business establishments grew from 120 in 1950 to almost 900 in 1976. Most of these Indian establishments involve light manufacturing and specialize in clothing and footwear. But there are a number of larger enterprises that are able to bid on government contracts and export their products.[39]

Residential Segregation and Reality

The Bantu Land Act (1913), the Bantu Trust and Land Act (1936), the Bantu Consolidation Act (1945), the Bantu (Abolition of Passes and Documents) Act (1952), the Group Areas Act (1966), and many of the other components of the apartheid apparatus had as their objective "separate development." The supporting ideological rhetoric was that blacks were not citizens of South Africa, and therefore could not live and enjoy rights within its borders. They could only be "temporary sojourners." The reality is very different: The black urban population has steadily grown since 1936, as seen in Table 5.3.

The reason for black urban population growth is quite simple. Urban areas like Johannesburg, Durban, Natal, and Cape Town—and others—are centers of thriving commercial and industrial activity. Hotel clientele, for example, want their breakfast served and their rooms cleaned at a reasonable hour; they have little sympathy for an excuse like, "The workers are having some transportation problems getting in to work from the black areas." Households want their servants and chauffeurs—and businesses want their workers—available at conventional hours. All of this has led people to seek special exemptions as well as other ways to contravene apartheid law and its spirit.

In response to economic reality and in violation of the Group Areas Act, about one-half of the black population—it has been estimated—resides in white-designated areas.[40] A 1986 report by the Department of Development Studies of the Rand Afrikaans University in Johannesburg found,

> Pockets of integrated residential settlements have become characteristic of most of the large South African cities. Examples are the suburbs of Salt River, Landsdowne, Wynberg, Observatory and Woodstock in Cape Town, Clairwood and Greyville in Durban, North End and Korsten in Port Elizabeth, and Hillbrow, Berea and Joubert Park as well as Mayfair in Johannesburg."[41]

An even more recent increase in interneighborhood mobility, resulting from contravention of the Groups Areas Act has been due mainly to a South African Supreme Court ruling in the case of *S. v. Govender* (1986 (3) T69). The court held that—since the original Group Areas Act (Act 41: 1950) provided that, on issuing a conviction, the court "shall" order a convicted person to vacate the premises being illegally occupied—the court had no discretion under the act at that time. However, when the Group Areas Act was amended in 1966, the word "shall" was replaced with "may." Therefore, today's court interprets the act as providing for discretionary jurisdiction. In *S. v. Govender*, the following considerations were enumerated to be taken into account in the exercise of the court's discretion: the nature of the area concerned; the attitude of the neighbors; the policy and views of relevant state departments; the attitude of the landlord; the prospect of a permit being issued for lawful occupation of the said premises; the personal hardship that such an eviction might cause; and the availability of alternative accommodation.

While white attitudes are changing toward greater acceptance of nonwhites residing in white areas, there are some strong reinforcing market forces at play, as well. The Council for Scientific and Industrial Research found that there was a *surplus* of 37,000 housing units for whites in urban areas in 1985. That same year, there was a *shortage* of urban housing for blacks, amounting to 538,000 units; for coloreds, 52,000; and for Asians, 44,000. A similar study by the Johannesburg City Council found "that a total of 740 flats in the CBD-area of that city alone are at present unoccupied whilst the waiting list for housing for Coloureds and Asians is 4,970 and 8,062 respectively."[42]

The surplus of housing for whites and the shortage of housing for nonwhites acts—as it would for any other commodity—as a strong inducement for transactions. De Coning, Fick, and Olivier conclude from their countrywide survey of "grey areas"—places where whites and nonwhites reside together in violation of the Group Areas Act—that there is an apparent discrepancy between the politically motivated view of some residents (flowing from association with right wing political parties) and the financial advantages these same persons are taking due to the character change their neighborhood is undergoing (e.g., their political sympathy lies with the CP or HNP but they enthusiastically sell their houses at above market prices to eager Indian buyers or even, for a handsome fee, in order to circumvent the Group Areas Act, operate as so-called Nominees for well-to-do Indians).[43]

A white person becomes a nominee by having his or her name on the title transfer and, in a separate transaction, selling that title to a nonwhite for a nominal fee—frequently, the equivalent of US$1.00.

While houses sold to nonwhites in white areas may trade at a premium, they often turn out to be bargains in comparison to houses for sale in the black townships. An article entitled "Cheaper to Buy a Home in the Northern Suburbs than in Soweto," in *New Dawn's SA Black Enterprise* (vol. 4, p. 5), said,

Those who are buying houses in Johannesburg's suburbs these days are getting them for a song because many of them have dropped in value, yet in Soweto houses fetch unbelievable prices.... A house in the northern suburbs [white] whose value was R85,000 might be sold for R60,000 simply because very few people were competing for a house. But in Soweto the story is the other way round. Houses whose value is around R50,000 are easily fetching around R80,000 to R90,000.

The result of these economic forces is that whites are becoming the minority population in some areas specified under the Group Areas Act as "white." Although there are no official statistics because of the illegality involved, the Housing Department of the Johannesburg City Council estimates that, based on informal counts, the Johannesburg white suburb of Mayfair houses 5,645 Indians, 936 other nonwhites, and 6,321 whites.[44]

The government's decision not to press for full enforcement of the Group Areas Act is seen in an announcement by the attorney general of the Transvaal that he has not been instituting any prosecutions under the act. Furthermore, in October 1986, State President P. W. Botha told a Cape congress of National party members that he does not think of the Group Areas Act as a "holy cow," and that the government is prepared to consider amendments. Some of the contraventions of the act can be made legal—Botha said—through the use of special permits. Botha added that special protection may be needed, especially by lower income groups. However, the opening of higher income suburbs to all races would be considered. Botha said that as many South Africans of all groups as possible should be put in a position to own their own homes.[45] High government officials are just now reluctantly accepting what has for some time been an economic reality.

A part of this official acceptance of economic reality—and rejection of one of the basic tenets of apartheid: that blacks are temporary sojourners in white areas—is the 1984 Development of Black Communities Act. Under this act, blacks have the choice of buying or selling property (in urban black townships) by 99-year leasehold rights or full property ownership—giving them the same common-law rights as whites, coloreds, and Asian homeowners. The new regulations also permit any person, regardless of race, to participate in the development of black residential areas. Therefore, black townships are now open to outside land developers without the former proviso that a black person must hold the controlling interest.

REALITY ON THE RAND

The Industrial Conciliation Act of 1924 and its subsequent amendments allowed the minister of labor to make "determinations" specifying certain jobs as white only, in order to "safeguard against interracial competition." Ever since that time, the Chamber of Mines has been working to undermine these job reservation laws—by political efforts to win their repeal, by petitions for exemption, by negotiations with white unions, and by stealth.

The presence of apartheid labor law, the unions' power to strike, and the country's memory of the violent 1922 Rand Rebellion gave to the white trade unionists considerable leverage in maintaining the color bar. Despite this power, the color bar legislation has been continually violated. According to the government's 1936 annual report, hardly a year went by without the government mining engineer blaming white miners for "inciting" blacks—who did not hold blasting certificates of competency—to charge drill holes in the mines. In 1936, the fine for such a violation was R25 for each black miner so employed; by 1967, the find had risen to R60.[46]

Sometimes a mine could get around the color bar by seeking an exemption. This would require that the mine demonstrate to the government mining engineer the unavailability of suitable, unemployed, and qualified white men. Scarcity of white skilled labor has indeed been the driving force for relaxation of the color bar during periods of economic growth in South Africa.

This is reflected in the Chamber of Mines primary means of assaulting the color bar: negotiation with white trade unionists. White workers were promised that, if they would allow some blacks to do white jobs, their positions would not be in danger and there would be no undercutting of their wages. Despite these kind of adjustments to the color bar, a skilled labor shortage persisted in the mines.

In 1964, a dozen mines—with the backing of white trade unions—sought and obtained permission to relax temporarily the government's regulation regarding "early examination." This regulation required that, before black men could go to work at a shaft position, the site had to be declared safe by a white miner. This regulation was a source of large losses in man-hours, because gangs of black workers had to wait at the bottom of a shaft for an area to be declared safe. The government responded by allowing experiments that permitted the use of a "nonscheduled" person—a black who bore the title of "bossboy"—to inspect the site.

The mines' management staffs were satisfied with the experiment because they were able to use the available labor more productively. The black miners were satisfied because the change meant wage increases and advancement for them. Finally, the white miners—now on a monthly salary—had more pay and less work. Moreover, production increased, and the accident rate fell.

Some of the driving force behind such experimentation with relaxing certain features of the color bar was a fear on the part of the Mine Workers Union that marginal mines would have to shut down, and that union workers would lose their jobs.[47]

While the experiment was a success on purely economic grounds, it was called off because of dissatisfaction among some of the white miners who had not taken part in the agreement; they resurrected the memory of the 1922 Rand Rebellion. They warned of unfair competition and raised the specter of blacks taking over white jobs. The government-sanctioned experiment was then investigated, and was found to be an economic success. Still, it was called off after a year because of its political risks.[48]

The shortage of skilled mineworkers persisted. In February 1966, the government's minister of mines testified in the House of Assembly that the mining industry was short of 2,000 white miners. This shortage led to negotiations between the Federation of Mining Unions and the Chamber of Mines. The negotiations were greeted with skepticism by many white miners not only had they been seeing a rise in black to white employment ratios (see Table 5.4)—and the Chamber of Mines again trying to erode the color bar—but they also saw their union leaders as being weak and unwilling to combat the chamber's onslaught against the "white man's preserve."

Suspicion of the chamber's design caused a wave of wildcat strikes. The members of the Mine Workers Union threw out their secretary and elected one who was sworn in on the oath that he would resist "the onslaught of Kaffir, Moor and Indian on the White working community."[49] Striking MWU members were told, "Your jobs in the gold mining industry are in danger. Certain types of work are being taken over by the Kaffir, and you are gradually being pushed out of the industry."[50]

Despite the protests, however, an agreement between the union federation and the mineowners' chamber was reached in April 1967. Black workers would be allowed to handle explosives; they would be permitted to operate underground locomotives that carried whites, so long as the speed was no greater than 10 miles per hour; and, with certain stipulations, they would no longer have to wait for a white miner to declare a mine area safe.

For their part in the agreement, the 22,000 white miners were given the largest part of the expected productivity gains resulting from their concession. They were put on a monthly salary basis with increased pension, accident, and sick pay benefits—all of which raised their wages by 11 percent.[51]

The sheer weight of economic reality had taken its toll on some of the strongest preserves of apartheid. Prestigious people were speaking out against it. D. A. J.

Table 5.4
Employment on Gold Mines[a]

Date	White[b]	Black[c]	Index |1936=100| White	Index |1936=100| Black	Ratio Black:White	Remarks
1910	23,621	183,793	67	62	7:8:1	
1911	24,746	190,137	70	64	7:7:1	Mines and Works Act
1912	23,867	192,767	67	65	8:1:1	
1913	23,179	184,812	66	62	8:0:1	White miners'strike
1914	21,164	169,385	60	57	8:0:1	Black labour unrest
1915	22,080	195,426	62	66	8:9:1	
1916	22,329	203,666	63	69	9:1:1	
1917	22,475	183,304	64	62	8:2:1	
1918	22,764	179,628	64	60	7:9:1	*Status Quo* Agreement
1919	23,179	171,326	66	58	7:4:1	
1920	22,198	176,057	63	59	7:9:1	Black miners' strike
1921	21,036	172,694	59	58	8:2:1	
1922	14,207	161,351	40	54	11:4:1	Rand rebellion
1923	17,727	177,855	50	60	10:0:1	
1924	18,457	178,395	52	60	9:7:1	
1925	19,263	174,539	54	59	9:1:1	
1926	19,713	181,577	56	61	9:2:1	
1927	20,765	186,407	59	63	9:0:1	
1928	21,701	196,660	61	66	9:1:1	
1929	21,949	193,221	62	65	8:8:1	
1930	22,112	202,118	63	68	9:1:1	
1931	22,654	210,238	64	71	9:3:1	
1932	23,448	217,774	66	73	9:3:1	Sharp increase in gold price
1933	25,218	229,696	71	77	9:1:1	
1934	28,334	249,200	80	84	8:8:1	
1935	31,898	273,218	90	92	8:6:1	
1936	35,393	297,441	100	100	8:5:1	
1937	38,327	303,087	108	102	8:0:1	
1938	40,793	316,862	115	107	7:9:1	
1939	43,183	321,400	122	108	7:5:1	
1940	42,852	351,826	121	188	8:3:1	Increase in black labour supply
1941	41,424	368,417	117	124	9:0:1	
1942	40,555	357,573	115	120	8:9:1	
1943	38,508	306,285	109	103	8:0:1	
1944	37,166	297,591	105	100	8:1:1	
1945	36,328	307,291	103	103	8:5:1	
1946	39,642	304,782	112	103	7:7:1	Black miners' strike
1947	38,829	295,867	110	100	7:7:1	
1948	39,019	279,218	110	94	7:3:1	

Table 5.4 (continued)

			Index |1936=100|		
					Ratio	
Date	White[b]	Black[c]	White	Black	Black:White	Remarks
1949	39,527	294,180	112	99	7:5:1	Sharp increase in gold price
1950	43,109	305,165	122	103	7:2:1	
1951	44,291	298,754	125	100	6:9:1	Acute shortage of black labour
1952	45,105	298,980	127	101	6:8:1	
1953	46,355	290,962	131	98	6:4:1	
1954	47,967	314,399	136	106	6:7:1	
1955	49,266	327,475	139	110	6:7:1	
1956	49,469	336,215	140	113	6:8:1	
1957	47,903	335,098	135	113	7:0:1	
1958	47,303	339,867	134	114	7:2:1	
1959	48,600	380,473	137	128	7:7:1	Large influx of black labour
1960	49,688	387,577	140	130	7:7:1	
1961	49,144	399,009	139	134	8:1:1	
1962	48,639	392,733	137	132	8:1:1	
1963	47,352	381,440	134	128	8:1:1	
1964	45,774	380,949	129	128	8:3:1	First official attempt to ease colou bar (since 1922)
1965	44,181	375,329	125	126	8:5:1	
1966	43,439	370,469	123	125	8:5:1	
1967	42,296	361,893	120	122	8:6:1	
1968	40,491	368,135	114	124	9:1:1	
1969	39,660	364,151	112	122	9:2:1	

Source: Francis Wilson, *Labour in the South African Gold Mines* (London: Cambridge University Press, 1972), pp. 157-158.

Notes: (a) Members of the Chamber of Mines. (b) Figures for 1940-45 exclude some 5,000 men on full-time national service. (c) These figures include small numbers of Coloured and Indian workers. In 1936, 0.6% of the total labour force was Coloured and 0.05% was Indian. In 1968 the figures were 0.09% and 0.007% respectively.

Norval, former chairman of the Board of Trade—addressing the Institutue of Bankers annual meeting in 1968—said that, if the gold-mining industry were to survive, blacks would have to replace 70 percent of the white workers. Needless to say, this statement incurred the anger of the white unions, and the government disassociated itself from Norval's statement. However, there is some evidence that such a view had National party support. Federale Mynbou—chairman of the General Mining Group, and brother of a cabinet minister—argued that the status and material well-being of the white worker is enhanced by allowing blacks to do the work traditionally done by whites. Mynbou added that this would free the white man to do more responsible and productive work.[52]

White Protest

Economic realities, along with added international and domestic pressures, continue to threaten the political protections that whites had enjoyed for decades.

Through their unions, white miners have expressed considerable concern with what they see as betrayal by the government. Studying the responses and complaints of the unions in recent years can lead us to a valuable understanding of the forces for discrimination, in South Africa and elsewhere. Moreover, these white worker protests seriously call into question the Marxist rhetoric that portrays apartheid as a tool of capitalist enrichment.

The *Financial Mail* (November 11, 1983) reported that Tom Neething, general secretary of the whites-only Amalgamated Engineers Union (AUE), had urged the manpower minister, Fanie Botha, to meet with unions and provide "a specific, categoric and unambiguous undertaking that the goverment will step in where necessary to protect the rights of minority groups." To Neething, "minority groups" meant white miners. He added, "On the workshop floor it is the black, who by virtue of his exploitability and his numbers, poses the biggest long-term threat to the future of all workers." Neething did not oppose "the principle of orderly advancement of any race to the limits of the capabilities of its members," but he felt that white workers' futures were being threatened. In response to relaxation of some of the legalized discrimination against black workers, Neething said, "Our experience since then has been that we are under a constant state of siege from employers who have seized the new-found freedom of movement granted to them in terms of the new legislation, to introduce changes without consultation with those affected by such change." Neething's complaint was that employers were hiring "too many" blacks, thereby threatening the jobs of white union members.

The Wiehahn Commission

A considerable part of the controversy in the mining industry concerns the 1979 Wiehahn Commission recommendation that the regulations on the definition of "scheduled person" in the Mines and Works Act be replaced by the nonracial epithet "competent person." According to the Mines and Works Act of 1911, as amended by the Amendment Act of 1925:

(i) The regulation under paragraph (n) [see below] may provide that in such provinces, areas or places as may be specified in the regulations, certificates of competency in any occupation referred to in that paragraph shall be granted only to the following classes of persons, namely—
    (a) Europeans:
    (b) persons born in the Union and ordinarily resident in the Province of Good Hope who are members of the class or race known as "Cape Coloured" or of the class or race known as "Cape Malays";
    (c) persons born in the Union and ordinarily resident in the Union elsewhere than in the Province of the Cape of Good Hope who would if resident in that Province, be regarded as members of either of the classes or races known as "Cape Coloured" or "Cape Malays"; and

(d) the people known as Mauritius Creoles or St. Helena persons or their descendants born in the Union.
(ii) The regulations under any other paragraphs of this subsection may restrict particular work to, and, in connection therewith, impose duties and responsibilities upon the classes of person mentioned in (a), (b), (c) and (d) of part (i) of this subsection; may apportion particular work as between those classes and other persons; and may require such proof-of-efficiency as may be prescribed.

Through these provisions, blacks are omitted from the list of scheduled persons, which means that they cannot receive certificates of competency and are prohibited from 13 categories of mine employment as specified in Section 4(n) of the Mines and Works Act. Section 4(n) empowers the governor-general to

make regulations, not inconsistent with this Act, in respect of or in connection with all or any of the following matters or things, namely—
(n) the grant, cancellation, and suspension of certificates of competency to—
(1) mine managers,
(2) mine overseers,
(3) mine surveyors,
(4) mechanical engineers,
(5) engine drivers,
(6) miners entitled to blast,
(7) such other classes of persons employed in or about mines, works, and machinery as the Governor-General may from time to time deem it expedient to require to be in possession of certificates of competency.

The 13 different categories of mine work for which blacks are denied certificates of competency are indeed the highest paid jobs.

While the South African government has written a white paper in support of the changes recommended by the Wiehahn Commission, it prefers that the matter be left to negotiation between the Chamber of Mines and the white unions. The government wishes to avoid imposing its will in this politically explosive area, where white unions often raise the specter of the violent 1922 strikes on the Rand. The Mine Workers Union—represented by its secretary, Arrie Paulus—has been very vocal in its opposition to proposed changes in the Mines and Works Act because most of its members have not risen above the status of blasting certificate holder. This is particularly threatening in face of the fact that "black miners actually perform many of the functions of blasting certificate holders in terms of the exemptions of the Mines and Works Act."[53]

What clearer evidence do we need that apartheid labor laws are mostly the result of union pressures for government to grant them special monopoly privileges?! The fact that business officials rebel against union monopolies—and vice versa—stems from neither vice nor virtue. People always want a free market when they are buying and a monopoly when they are selling, for the simple reason that a free market results in lower prices and a monopoly results in higher prices. That is why unions—as sellers of labor services—always want to close their market to potential competitors.

But just as important to us is recognizing the issue of racial restrictions as but a special case of union monopoly strategy. Consider the above quotation of Mr. Neething: "On the workshop floor it is the black, who by virtue of his exploitability and his numbers, poses the biggest long-term threat to the future of all workers." With minor word changes here and there, that remark could come from the mouth of some union official in the United States—who professes a concern *for* blacks. For example, this U.S. union official might say, "On the workshop floor it is the *teenager*, who by virtue of his exploitability... poses the biggest long-term threat to the future of all other workers." Just as easily, we could substitute "illegal alien" and express the same sentiment. The union definition of "exploitability" often boils down to one class of workers accepting a wage lower than the union's, which threatens the likelihood that the union wage can be sustained. Therefore, unions can be predicted to seek legislation that will reduce their competition—no matter whether the competition comes from blacks, teenagers, illegal aliens, or machinery. Thus, the general case for union strategy is to close the labor market to competition from those who would accept a lower wage. In South Africa, it happens to be blacks, coloreds, and Asians. Elsewhere, it might be teenagers, illegal aliens, or housewives working at home.

THE ECONOMIC GENERALITIES OF APARTHEID

It is important in understanding some of the forces at play in South Africa to develop a framework in which one can decide who benefits from apartheid and who is harmed. The conventional wisdom says that all whites are apartheid beneficiaries, and all nonwhites are apartheid losers. The truth of the matter is probably a mixture of the two.

Be they housewives hiring domestic servants, farmers hiring field hands, or factories hiring labor, South Africa's white employers (buyers of labor) benefit from having a large number of blacks available to work. Competitive pressures lead to lower market wages. On the other hand, sellers of labor benefit from restrictions that reduce the supply of available workers.

The influx control laws, which restricted the supply of black workers in white urban areas, did several things. First, they raised the labor costs of employers in urban areas, by reducing the supply and mobility of labor. Also, to the extent that the influx control laws were effective, they depressed wages in rural areas—where blacks were crowded in—and denied to blacks the option for higher urban wages and training opportunities. Thus, the beneficiaries of the restrictions on black mobility were the rural area employers, who were able to pay lower wages. The losing class of employers were those in urban areas: They had to pay higher wages. The unintended beneficiaries of influx control were those blacks who did have legal permission to work in urban areas. They benefited in the form of higher wages, as a result of the smaller number of blacks in the urban designated townships.

We can use this depiction of apartheid winners and losers—assuming that it is correct—to gain insight into some of the political forces at work in South Africa's history. For example, urban interests supported and benefited from the Native Land Act of 1913 and other measures that sought to drive blacks off the land. Eliminating or reducing rural self-employment forced more blacks into the urban labor market.

Driving blacks off the land also benefited white rural interests. First, it reduced the competition that white farmers were getting from blacks in the agricultural products market. Second, it made more blacks available for hired labor. But with fewer self-employment opportunities in rural areas and higher wages available in urban areas, blacks left for the cities in droves. Therefore, it was beneficial to the rural interests to restrict that mobility—hence, the rural support for influx control and other impediments to black urban mobility.

Urban employers did not share the rural employers' enthusiasm for influx control. They constantly sought special exemptions and evaded, contravened, and violated influx control law in order to hire blacks.

The fact that urban employers sought to violate and contravene the apartheid law that was benefiting another class of whites does not require that we assess whether they had more or less feelings of white supremacy than anyone else. Their financial interests were served by having a larger supply of black workers to work in the mines, textile factories, and other urban-oriented businesses.

Similarly, we need not assess whether the labor unions were full of white supremacists when they supported influx control. It was in their financial interest to restrict the supply of competing workers. Race and the ideology of white supremacy turned out to be a convenient exclusionary device. Thus, economic theory predicts that the conjunction of their mutual interests would lead to a political coalition between urban white workers and white farmers in support of influx control laws.

A similar economic analysis can be applied to the job reservation laws. Job reservation raises wages by restricting the supply of potential applicants. As such, it benefits the seller of labor services, and not the buyer. Identifying the sector of the economy were job reservation flourished can tell us something about the distribution of political power among the various classes of labor buyers. The labor buyer with political clout will seek ways to avoid the high-cost labor policy of job reservation, the buyer with less political clout will have to suffer. In South Africa, the white Afrikaner farmer has traditionally been the backbone of the powerful National party. Predictably enough, it has been precisely the farmers who have escaped most of the high costs of apartheid labor law. The South African industrialist—predominantly English, up until quite recently—has had little political power, and hence little power to fight the labor market interests of the farmers and unionists. The industrialists have borne the high costs of apartheid labor law.

SUMMARY

On top of the general agreement that South Africa's apartheid laws are offensive to the principle of human rights, we have also found that the achievement of apartheid's goals are elusive in any case. Governments can legislate market restrictions, but—try as they may—governments cannot legislate market forces completely out of existence. There will always be a tendency for people to seek mutually advantageous exchanges. In South Africa, it is a matter of contravention of the apartheid laws; but in other places, it is evasion of price controls, rent controls, or other government hindrances to voluntary exchange.

Many of the socioeconomic advances made by blacks, coloreds, and Asians in South Africa have been due to the market forces that produce this search for mutually advantageous exchange. These advances come as a result of the non-European's ability to underprice the European—leading the former not only to a higher income than would otherwise be possible, but to the acquisition of skills, as well.

If market forces act as a friend to South Africa's non-European population, we can begin to understand what kind of policies will promote the well-being of this disadvantaged majority. That idea will be one of the issues discussed in the following chapter.

NOTES

1. George V. Doxey, *The Industrial Colour Bar in South Africa* (London: Oxford University Press, 1961), p. 180.
2. Doxey, *Industrial Colour Bar*, p. 182.
3. Ibid., pp. 183–84. Black compensation is understated to the extent that they received nonmoney wages in the form of "free" housing and food. In 1969, food subsidies to blacks averaged R56.30 ($40.50) and R.72 ($7.00) for whites. Whites received housing subsidies that, in 1965, ranged from R40 ($29) for a junior employee to R330 ($238) for a mine manager. See Francis Wilson, *Labour in the South African Gold Mines 1911–1969* (London: Cambridge University Press, 1972), pp. 166–68.
4. Merle Lipton, *Capitalism and Apartheid: South Africa, 1910–84* (Totowa, N.J.: Rowman and Allanheld, 1985), p. 138.
5. Ibid., p. 140.
6. Ibid., p. 142.
7. See A. B. Lumby, "Tariffs and the Printing Industry in South Africa, 1906–1939," *South African Journal of Economics* 45, 2 (February 1977); Arnt Spandau, "South African Wage Board Policy: An Alternative Interpretation," *South African Journal of Economics* 40, 4 (December 1972): 377–87.
8. Lipton, *Capitalism and Apartheid*, pp. 152–56.
9. Ibid., p. 152.
10. Alex Hepple, *South Africa: Workers under Apartheid*, 2nd ed. (London: International Defence and Aid Fund, 1971), p. 46. See also Leo Marquard, *The People and Policies of South Africa* (London: Oxford University Press, 1969), p. 141.

11. Lawrence Schlemmer, *Employment Opportunities and Race in South Africa* (Denver, Colo.: University of Denver, 1973), p. 28.
12. G. M. E. Leistner and W. J. Breytenback, *The Black Worker of South Africa* (Pretoria: Africa Institute of South Africa, 1975), p. 26.
13. Schlemmer, *Employment Opportunities*, p. 28.
14. Ibid.
15. Hepple, *South Africa*, p. 47.
16. Ibid., p. 79.
17. S. Busheunel, "Black Industrial Labour in South Africa," *South African Journal of Economics* 42, 3 (September 1974): 297.
18. Leistner and Breytenback, *Black Worker*, p. 27.
19. Ibid.
20. Ibid., p. 29.
21. Ibid.
22. Gavin Maasdorp and Nesen Pillay, "Indians in the Political Economy of South Africa," in *South Africa's Indians: The Evolution of a Minority*, edited by Bridglal Pachi (Washington, D.C.: University Press of America, 1979), p. 211.
23. Ibid., p. 219.
24. Ibid., p. 303.
25. Dan O'Meara, *Volkskapitalisme: Class, Capital, and Ideology in the Development of Afrikaner Nationalism, 1934–1948* (London: Cambridge University Press, 1983), pp. 167–68.
26. "Notes," *South African Law Journal* 6 (1939): 345–46.
27. O'Meara, *Volkskapitalisme*, p. 168. Emphasis in original.
28. Ibid., p. 169.
29. *Weekly Newsletter*, 484 (March 12, 1949): 7, cited in Eugene P. Dvorin, *Racial Separation in South Africa: An Analysis of Apartheid Theory* (Chicago: University of Chicago Press, 1952), p. 161.
30. Maasdorp and Pillay, "Indians in the Political Economy," p. 303.
31. *Weekly Newsletter*, 460 (September 27, 1948): 6, cited in Dvorin, *Racial Separation*, p. 163.
32. *Weekly Newsletter*, 465 (November 1, 1948): 8, cited in Dvorin, *Racial Separation*, p. 166.
33. Cited in Dvorin, *Racial Separation*, p. 169.
34. Ibid., p. 170.
35. O'Meara, *Volkskapitalisme*, p. 170.
36. *Die Burger* (March 29, 1948), cited in O'Meara, *Volkskapitalisme*, p. 171.
37. Gwendolyn Carter, *The Politics of Inequality: South Africa since 1948* (London: Thames and Hudson, 1959), p. 86.
38. Maasdorp and Pillay, "Indians in the Political Economy," p. 305.
39. Ibid., p. 239.
40. "The Crumbling of Apartheid," *Leadership* 4, 4 (1985): 57.
41. Christo de Coning, Johan Fick, and Nellie Olivier, "Residential Settlement Patterns: A Pilot Study of Socio-political Perceptions in Grey Areas of Johannesburg," unpublished working paper, Department of Development Studies, Rand Afrikaans University, Johannesburg, 1986, pp. 3–4.
42. Ibid., pp. 4–5.
43. Ibid., p. 34.

44. Ibid., p. 7.
45. Ibid., pp. 9–10.
46. Wilson, *Labour in the Gold Mines*, p. 114.
47. Marquard, *People and Policies*, p. 141.
48. Wilson, *Labour in the Gold Mines*, p. 115.
49. Ibid., p. 116.
50. Ibid., p. 226.
51. Ibid., pp. 116–17.
52. Ibid., pp. 117–18.
53. "Behind the Pact," *Financial Mail*, June 7, 1985, p. 58.

6
Apartheid: A Triumph over Capitalism

The dominant black opinion in South Africa is that apartheid is an outgrowth of capitalism. Business people are often seen as evil forces seeking racially discriminatory laws as a means to higher profits through the economic exploitation of non-Europeans. Therefore, in the eyes of many black Africans and their benefactors in Europe, the United States, and elsewhere, a large part of the solution is seen as being—inter alia—in the promotion of socialistic goals, such as state ownership and income redistribution, as a means to bring about a more just society.

The indictment of capitalism and market forces are reflected in statements by Bishop Desmond Tutu, South Africa's Nobel laureate, who wrote in *Frontline* (September 1980): "At the outset I must say that I am opposed to capitalism. ... It is due to abhorrence at what I believe to be an essentially exploitative economic order.... What I have seen of capitalism in my 48 years, and all over the world, has convinced me that no amount of plastic surgery can alter its basically ugly face." After accepting $232,000 in Nobel prize money—from the estate of a capitalist made rich through the sales of explosives—Bishop Tutu reiterated his assessment in London's *Sunday Telegraph*: "I myself *hate* capitalism."[1]

There are some South African whites who—wanting a better life for blacks—also share this view of capitalism. Raymond Sutter, an anti-apartheid activist, wrote in *Business Day* (August 22, 1985) that "The struggle for the Charter is therefore an anti-capitalist programme, because any programme to end racial oppression in South Africa must be anti-capitalist." Winnie Mandela—wife of the imprisoned black leader, Nelson Mandela—was quoted in *Pravda* (February 14, 1986) as saying, "The Soviet Union is a torch bearer for all our hopes and aspirations. In Soviet Russia genuine power of the people has been transformed from dreams to reality." Chris Dliami—vice-president of COSATU, a black labor union—said, "The unholy alliance apartheid and capitalism has become obvious and concrete. One cannot expect to eradicate it simply by removing apartheid.... What we are talking about is the total change of the present system."[2]

Contributing to the apartheid–capitalist connection in the minds of many South Africans are statements by South African government officials who refer to their economy as "our free market system." As President P. W. Botha said in his January 31, 1986, address to the South African Parliament: "Our country today is a symbol of . . . free enterprise."

Contrary to these mutually reinforcing sets of beliefs, the major premise of this book is that South Africa's apartheid is *not* the corollary of free-market or capitalistic forces. Apartheid is the result of anticapitalistic or socialistic efforts to subvert the operation of market (capitalistic) forces. Indeed, it is the free play of market forces—with no intervention by political forces—that has always been seen as the enemy of white privilege and that apartheid ideology has always sought to defeat.

South Africa's history is riddled with white contempt for market forces, from the highest levels of government on down. Prime Minister Jan Christiaan Smuts—in *A Century of Wrongs* (London: Review of Reviews, 1900)—said, "It is ordained that we [Afrikaners], insignificant as we are, should be amongst the first people to begin the struggle against the new world tyranny of capitalism."

Similar anticapitalist sentiment was echoed by Daniel F. Malan, who was later to lead the Afrikaner National party to victory at the polls in 1948. Addressing the Volkskongres in October 1934, Malan said,

If war should come, it will mean, in my opinion, the end of the capitalist system . . . but whether this happens with or without war, by revolution or evolution, the capitalist system which is based on self-interest and the right of the strongest is in any case doomed. For us to work together until the correct adjustment has been made will also be South Africa's task in the future.[3]

Later, *Volkshandel* (September 1941)—an Afrikaner business publication—carried more of the same:

Every sober-minded, thinking Arikaner is fed up to the top of his throat with so-called laissez faire—let-it-be—capitalism, with its soul destroying materialism and the spirit of "every man for himself and the devil for us all." We are sick of it because of its legacy of Afrikaner poor whiteism and the condition which makes the Afrikaner a spectator in the business of his own country.

One particularly crucial step in understanding the complexities of South Africa is to identify correctly just what the economic system of South Africa is. A good general place for us to begin is with a thumbnail description of capitalism contrasted to socialism.

CAPITALISM VERSUS SOCIALISM

Capitalism—or its synonyms: free enterprise, laissez-faire, and free markets—refers to a system where people hold private property rights to goods and services.

As owners, they have exclusive rights to decide on the uses of these goods and services in ways that do not violate the property rights of others. Private property rights include the right of individuals to keep, acquire, or dispose of goods and services with others on mutually agreeable terms without third party interference.

By contrast, socialism refers to a system where there is extensive government ownership and/or control over the means of production. The right of individuals to exchange property privately on mutually agreeable terms is severely limited by the state.

While there is no purely socialistic or capitalistic society in the world, one can arrange the various social orders along a continuum connecting the polar opposites of capitalism and socialism. Where South Africa fits along this continuum may be a matter for contention, but all must agree that socialism—along with its extensive government control over economic transactions—has been and continues to be a major feature of South African economic life. The fact that it masks itself as "nationalism" does not alter this description.

Government-owned monopolies in South Africa include the Electricity Supply Commission (ESCOM); the Iron and Steel Corporation (ISCOR); in telecommunications, the South African Broadcasting Corporation (SABC); railroad services (SATS); airlines (SAA); and many quasi-government entities. Through the National Marketing Council, the government has extensive control over agriculture. It controls hundreds of prices through the Price Control Act of 1964. Through legislation like the Mines and Works Act of 1926, the Native Building Workers Act of 1951, and the Industrial Conciliation Act of 1956, the government maintains extensive control over labor market transactions. Through the Group Areas Act of 1950, the government controls housing market transactions. In fact—as discussed throughout this book—the South African government controls many other economic transactions, as well.

MAKING RACE COUNT

The South African government's extensive control over the racial aspects of economic transactions in order to confer special privileges on whites stands as solid evidence that free market forces do not confer privileges based on race or other market-irrelevant attributes of the transactors. The mere existence of South Africa's extensive racial regulatory laws is evidence enough that racial privilege is difficult through free market forces. Consider South Africa's job reservation laws, which mandate that certain jobs be performed by whites only—like the Section 77 determination of the Industrial Conciliation Act requiring that underground steam engines used for transporting men be operated only by whites. South Africa's mines are owned and controlled by whites. The question is: If white mineowners would voluntarily discriminate against black workers as steam engine drivers, why would a law mandating that they do so be necessary?

The presence of job reservation laws suggests that at least some employers *would* hire blacks in the "white jobs." The fact that they would hire blacks to do white jobs neither requires nor suggests that these employers be necessarily any less white supremacist than anyone else. It does suggest that those employers who would hire blacks considered such a course of action to be an attractive alternative because blacks were willing to work for lower wages—"uncivilised wages"—than white workers. The business pursuit of profits—which caused employers to be less ardent supporters of the white supremacist doctrine—has always been the enemy of white privilege. This is why South African white workers resorted to government. The political arena allows one to achieve privilege that would be impossible—or very costly—in the market arena because market forces have little respect for status attributes like race, sex, and nationality. The political arena does—or can be made to—have respect for status attributes.

It is precisely these socialistic features of South African society that constitute the most important source of blacks' grievances. To make this assertion more concrete, the author wishes to relate an experience that he had at the University of the North—a black university near Pietersburg—during a ten-week lecture tour in 1980. During the discussion period that followed the lecture, a black student rose to announce that he was against capitalism and believed in socialism. The author proceeded to ask this young man a series of questions: (1) Do you believe that you ought to be free to purchase property wherever you please, without government interference? (2) Do you believe that you ought to be free to start up any type of business wherever you want, without government interference? (3) Do you believe that you ought to be free to work for any employer in any capacity commensurate with your skills, under mutually agreeable terms, without government interference? After the student answered yes to these and several similar questions, the author informed the student that his sentiments were actually closer to laissez-faire capitalism than to socialism. The author then went on to explain that it was the socialistic features—the extensive government control—of South African society that were the chief sources of black suffering.

APARTHEID ON THE DECLINE

South African apartheid is falling victim to domestic political and economic forces and to international opinion. The 1980s have seen dramatic changes that have struck at the very foundations of apartheid principles as envisioned by its architects, Prime Ministers Malan and Verwoerd.

In 1976, sports and athletics were desegregated, though the complaint remains that the facilities in black areas are not equal to those in white areas.

The Abolition of Influx Control Act No. 68 of 1986 abolished 32 individual enactments including the old passbook law, which was replaced with a uniform identity document for both blacks and whites (coded according to race). The act removed a very serious obstacle to the economic mobility of millions of blacks, and it removed what blacks saw as one of the most offensive features of apartheid. This measure, along with the repeal of the influx control measures imposed by the Black Labour Act of 1964 and the Black Urban Areas Consolidation Act of

1945, eases restrictions on blacks whom the government consider citizens of South Africa.

The impact of these changes on the more than nine million black "noncitizens"—officially citizens of Transkei, Boputhatswana, Venda, and Ciskei (TBVC)—is not clear. In order for them to legally work and reside in urban areas of South Africa, work permits are required. The government promises to restore South African citizenship to these people; but—for better or worse—doing so may destroy whatever political meaning can be attached to the "independent" status of the TBVC homelands. Conceding citizenship rights in this case might have implications similar to the United States passing a law granting U.S. citizenship to all Canadians and Mexicans.

The Industrial Conciliation Amendment Acts of 1979 and 1981 repealed Section 77 of the Industrial Conciliation Act of 1956, which had established discriminatory job reservation laws. The new acts repealed job reservation in every area of employment except for five categories of work in the mining industry. This exception reflects the government's fear of intrusion into an area that is very sensitive to the politically powerful white mining unions. In 1987, the government moved to abolish job reservation in the mining industry through enactment of the Mines and Works Amendment Act No. 38.

The Labour Law Amendment Act No. 57 of 1981 was another key change in labor law. It removed racial bars to unionism—giving black unions the right to collective bargaining and the right to strike.

The Liquor Act, of 1927 as amended, had been a major support legislation for racial segregation of hotels, clubs, and restaurants. The violation of racial codes could lead to fines and possible nonrenewal of licenses. The Liquor Act Amendment of 1986 repealed all racially discriminatory provisions—thus permitting (but not requiring) hotels, bars, private clubs, and restaurant owners to serve a racially mixed clientele.

The Group Areas Amendment Act No. 101 of 1985, along with Proclamation R17 of 1985, permitted the minister of constitutional development and planning to establish mixed business districts in exclusively white areas. By 1986 integrated business districts were already established in 55 municipalities.

Through the Immorality and Mixed Marriages Amendment Act No. 72 of 1985, the South African Parliament repealed the Mixed Marriages Act of 1949, which had prohibited marriages between members of different races. It also repealed the provisions of the Immorality Act that prohibited sexual relations between members of different races.

The Black Communities Development Act No. 74 of 1986 and Proclamations Nos. 1538 and 1898—both in 1986—repealed the prohibition against black ownership of immovable property in areas designated for them under the Group Areas Act. Furthermore, it permitted blacks the right to convert their recently won 99-year leasehold rights (under the Black Communities Development Act of 1984) into absolute ownership rights—like those of the average U.S. homeowner.

Moreover, Sections 33 and 41(1) of the Black Communities Development Act

No. 74 of 1986 and the Township Establishment and Land Use Regulation No. 1897 of 1986 transferred full ownership of land to the black municipal administrations and local authorities. The Constitutional Affairs Act No. 104 of 1985 repealed the Prohibition of Political Interference Act of 1968, which had prohibited racially mixed political parties.

As of this writing, the Separate Amenities Act—another major cornerstone of apartheid—has been suggested for repeal by some government officials. Currently, many of its provisions—such as the segregation of theaters, hotels, and restaurants—are either left up to the discretion of local authorities through Proclamation R71 of 1986, or else are not being enforced at all.

At this time, the remaining major legalized forms of discrimination in South Africa are the Population Registration Act, the Group Areas Act, the Separate Amenities Act, the Land Act, and the fact that blacks do not have the political franchise. Even the Group Areas Act has been weakened through Proclamation No. 112 of 1986 and Notice No. 524 of 1986. These new standards relax the procedures for blacks, coloreds, and Asians in obtaining special permits to legally reside in white areas, and they restrict the prosecution of nonwhites who are residing illegally in white areas in violation of the Group Areas Act of 1966. In *The Dismantling of Apartheid*, Andre E. A. M. Thomashausen cities other apartheid laws, too, that have been either repealed or relaxed.[4]

KWAZULU/NATAL INDABA

A major effort at racial reconciliation in South Africa—one that has been grossly underreported in the international arena—is the KwaZulu/Natal Indaba. In the spring of 1982, Chief Mangosuthu Buthelezi, chief executive officer of KwaZulu, issued a two-volume work that has become known as the "Buthelezi Commission Report." The Buthelezi Commission was constituted by a broad cross-section of interests including union leaders, business people, politicians, and professionals of all races: black, colored, Indian, Afrikaner, and English. The commission's charge was to enquire into the social, political, and economic conditions of KwaZulu and Natal, and to make constructive proposals for stability and development. A major proposal of the Buthelezi Commission Report was a call for a KwaZulu/Natal Indaba. The charge for the Indaba (a Zulu word for the meeting of wise men on important matters) was to study the requirements for joining Natal—a white province that includes Indians, coloreds, and blacks—with KwaZulu—a black homeland—into a single political jurisdiction with a nonracial constitution.

Natal Province lies adjacent to the Indian Ocean with the port city of Durban as its major metropolitan area. KwaZulu consists of 50 fragmented—half of them quite small—noncontiguous areas of land within the geographical boundaries of Natal, with its capital in Ulundi. According to the 1980 census, Natal Province's population consists of 560,000 whites, 91,000 coloreds, 661,000 Indians (80 percent of South Africa's Indian population), and 1.4 million blacks.

KwaZulu's population consists of 3.5 million blacks, 17,000 whites, 2,500 coloreds, and 8,300 Indians.

The fact that an indaba was actually formed among the diverse—and often antagonistic—population of KwaZulu and Natal is in itself a miracle of sorts. First of all, the fears and suspicions between the Zulus and the Indians that culminated in the 1949 Zulu/Indian riots have not been entirely eliminated. Second, Indian/white relations have traditionally been one of mutual contempt. Third, the English-speaking population and the Afrikaans-speaking population have always viewed each other with suspicion, and many Afrikaners still remember what they consider to have been English atrocities during the Boer War. Moreover, Afrikaners see the English, who are eligible to take up citizenship in British Commonwealth countries, as willing to sell the rest of the whites down the river into "black domination."

Despite all these differences and suspicions, the KwaZulu/Natal Indaba managed to agree on several major recommendations of the Buthelezi Commission: (1) that a single legislative body be set up to administer the KwaZulu/Natal area; (2) that the type of legislative body chosen would *not* be constructed on the Westminster model in which the ruling party has inordinate power; (3) that the combined KwaZulu/Natal area would remain a part of the Republic of South Africa; (4) that the collective fear of political domination by any one group would be honestly acknowledged by rejecting a system of universal suffrage for the unitary state.[5]

The KwaZulu/Natal Indaba met for most of 1986 and fashioned a constitution that provides for the appointment of a governor and two legislative houses. In both houses, the Indaba proposes proportional representation according to race, with its members elected on the basis of universal suffrage. Moreover, the Indaba has written and agreed on a U.S.-style Bill of Rights, which is reproduced in Appendix 6.A.

As of this writing, the South African government has not endorsed the KwaZulu/Natal Indaba proposals. But neither has it totally rejected them. If the government were to reject the Indaba proposals, the results would be tragic. It would be weakening the hand of decent South Africans in pursuit of a peaceful resolution of the nation's racial problems. And it would energize the extremists—both black and white—who seek violent confrontation and racial domination.

CANTONAL GOVERNMENT

One of the more interesting solutions to South Africa's racial problems has been put forward in a 1987 book by Leon Louw and Frances Kendall—*After Apartheid*[6]—which is an all-time best seller in South Africa and has won the endorsement of such widely divergent people as Winnie Mandela, Chief Mangosuthu Buthelezi, the white South African writer and liberal politician Alan Paton, and the U.S. civil rights leader Bayard Rustin. Louw and Kendall assert that the powers of South Africa's central government are so awesome that no ethnic group can trust putting those powers into the hands of another ethnic group—which is what would happen under a one-person-one-vote system in a unitary state. The whites who currently hold the political power at the exclusion of blacks would not trust putting the power into the latter's hands. On the other hand, blacks—who do not have the power—do not like it or trust it in the hands of whites. But just as importantly, if it were to turn out as the result of an election that the Zulus—who are the most numerous single ethnic group—won the power of the central government, the Xhosas would not feel as though they could trust the Zulus with that power.

What Kendall and Louw propose—which can only be highlighted here—is that South Africa be split into numerous autonomous cantons, linked by a central government whose functions would be strictly limited (to matters like national defense, foreign affairs, and finance) by a constitution that must entrench equality before the law for every individual and must not subjugate minorities.[7]

The key feature of the Kendall and Louw proposal is that it would devolve power from the central-government level down to numerous cantonal levels. The focus of political activity would be at the cantonal level; different political groupings would form in different areas. According to Kendall and Louw, each canton would determine its own economic policy and its own labor, transport, education, tax, subsidization, welfare, and race policies.[8] In each canton, the political franchise would be exercised as one-person-many-votes: People would vote on community issues, cantonal issues, and in national referendums on national issues. A constitutional bill of rights would guarantee freedom of movement, protection of property, rights of association, rights to call for a referendum, and protection from victimization and intimidation of minorities.

The major benefit of the Kendall and Louw canton-system concept is that it accommodates the wide diversity found in South Africa while minimizing the probability that any one group would be able to impose its values and customs on another. Or, as Kendall and Louw put it:

Ultimately, the only way to avoid group domination is by allowing people to govern themselves. Given self-government, even without all the constitutional guarantees we have included, we can safely rely on the most meaningful protection of all: the goodwill of most South Africans—black, white, Indian and Coloured alike.[9]

PRIMUM NON NOCERE

South Africa's recent measures to enhance the civil rights of its nonwhite population fall far short of what its citizens are demanding and what the Western world expects. At the same time, however, the government's efforts at reform are moving in the right direction. While no one would wish to justify South Africa's status quo, a sense of compassion demands that we acknowledge some undeniable facts about the country and its nonwhite population.

If South Africa—or any other country, for that matter—were compared to our

Table 6.1
Approximate Work Time Required for Average Manufacturing Employees to Buy Selected Commodities in Retail Stores in Washington, D.C., and London and at State-fixed Prices in Moscow and Johannesburg during May 1976

Commodity	Washington	London	Moscow	South Africa: Witwatersrand Area		
				Artisan (White)	Machine Operator (Black)	Labourer (Black)
White bread, 1kg	21 min	10 min	20 min	4 min	12 min	19 min
Beef, 1kg	34 min	76 min	3.5 hrs	52 min	2.5 hrs	4 hrs
Pork sausages, 1kg	71 min	60 min	2.6 hrs	36 min	1.8 hrs	2.8 hrs
Potatoes, 1 kg	8 min	23 min	7 min	6 min	18 min	28 min
Apples, 1kg	16 min	24 min	5.4 hrs	10 min	30 min	47 min
Sugar, 1kg	9 min	15 min	65 min	4 min	12 min	19 min
Milk, 1 litre	7 min	11 min	21 min	5 min	15 min	23 min
Eggs (10)	10 min	13 min	97 min	8 min	24 min	37 min
Vodka (0.7 litres)	67 min	3.4 hrs	9.8 hrs	1.5 hrs	4.5 hrs	6.6 hrs
Cigarettes (20)	10 min	27 min	23 min	8 min	24 min	37 min
Soap, toilet, 150 gr	5 min	10 min	72 min	8 min	24 min	37 min
Lipstick	31 min	54 min	7.8 hrs	32 min	1.5 hrs	2.5 hrs
Panty hose	17 min	15 min	9 hrs	15 min	44 min	70 min
Men's shoes, leather	6.7 hrs	7.7 hrs	36 hrs	8.6 hrs	25.5 hrs	40.3 hrs
Men's business suit	25 hrs	40 hrs	106 hrs	34.6 hrs	102.6 hrs	162.1 hrs
Refrigerator, 150 ltr	47 hrs	50 hrs	168 hrs	79.3 hrs	235.1 hrs	371.5 hrs
Small car	6.9 mo	11.1 mo	3.1 yrs	6.5 mo	1.7 yrs	2.6 yrs

Source: Arnt Spandau, *Economic Boycott against South Africa: Normative and Factual Issues* (University of the Witwatersrand, Labour Research Programme, Johannesburg, 1978), p. 83.

visions of utopia, it would fail miserably. Even if we compare it to most countries in the Western world, it comes up quite short. However, if we compare South Africa to the non-Western world—particularly, to its neighbors on the African continent—it fares quite well by comparison.

Two Africanists, Lewis Ganns and Peter Duignan, give this report: "There is indeed much poverty in Soweto. But there is no misery of the kind found in say, Addis Ababa, Kinshasa or Karachi."[10] The standard of living of a Soweto worker might look good to an unskilled Soviet worker in Kiev, not to mention a slum dweller in Delhi or in the shantytowns that surround Lusaka, Nairobi, or Algiers. (See Table 6.1.)

Another point of comparison is suggested by the activities of South Africa's opposition leaders. Chief Mangosuthu Buthelezi, Mrs. Winnie Mandela, Bishop Desmond Tutu, Mr. Allan Boesak, and many others are often seen and quoted in Western news media roundly criticizing and condemning the South African government as fascist and racist. They do this whether they are being interviewed in South Africa or elsewhere. Within days, weeks, or months, we see them denouncing their government once again. In light of this observation, we might insightfully ask whether other government critics like Lech Walesa and Zbignew Bujak have the freedom to do the same in Poland; did Sakharov, in the Soviet Union; or Bishop Muzorewa and Joshua Nkomo, in Zimbabwe. Clearly, South African blacks do not have the freedom of speech that Americans have come to take for granted, but it is possible that they have far more than most people in the world. Moreover, the fact that South Africa's opposition leaders do visit foreign countries—to condemn their own—points to a relative freedom of travel that is envied by the opposition leaders of East Germany, the Soviet Union, Poland, China, and elsewhere.

In addition to the state of relatively free speech in South Africa, there are no walls at its borders, as in some communist countries. There has been no mass exodus of South Africans, as in Ethiopia, East Germany, Cuba, and Cambodia. In fact, an estimated 1.5 million people—including illegal immigrants—voluntarily go to South Africa each year. Moreover, South Africa has not expelled whole racial groups, as have Angola, Mozambique, Ghana, Nigeria, Uganda, Kenya, and Tanzania. While South Africa's Indian businesspeople do face numerous racial restrictions few of them would prefer the black rule of Tanzania or Uganda, where Indian property has been expropriated and owners expelled.

Since 1900, fewer than 7,000 South African blacks have died in all civil conflicts with government.[11] While the loss of human life is always a tragedy, South Africa's experience compares favorably with the untold millions who have lost their lives in civil conflicts in Uganda, Ethiopia, Mozambique, Nigeria, the Soviet Union, China, and Cambodia. As recently as August 1988, as many as 30,000 Hutus lost their lives at the hands of the Tutsi in Burundi.

Acknowledging the fact that South African blacks enjoy freedoms and living standards envied elsewhere should in no way provide justification for—or turn our attention away from—the immorality of apartheid. On the contrary, our acknowledgment should include this important admonition given to new physicians: *Primum non nocere*. First, do no harm. In other words, if black South Africans were in such a state of desperation that they could not be made worse off, then there would be little downside risk to any domestic or international policy aimed at helping them. If they can be made worse off, however, then it behooves us to be a little more thoughtful about policy prescriptions. All of Africa's postcolonial experience should have taught us to ask: When one kind of oppression is eliminated, what is going to take its place?

SANCTIONS AND DISINVESTMENT

International revulsion with South Africa's legalized racial discrimination has led to calls for economic sanctions and disinvestment in companies that do business in South Africa. The U.S. Congress overrode a presidential veto and passed the Comprehensive Anti-Apartheid Act of 1986 (CAAA), which prohibits new loans to the government and new investment in South Africa; forbids the export to South Africa of crude oil, petroleum products, and computers; prohibits the import from South Africa of agricultural products, Krugerrands, food, iron, steel, and sugar; and terminates direct flights to and from South Africa. The disinvestment movement—a popular cause on many U.S. college campuses—calls for churches, universities, and other institutions to purge their portfolios of stockholding in companies that do business in South Africa. Several U.S. cities—including the nation's capital, San Francisco, and Philadelphia—have passed laws to purge city retirement portfolios of holdings in these companies.

The stated purpose of the disinvestment and sanctions campaign is to put economic pressure on the South African government to eliminate racially discriminatory laws and give blacks the political franchise. Other supporters—believing that disinvestment and sanctions would not produce so ambitious a result—argue disinvestment and sanctions will at least "send a signal" of U.S. dissatisfaction with South Africa's human rights abuses.

Analysis of Results

Economic analysis as well as historical evidence place considerable doubt on the efficacy of disinvestment and sanctions in achieving any of their proponents' goals. The first sanctions against South Africa took the form of a U.N. Security Council voluntary arms embargo in 1963, which became a mandatory arms embargo in 1977. The arms embargo prohibited all member states from shipping arms and other war-related materials to South Africa. The result was the rapid development of the Armaments Corporation of South Africa (Armscor). Through Armscor, South Africa has become virtually self-sufficient in arms production and produces some of the world's most technologically advanced weapons systems. Moreover, it has become one of the world's top ten exporters of weapons.

The United States imposed a trade embargo against Cuba in 1960 in order to topple the Castro government. Today, Castro appears to be well entrenched, showing little signs of losing power. Similarly disappointing results of sanctions and trade embargoes have been seen in Rhodesia (now Zimbabwe), Germany, Japan, Poland, the Soviet Union, and the People's Republic of China.

Disinvestment has been a disappointing strategy, also. At the urging of anti-South African activists, U.S. companies like IBM, Coca-Cola, Proctor & Gamble, and Kodak have decided to pull up stakes and leave South Africa. U.S. corporations might leave South Africa, but they are not likely to dismantle their productive assets and bring them home, as well. That means that the production units wind up being sold to South Africans—mostly white South Africans.

U.S. companies have had to sell out "frequently to incumbent managers in the form of leveraged buyouts, often for a fraction of market value, because everybody knew they were desperate."[12] Anglo-American, the largest mining house and one of the largest sources of capital in South Africa, acquired South

Africa's largest bank, Barclays National, from its British parent—a long-standing target of antiapartheid protesters. Anglo-American paid R16.79 ($8.06) for Barclays stock, which was trading at R21.46 ($10.30).[13] What makes the transaction even more costly to the parent bank, Barclays Bank, is that, "because of the machinations of South Africa's ingenious two-tier foreign exchange system,"[14] Barclays Bank will actually get only about half of the sale proceeds. Moreover, South Africa will save about 29 million rand ($14 million) annually in foreign dividend payments.

Another boon to South Africans who are purchasing foreign companies is that they can eliminate costly "social responsibility" programs implemented to conform to the "Sullivan Principles"—a code of conduct developed for U.S. corporate subsidiaries by the Reverend Leon Sullivan, a Philadelphia minister. Under the Sullivan code, many U.S. and European firms were developing training programs, adopting black schools, and building housing and medical facilities for black workers and their families. It is unlikely that South African purchasers will feel the same pressure to uphold the Sullivan Principles.

A moral dilemma also confronts the proponents of disinvestment. Church and college officials disinvest when they sell their asset portfolio holdings of companies with subsidiaries in South Africa. After the transaction has been made, the stock certificate still exists; only its ownership has been changed. The church or college no longer owns it; somebody else does. Therein lies the moral dilemma: Is it moral to cleanse your soul when—of necessity—to do so requires that you get somebody else to dirty his soul? In other words, a minister can purge the church's holdings of "evil" IBM stock *only* by selling to somebody else that "evil" stock.

We might ask whether such a course is appropriate for the socially conscientious. This moral dilemma facing disinvestors is analogous to the repentant slaveowner who satisfies an awakened craving for justice by selling his slave to another slaveowner. The more moral action would be to *free* his slave. The loss of wealth incurred would stand as good evidence of the owner's moral commitment. Disinvestors could make a similar show of moral commitment by "freeing" their stock certificates—for example, putting them in a shredding machine or the fireplace. So far, disinvestors have shown no tendency for this kind of personal-wealth-reducing moral commitment.

Do Black South Africans Want Sanctions and Disinvestment?

Aside from questions concerning the efficacy of sanctions and disinvestment, we might ask whether black South Africans want them. Are blacks willing to sacrifice their jobs on the altar of economic warfare? John Kane-Berman, executive director of the South African Institute of Race Relations, reports that—while blacks do favor some international pressures on the South African government—by and large, they are opposed to disinvestment and sanctions. Kane-Berman came to this conclusion after examining 14 opinion surveys on the

Table 6.2
Surveys on Disinvestment and Sanctions

Publication Date	Conductor/ Sponsor	Sample Number	Area/ Sample	Antidis- investment/ Sanctions	Pro	Other
June, 1984	Schlemmer	551	Urban	74%	26%	—
July, 1984	HSRC	1,478	PWV	82%	10%	8% don't know
Nov., 1984	Schlemmer	1,000	Urban	84%	14%	2% don't know
Feb., 1985	HSRC	736	?	48%	18%	34% don't know
Feb., 1985	HSRC	736	?	65%	30%	5% don't know
Feb., 1985	Star	459	Johannesburg	51%	?	?
May, 1985	HSRC	1,200	PWV	76%	16%	4% don't know
Aug., 1985	London Sunday Times	400	Urban	?	77%	?
Sept., 1985	CASE	800	Urban	26%	24%	49% conditional
May, 1986	HSRC	1,338	PWV	68%	?	?
May, 1986	London Sunday Times	615	Urban/ rural	32%	29%	39% no view
April, 1987	Bureau for Information	4,500	Urban/ rural	79%	13%	8% don't know
Oct., 1987	German Africa Foundation	1,004	Miners	70%	21%	9% undecided
Oct., 1987	CASE	800	Urban/ rural	26%	21%	46% conditional 6% noncommittal

Source: South African Institute of Race Relations, *Race Relations News* Vol. 49 No. 4 (December, 1987), p. 8.

question. Table 6.2 shows that, in nine of the 14 surveys, an absolute majority of black respondents was against disinvestment and sanctions.[15] In four other surveys, more blacks were against disinvestment and sanctions than were in favor. In two of the surveys, blacks were for foreign investment on the condition that it be used to dismantle apartheid.

These findings stand in stark contrast to the opinions spread abroad by Western supporters of sanctions and disinvestment. Senator Ted Kennedy—for instance—has said, "Throughout South Africa, the sanctions were warmly welcomed by those they were intended to assist."[16]

SOUTH AFRICA'S ECONOMIC NEIGHBORS

While some of South Africa's neighbors do call for Western sanctions, they themselves conduct a robust economic trade with her. This can be expected since, among South Africa's neighbors in southern Africa—Angola, Botswana, Lesotho, Malawi, Mozambique, Namibia, Swaziland, Zambia, and Zimbabwe—she produces (out of the total produced by them all) 94 percent of the wheat, 77 percent of the electricity, 84 percent of all cereals, 82 percent of the motor vehicles, and the highest percentages of other critical goods and services. South

Africa's 41 percent of the population of southern Africa had a gross national product in 1985 of R156 billion ($75 billion) which was more than three times the combined total of her neighbors.

South Africa's productive capacity relative to the continent as a whole is no less impressive. Occupying slightly more than 4 percent of the surface area of the continent, South Africa carries 81 percent of the freight, and produces 54 percent of the electricity, 47 percent of the motor vehicles, 37 percent of the steel, 22 percent of the cereals, and 23 percent of the wheat, specifically.[17]

In 1985, South Africa exported $705 billion in goods and services to her neighbors in southern Africa, while importing just over $207 billion from them. South Africa supplies 100 percent of Lesotho's electrical power, 44 percent of Mozambique's, 42 percent of Swaziland's, and 35 percent of Botswana's.[18] In addition, South Africa provides airfreight and passenger services to many of her neighbors, whose stated official policy is that of denying overflight rights to South African Airlines. South Africa is a place of employment for more than 500,000 foreign workers—not counting the estimated hundreds of thousands more who enter South Africa illegally to work.

Without a doubt, there is considerable interdependency between South Africa and her neighbors—an interdependency made even more critical by the fact that, as Ali Mazrui puts it,

> Africa is in the process of decay or social decomposition. Instead of African economies growing, they show signs of shrinking. Instead of Africa's per capita production expanding, it betrays a tendency to diminish. Instead of greater experience leading to greater efficiency, Africa's experience paradoxically seems to result in *decreasing* competence. . . . Infrastructures are decaying. The curse of its ancestors is upon the continent.[19]

All of this suggests that Western policy toward South Africa cannot be viewed in isolation for, if the West were to damage South Africa economically, its neighbors—who have tottering economies, at best—would feel considerable pain, and possibly total collapse.

SUMMARY

Free markets—laissez-faire capitalism—along with limited government power has generally served the interests of discriminated-against people everywhere. The architects of South Africa's apartheid ideology sought to eliminate the parity of the marketplace. They found that white privilege could best flourish with massive government intervention into and control of the economy. In many ways, South Africa's apartheid system is a triumph over capitalism. The gains made by South Africa's nonwhite population—that is, when employers have chosen to evade and contravene legal discrimination—were the result of strong market forces seeking to override apartheid ideology.

The evidence marshalled in this book strongly suggests that whatever strengthens market forces and weakens government power will best serve the interests of South Africa's nonwhite population. Such a proposition is not unique to South Africa; it is generally applicable to people anywhere who can be characterized as low skilled, unpopular, and discriminated against.

APPENDIX 6.A: RIGHTS DOCUMENT OF THE KWAZULU/ NATAL INDABA

KWAZULU NATAL INDABA BILL OF RIGHTS GUARANTEES

to everyone the equal protection of the law, without regard to race, colour, ethnic origin, political opinion or economic status and, in particular

ENSHRINES

the right to life and liberty
the right to own and occupy property anywhere
the principle of administrative justice
the right of public education
ethnic, linguistic and cultural rights

WILL BE

part of the constitution of the new Province of Natal
binding on provincial and local government in Natal
enforced by the Supreme Court of South Africa

BILL OF RIGHTS

Human dignity and equality before the law

1. (1) All human beings are born free and equal in dignity and rights.

(2) Everyone is equal before the law, and shall be entitled to equal protection of the law, without any distinction on the basis of race, colour, language, sex, religion, ethnic or social origin, property, birth, political or other opinion, or economic or other status.

Right to life

2. (1) Everyone's right to life shall be protected by law, and no one may be deprived of his life intentionally save in the execution of a sentence of a court following his conviction of a crime for which this penalty is provided by law.

(2) Deprivation of life shall not constitute a contravention of this article when it results from the use of such force as is absolutely necessary and justified in the circumstances—

(i) in defence of any person against unlawful violence;

(ii) to effect a lawful arrest in order to prevent the escape of a person lawfully detained for a serious offence;

(iii) in action lawfully taken for the purposes of quelling a riot or insurrection.

Punishment

3. No one shall be subjected to torture or to inhuman or degrading treatment or punishment.

Right of liberty

4. (1) No one shall be held in slavery or servitude.

(2) No one shall be required to perform forced or compulsory labour; Provided that this does not include—

(a) any normal work required to be done in the ordinary course of detention under the provisions of subsection (3) or during conditional release from such detention;

(b) any service of military character in terms of a law requiring citizens to undergo military training;

(c) any service exacted in case of emergency or calamity threatening the existence or well-being of the Province;

(d) any work or service which forms part of normal civic obligations imposed by law.

(3) Everyone has the right to liberty and security of person and no one shall be deprived of his liberty save in the following cases and in accordance with a procedure prescribed by law which does not deny his basic rights to physical and mental health and integrity—

(a) the lawful detention of a person after conviction by a competent court;

(b) the lawful arrest or detention of a person for non-compliance with the lawful order of a court;

(c) the lawful arrest or detention of a person effected for the purpose of bringing him before a competent legal authority on reasonable grounds of having committed an offence or when it is reasonably considered necessary to prevent his committing an offence or fleeing after having done so;

(d) the lawful detention of a person for the prevention of the spreading of infectious diseases, of a person of unsound mind, an alcoholic or a drug addict;

(e) the lawful arrest or detention of a person to prevent his effecting an unauthorised entry into the Province or of a person against whom action is being taken with a view to deportation or extradition.

(4) Everyone who is arrested shall be informed promptly, in a language which he understands, of the reasons for his arrest and of any charge against him.

(5) Everyone arrested or detained in accordance with the provisions of subsection (3)(c) shall be brought promptly before a judge or other officer authorised by law to exercise judicial power and shall be entitled to trial within a reasonable time or to release pending trial, which may be conditioned by guarantees to appear for trial.

(6) In the determination of his civil rights and obligations or of any criminal charge against him, everyone shall be entitled to a fair and public hearing within a reasonable time by an independent and impartial court established by law; judgment shall be pronounced publicly but the press and public may be excluded from all or part of the trial in the interests of morals, public order or national security in a democratic society, where the interests of juveniles or the protection of the private life of the parties so require, or to the extent strictly necessary in the opinion of the court in special circumstances where the publicity would prejudice the interests of justice.

(7) Everyone charged with a criminal offence should be presumed innocent until proved guilty according to law.

(8) Everyone charged with a criminal offence shall have the right—

(a) to be informed promptly, in a language of his choice which he understands and in detail, of the nature and cause of the accusation against him;

(b) to have adequate time and facilities for the preparation of his defence;

(c) to defend himself in person or through legal assistance of his own choosing or, if he has not sufficient means to pay for legal assistance, to be given it at no cost to himself when the interests of justice so require;

(d) to examine or have examined witnesses against him and to obtain the attendance and examination of witnesses on his behalf under the same conditions as witnesses against him;

(e) to have the free assistance of an interpreter if he cannot understand or speak the language used in the court, or if he so requests.

(9) Everyone who is deprived of his liberty by arrest or detention shall be informed promptly in language of his choice which he understands, and in detail, the reasons for his arrest and detention, and shall be entitled to take proceedings by which the lawfulness of his detention is decided speedily by a court, and to be released if the detention is not lawful: Provided that if he has not sufficient means to pay for legal assistance, he will be given it at no cost to himself.

(10) Everyone who has been the victim of unlawful arrest or detention shall have an enforceable right to compensation.

(11) No one who is tried for a criminal offence shall be compelled to give evidence at the trial.

(12) No one who shows that he has been tried by a competent court for a criminal offence and either convicted or acquitted shall again be tried for that offence or for any other criminal offence of which he could have been convicted at the trial for the offence, save upon the order of a superior court in the course of appeal or review proceedings relating to the conviction or acquittal.

(13) No one shall be found guilty of any penal offence on account of any act or omission which did not constitute a penal offence at the time when it was committed.

Right to administrative justice

5. (1) All administrative tribunals, public authorities and officials shall follow rules of fundamental fairness in coming to their decisions and they shall, unless inappropriate, be required to furnish reasons for such decisions.

(2) Delegated legislation shall be drafted with a reasonable allowance for public comment and participation.

(3) Everyone who has suffered damage as a result of unlawful action by public authorities shall have an enforceable right to compensation.

Right of privacy and protection of the family

6. (1) No one shall be subjected to arbitrary interference with his privacy, family, home or communications, nor to attacks upon his honour and reputation.

(2) The widest possible protection and assistance shall be accorded to the family, which is the natural and funadmental group in society, and the care and upbringing of children are recognised as a natural right of, and a duty primarily incumbent on, the parents.

Right of property

7. (1) Everyone has the right to lawfully own and occupy property anywhere in the Province.

(2) No one is to be deprived of his property without due process of law, and expropriation may only be authorised in terms of a law if it is for the public benefit and if equitable and fair compensation is promptly paid.

(3) Land and natural resources shall not be expropriated except for the common good and in accordance with laws providing for equitable compensation.

Ethnic, religious, linguistic, cultural and educational rights

8. (1) A person belonging to an ethnic, religious or linguistic group shall not be denied the right to enjoy his own culture, to profess and practise his own relgiion or to use his own language.

(2) Everyone shall have the right freely to participate in the cultural life of the Province, to enjoy the arts, to share in scientific advancement and its benefits, and to the free and full development of his personality.

(3) In all proceedings involving customary law followed by persons in the Province, such law may be applied except insofar as the court finds that it has fallen into disuse or is contrary to the principles of natural justice and morality.

(4) Every person shall have the same right to public education in an institution that will cater for his interests, aptitudes and abilities and the Province shall make provision for this right without discrimination: Provided that, notwithstanding the provisions of section 1(2), it may, in providing facilities, distinguish between persons on grounds of language or sex.

Freedom of movement

9. Everyone lawfully present in the Province, shall be entitled to freedom of movement and residence within the borders of the Province.

Freedom of thought, conscience and religion

10. (1) Everyone shall be entitled to freedom of thought, conscience and religion and to change his religion or belief, to manifest his religion or belief in worship, teaching, practice and observance, whether alone or in community with others, in public or in private.

(2) No one shall be compelled against his religious convictions to render military service involving the use of arms but shall be required to perform national service as required by law in lieu thereof.

Freedom of opinion and expression

11. (1) Everyone shall be entitled to freedom of opinion and expression, which includes the freedom to hold opinions without interference and to seek, receive and impart information and ideas.

(2) Any advocacy of national, racial or religious hatred and aggression between groups that constitutes incitement to discrimination, hostility, violence or political animosity is prohibited.

Freedom of association

12. (1) Everyone shall be entitled to freedom of peaceful assembly and to freedom of association with others, including the right to form and to join trade unions for the protection of his interests, and no one may be compelled to belong to an association.

(2) Everyone shall be free to form or to join political parties in order to participate in periodic and free elections, which shall be held by secret ballot or by equivalent free voting procedures.

Freedom of work and freedom of contract

13. (1) Everyone shall be entitled to equal work opportunities and to free choice of employment.

(2) Everyone with legal capacity shall have freedom to contract and to conclude agreements with others in the voluntary exercise of his rights and freedoms and generally for the promotion of his interests.

Restriction of rights and freedoms

14. (1) The rights and freedoms recognised, under the provisions of this Bill of Rights may be restricted by a law of the Provincial legislature which has general application, for reasons which are necessary in a free and democratic society in the interests of public safety, for the prevention of disorder or crime, for the protection of health and morals, for the protection of the rights, freedoms and reputation of others, for maintaining the authority and impartiality of the judiciary and for the social, moral and economic well-being of all the inhabitants of the Province.

(2) Everyone's exercise of his rights and freedoms shall be subject to such limitations as are legally determined for the purpose of securing due recognition and respect for the rights and freedoms of others; and groups which by reason of their aims and the behaviour of their adherents, seek to impair or abolish the free democratic order or to endanger the security of the Province, are prohibited.

(3) A fundamental right and freedom protected in this Bill of Rights may not be abolished or in its essence be encroached upon by a law of the Province.

Enforcement of rights and freedoms

15. (1) The rights and freedoms protected in this Bill of Rights are binding on the legislature, the executive, the judiciary and all government institutions in the Province insofar as they fall within the purview of and flow from the powers and functions devolved on the Province and any person may forthwith apply to the Supreme Court or to other competent authorities provided for in the Constitution by appropriate proceedings or by petition to enforce these rights and freedoms.

(2) The Supreme Court shall have the power to make all such orders as may be necessary and appropriate to secure the applicant the enjoyment of any of the rights conferred by the provisions of this Bill of Rights; Provided that if at the commencement of this Constitution there are laws in existence in the Province which fall within the purview of the powers and functions bestowed on the Province and which are inconsistent with this Bill of Rights, such laws may, after the lapse of one year after the commencement of this Constitution and on application to the Supreme Court be declared void to the extent of such inconsistency.

NOTES

1. M. L. Truu, "Economics and Politics in South Africa Today," *South African Journal of Economics* 54, 4 (December 1986): 354.

2. As reported in Southern African Catholic Bishop's Conference, "Special Commission on Economic Pressures," mimeograph, n.d., p. 12. Emphasis in original.

3. Alexander Hepple, *Verwoerd* (Baltimore: Penguin Books, 1967), p. 28.

4. Andre E. A. M. Thomashausen, *The Dismantling of Apartheid* (Cape Town: Printpak Books, 1987), pp. 14–20.

5. Some of the details of the KwaZulu/Natal Indaba that are reported here were extracted from Alan Paton, "Indaba without Fear," *Optima* 35, 1 (March 1987): 2–10.

6. Frances Kendall and Leon Louw, *After Apartheid: The Solution for South Africa* (San Francisco: Institute for Contemporary Studies, 1987).

7. Ibid., pp. 124–25.

8. Ibid., p. 126.

9. Ibid., p. 160.

10. L. H. Gann and Peter Duignan, *Why South Africa Will Survive: A Historical Analysis* (New York: St. Martin's Press, 1981), p. 84.

11. Peter Duignan, *South Africa: What's to Be Done?* (Stanford, Calif.: Hoover Institution Reprint Series No. 111, n.d.).

12. Peter Brimelow, "Why South Africa Shrugs at Sanctions," *Forbes* (March 9, 1987): 101.

13. Ibid., p. 102.

14. Ibid.

15. South African Institute of Race Relations reporting in *Race Relations News* 49, 4 (December 1987): 8.

16. Washington *Post*, October 16, 1987, p. A 23.

17. "Overview of Interaction in Africa," *International Bulletin* 1, 3 (1987): 56. Published by the Africa Institute of South Africa, in Pretoria.

18. Ibid., p. 61.

19. Ali A. Mazrui, *The Africans: A Triple Heritage* (London: BBC Publications, 1986), p. 201. Cited in "Overview of Interaction in Africa," p. 41. Emphasis in original.

7

Postscript for South Africans

APARTHEID IN CAMOUFLAGE

South African blacks, Indians, and coloreds do not need anyone to define apartheid. They have suffered its insults and restrictions since the beginning of the twentieth century. As official apartheid declines and is ultimately eliminated, the victims of this state policy must be alert to the emergence of apartheid in camouflage. To this end, it might be useful to examine restrictions as a general phenomena.

Apartheid is a special case of the kind of restrictions that are achieved when one class of individuals acquires privilege through the use of state violence to deny another class of individuals the right to engage in voluntary and mutually agreeable exchanges. This can be accomplished in many ways. People can use the power of the state to impose statutory restraints on voluntary exchange—through laws, regulations, or ordinances prohibiting exchanges unsanctioned by the state. These might take the form of occupational or business licensing, where individuals have to be sanctioned by a state-approved body in order to carry on a trade. Another method is for one class of individuals to use the power of the state to set numerical limits on the number of practitioners in a particular trade. Yet another method of using state power is to set the money terms of exchange—that is, minimum or maximum prices.

These and other restrictions all have predictable discriminatory effects on classes of individuals who may be described as low skilled, low educated, latecomers, and politically impotent. Exchange restrictions discriminate against people who may be generally classified as less preferred in the eyes of buyers and sellers and these restrictions create monopoly power and monopoly income for individuals seen as more preferred.

Calls for exchange restrictions are frequently concealed by motives that seem quite noble. The most familiar of these motives include providing for the public health and safety, preventing unfair competition, setting up orderly markets, protecting jobs, preventing exploitation, and equalizing bargaining power. To accomplish these objectives, the proponents call for restrictions on exchange.

The essence of all the apartheid rules and regulations is restriction in one form or another. In South Africa's labor market, the basic motivation behind the various provisions of the Industrial Conciliation Act was the use of state power by one class of individuals to restrict entry—and hence, the labor supply and competition—by another class of people. As we have discussed throughout this book, similar restrictions were sought and attained through the Land Act, the Group Areas Act, the Mines and Works Act, the Trade and Customs Act, and many other South African laws. Apartheid meant that the restrictive criterion was race, but—again—this is in fact a special case of a much larger phenomenon where one class of people uses state power to promote their ends at the expense of others.

Let us briefly consider this larger phenomenon—which, for comparative purposes, can be called *apartheid in camouflage*—and speculate on the various forms in which it may appear.

MIGRATION RESTRICTIONS

Since 1979, the Industrial Conciliation Act has been amended to permit the recognition of black labor unions. The recognition of black labor unions in South Africa had long been denied, and indeed this was an important government concession to a long-standing legitimate complaint.

The job of any labor union is to seek better working conditions and higher pay for its members. Better working conditions and higher pay always translate into higher labor costs for the employer. The higher labor costs occur independent of whether or not people agree about the merit of higher wages and better working conditions; however, there are certain predictable employer responses to changes in the price of any input. In an effort to maintain profits while at the same time lowering costs, employers will seek substitutes for an input whose price has risen. In the case of higher prices for labor, firms typically substitute capital for labor. That is, they increase the use of machinery relative to labor.

When this happens, the output per worker rises, and so does the pay of the worker using the capital. Along with higher wages comes an increased attractiveness of that employment to other workers earning lower wages elsewhere. If all potential workers were granted unrestricted access to the higher paying employment, then supply and demand considerations would make the higher wages of the incumbent workers unsustainable. Therefore, it is in the pecuniary interest of incumbent workers—who may be unionized—to erect entry barriers.

One way to accomplish this is through migration restrictions or some other means of reducing the supply of foreign workers. Seeking and using state power to limit foreign workers does not require any kind of antipathy for foreigners as such. Quite simply, national origin—like race—is a convenient attribute on which to discriminate. It is likely that this kind of discrimination is becoming especially tempting to the mineworker unions in South Africa.

In 1984, some 350,000 blacks from the neighboring countries of Mozambique, Malawi, Swaziland, Botswana, Lesotho, and Zimbabwe were legally employed on contract by South Africa's mining industry. The government estimates that another 1.2 million blacks from other countries are living and working illegally in South Africa.[1]

As mine wages increase, there is greater incentive for South Africa's mining houses to substitute capital for labor. In turn—as employment continues to fall—there will be increasing pressures on the unions to ration jobs. The large noncitizen work force will probably be a tempting target. In other words, South Africa's unions—both black and white—may find themselves calling on the government to restrict immigration or reserve mine jobs (at least, the highest paid ones) for South Africans only.

Reserving jobs, on the basis of the citizenship of the worker differs little from job reservation on the basis of the race of the worker. Its results differ little, as well: One class of people will monetarily gain at the expense of another class of people. Apartheid in camouflage differs from traditional apartheid only in the selected discrimination criterion.

LICENSING AND REGULATION

Another potential apartheid camouflage is in the form of occupational and business regulation. The most frequently stated justification of government regulation—in every country—is to protect public safety and morals, provide for orderly markets, eliminate unscrupulous practitioners, and provide for a fair rate of return. For our purpose here in studying the actual effects of regulation, however, we need not evaluate—or even acknowledge—its proponents' stated justifications or intentions.

The economic effects of licensing and regulation are quite predictable. The most immediate effect is that the number of practitioners are smaller than without licensing and regulation. There are fewer practitioners because entry costs are made higher through such requirements as minimum education, apprenticeships, and installation of costly health and safety equipment, or the requirement to purchase a costly license. In some cases, the number of practitioners are fewer because the regulatory agency sets a numerical limit.[2] Most often, the conditions for entry are decided by agencies composed of, dominated by, or influenced by incumbents in the trade. Their incentive is to prevent the number of practitioners from getting so large that the income of the incumbent becomes threatened by newcomers who may charge lower prices or offer better services.

This behavior is already evident in some South African cities. For years, blacks were not permitted to enter the taxi industry in the metropolitan Johannesburg area. Black taxi owners—who have only recently been permitted to operate—are now opposing further deregulation, which would allow entry by other black taxi owners.

Business Day (March 27, 1987) reports,

Black taxi drivers, through their association (SABTA) [South African Black Taxi Association], are angry about proposals in the Transport White Paper to deregulate the taxi business. Their complaint is that deregulation will not bring "pirates" [illegal operators, called "gypsies" in the United States] into the fold "but will destroy them" [members of the SABTA] and it will "resuscitate the power of the white bus industry" which will remain regulated.

Business Day concludes that the members of SABTA "now want to establish a cozy little cartel" which is "not in the interest of their passengers."

Further deregulation of the taxi business would allow more entry. In turn, more entry would tend to moderate taxi price increases, provide greater customer options, and offer greater business opportunities for would-be taxi owner/operators. The South African Black Taxi Association sees further deregulation as a possible threat to the income of its members. Especially ironic is that before blacks were permitted to enter the business, white taxi owner/operators were against their entry for identical reasons, and used the state's apartheid tools to keep blacks out.

LEGISLATED WAGES

Government-regulated wages based on race offends the moral sensibilities in us all. The regulation of wages and other conditions of the workplace was one of the most important building blocks in the perfection of apartheid. An interesting pattern often emerged in the practice of this type of regulation. In some cases, apartheid supporters called for mandatory *increases* in wages paid to nonwhites; and in other cases, they were satisfied with the mere *restriction* of black employment (see Chapter 4 for details). Where black employment could be excluded in the form of outright bans or strict black/white employment ratios or by the fact that blacks did not have the requisite skills, white workers faced little wage competition from blacks. In that case, there would be very little threat to white employment from the large racial wage differential. However, in cases where it was more difficult to restrict the employment of blacks, the large wage differences for the same productivity posed a competitive threat to white employment. In those cases, apartheid supporters relied more on wage legislation as a means to preserve white privilege.

Apartheid wage legislation was based on evil intentions, but we should not be blind to the fact that the effects of wage legislation are independent of its proponents' intentions. Had apartheid supporters said—as they sometimes did—that they were supporting wage legislation to help prevent the exploitation of blacks, the legislation would have nonetheless had the effect of pricing blacks out of the market and lowering the cost of racial discrimination.

As South Africa emerges from under the yoke of apartheid, we should keep reminding ourselves that the effects of legislation are not necessarily determined by legislative intent. Consider the state president office's announcement that disparities in pay differences will be abolished in public service employment on March 1, 1988. Both the White Public Servant's Association and the Coloured (mixed race) Public Servant's League welcomed the announcement, which will affect about 600,000 employees.[3] It is estimated that implementation of the elimination of racial wage disparities will cost the government R135 ($65) million a year in added wage costs.

No doubt, eliminating the scheduled racial wage differentials is a worthy goal as part and parcel of eliminating apartheid. However, we should be wary because some ways of calling for equal wages can produce effects similar to apartheid. Most likely, the elimination of wage differentials will take the form of *raising* the wages of nonwhites to the same level as whites. The effect of this will be to increase the cost of hiring nonwhites. Raising the cost of hiring nonwhites will have the predictable effect of making managers more selective in hiring nonwhites than previously. One selective mechanism would be to require greater job qualifications or credentials—which, contrary to the spirit of the mandate to equalize wages, would tend to discriminate against the employment of workers who are low skilled. To the extent that blacks share this characteristic to a greater extent, they will suffer the greater burden of skills and credentials discrimination.

By contrast, if the call to equalize wages took the form of *lowering* white wages to the level now received by nonwhite public employees, the effects would be opposite and symmetrical to equalizing the wages upward. Not wanting to earn "black wages"—or perhaps having higher paying alternatives elsewhere—some whites would probably quit public service employment. Equalizing the wages downward would tend to increase the employment opportunities for low-skilled workers, among whom blacks are disproportionately represented.

There is nothing that an economist qua economist can advise as the best way to eliminate racial wage differentials. However, understanding the effects (costs) of alternative means of doing so can assist policymakers in developing the appropriate trade-offs.

CONCLUSION

Given a bit of careful analysis, one might imagine many other camouflages that apartheid could assume. All would take the form of government regulation of some aspect of the business and labor markets—regulating entry conditions and/or setting the terms of trade. While—after the demise of apartheid—the criteria for exclusion will be in terms of nonracial attributes, there could very well be exclusion, nonetheless, based on some other personal attribute; and no one should be surprised to find an implicit reinforcement of the previously explicit racial regulations.

South Africa's history should amply demonstrate that her people's general interests are best served by a greater dispersion of political power to local levels of government, freer markets, and a reduction in the government regulation of economic activity.

The whole ugly history of apartheid has been an attack on free markets and the rights of individuals, and a glorification of centralized government power. In 1900 when South African Prime Minister Jan Christiaan Smuts said, "It is ordained that we [Afrikaners], insignificant as we are, should be amongst the first people to begin the struggle against the new world tyranny of capitalism," he was recognizing that free markets along with their inherent dispersion of power have little respect for race. Therefore, South Africa declared war on capitalism. Now—in order to promote tranquility, dignity for the individual, and prosperity for all—South Africa's people must strengthen its beleaguered market forces, and declare war against centralized government power.

NOTES

1. South African Department of Public Affairs, *Official Yearbook of South Africa 1986* (Pretoria: Government Printer, 1986), p. 214.

2. See Walter E. Williams, *The State against Blacks* (New York: McGraw-Hill, 1982), chs. 5 and 6. Also see Simon Rottenberg, "Economics of Occupational Licensing," in *Aspects of Labor Economics: A Report of the National Bureau of Economic Research* (Princeton, N.J.: Princeton University Press, 1962), pp. 3–20.

3. "Parliament," *South African Digest* (September 18, 1987): 5.

Selected Bibliography

Abedian, I., and B. Standish. "Poor Whites and the Role of the State: The Evidence." *South African Journal of Economics* 52, 2 (June 1985): 141–65.
———. "Market Imperfections and Employment: A Model of the South African Labour Market 1900–1940." *South African Journal of Economics* 54, 4 (December 1986): 406–17.
Alchian, Armen A., and Reuben A. Kessel. *Competition, Monopoly, and the Pursuit of Money*. Princeton, N.J.: Princeton University Press, 1962.
Anonymous correspondent of the International Labor Organization. "The New Wage Act in South Africa." *International Labor Review* 13, 3 (March 1926): 327–43.
Becker, Gary S. *The Economics of Discrimination*. 2nd ed. Chicago: University of Chicago Press, 1971.
"Behind the Pact." *Financial Mail*. June 7, 1985, p. 58.
Brimelow, Peter. "Why South Africa Shrugs at Sanctions." *Forbes* (March 9, 1987): 101–2.
Brookes, Edgar. *Apartheid: A Documentary Study of Modern South Africa*. London: Routledge and Kegan Paul, 1968.
Brotz, Howard. *The Politics of South Africa: Democracy and Racial Diversity*. London: Oxford University Press, 1977.
Bunting, Brian. "The Origins of Apartheid." In *Apartheid: A Collection of Writings on South African Racism by South Africans*. Edited by Alex LaGuma. New York: International Publishers, 1971.
Busheunel, S. "Black Industrial Labour in South Africa." *South African Journal of Economics* 42, 3 (September 1974): 292–311.
Carter, Gwendolyn M. *The Politics of Inequality: South Africa since 1948*. London: Thames and Hudson, 1959.
Cell, John W. *The Highest Stage of White Supremacy: The Origins of Segregation in South Africa and the American South*. London: Cambridge University Press, 1982.
Congressional Record, 71st Congr., House, 3rd Sess., 1931: 6513.
Cope, John. *South Africa*. New York: Frederick A. Praeger, 1967.
"The Crumbling of Apartheid." *Leadership* 4, 4 (1985): 57.
de Coning, Christo, Johan Fick, and Nellie Olivier. "Residential Settlement Patterns: A Pilot Study of Socio-political Perceptions in Grey Areas of Johannesburg." Unpublished Working Paper. Department of Development Studies, Johannesburg; Rand Afrikaans University, 1986.

Demsetz, Harold. "Minorities in the Market Place." *North Carolina Law Review* 43, 2 (February 1965): 271–97.
de Villiers, René. "Afrikaner Nationalism." Pp. 365–423 in the *Oxford History of South Africa*, Vol 2. Edited by Monica Wilson and Leonard Thompson. New York: Oxford University Press, 1971.
Dicey, Albert V. *Introduction to the Study of the Law of the Constitution.* 10th ed. London: Macmillan, 1959.
Doxey, George V. *The Industrial Colour Bar in South Africa.* London: Oxford University Press, 1961.
Dreyer, Peter. *Martyrs and Fanatics: South Africa and Human Destiny.* New York: Simon and Schuster, 1980.
Dugard, John. *Human Rights and the South African Legal Order.* Princeton, N.J.: Princeton University Press, 1978.
Duignan, Peter. *South Africa: What's to Be Done?* Stanford, Calif.: Hoover Institution Reprint Series No. 111, n.d.
Dvorin, Eugene P. *Racial Separation in South Africa: An Analysis of Apartheid Theory.* Chicago: University of Chicago Press, 1952.
Fagan, Henry Allan. *Our Responsibility: A Discussion of South Africa's Racial Problems.* Stellenbosch: Die Universiteit Uitgewers-En-Boekhandelaars, 1960.
Gann, L. H., and Peter Duignan. *Why South Africa Will Survive: A Historical Analysis.* New York: St. Martin's Press, 1981.
Gavin, Lewis. *Between the Wire and the Wall: A History of South African "Coloured" Politics.* New York: St. Martin's Press, 1987.
Giniewski, Paul. *The Two Faces of Apartheid.* Chicago: Henry Regnery, 1965.
Gompers, Samuel. *Samuel Gompers' Papers*, Vol. 1: *The Making of a Union Leader, 1850–86.* Edited by Stewart B. Kaufman. Chicago: University of Illinois Press, 1986.
Hepple, Alexander. *South Africa: A Political and Economic History.* New York: Frederick A. Praeger, 1966.
———. *Verwoerd.* Baltimore: Penguin Book, 1967.
———. *South Africa: Workers under Apartheid.* 2nd ed. London: International Defence and Aid Fund, 1971.
Higgs, Robert. *Competition and Coercion: Blacks in the American Economy 1865–1914.* London: Cambridge University Press, 1977.
Hutt, William H. *The Economics of the Colour Bar.* London: Andre Deutsch, 1964.
Johnstone, Frederick A. *Class, Race, and Gold: A Study of Class Relations and Racial Discrimination in South Africa.* London: Routledge and Kegan Paul, 1976.
Katz, Elaine. "White Workers' Grievances and the Industrial Colour Bar." *South African Journal of Economics* 42, 2 (June 1974): 127–56.
Kavalsky, S. "Validity of Municipal Bye-laws." *South African Journal of Law* 53 (1936): 170–85, 287–301, and 446–57.
Kendall, Frances, and Leon Louw. *After Apartheid: The Solution for South Africa.* San Francisco: Institute for Contemporary Studies, 1987.
Legassick, Martin, and Duncan Innes. "Capital Restructuring and Apartheid: A Critique of Constructive Engagement." *African Affairs* 76, 305 (October 1977): 437–82.
Leistner, G. M. E., and W. J. Breytenback. *The Black Worker of South Africa.* Pretoria: Africa Institute of South Africa, 1975.

Leys, Roger. "South African Gold Mining in 1974: The Gold of Migrant Labour." *African Affairs* 74, 295 (April 1975): 196–208.
Liebenberg, B. J. "Hertzog in Power." In *Five Hundred Years: A History of South Africa*. Edited by C. F. J. Muller. Johannesburg: Academia Press, 1981.
Lipton, Merle. *Capitalism and Apartheid: South Africa, 1910–84*. Totowa, N.J.: Rowman and Allanheld, 1985.
Locomotive Firemen's Magazine (August 1899): 203.
Louw, Leon, and Frances Kendall. *South Africa: The Solution*. (Bisho, Ciskei: Amagi Publications, 1986).
Lumby, A. B. "Tariffs and the Printing Industry in South Africa, 1906–1939." *South African Journal of Economics* 45, 2 (February 1977): 129–46.
Lundahl, Mats, and Eskil Wadensjo. *Unequal Treatment: A Study in the Neoclassical Theory of Discrimination*. New York: New York University Press, 1984.
Maasdorp, Gavin, and Nesen Pillay. "Indians in the Political Economy of South Africa." Pp. 209–54 in *South Africa's Indians: The Evolution of a Minority*. Edited by Bridglal Pachi. Washington, D.C.: University Press of America, 1979.
Magubane, Bernard M. *The Political Economy of Race and Class in South Africa*. New York: Monthly Review Press, 1979.
Marquard, Leo. *The People and Policies of South Africa*. London: Oxford University Press, 1969.
May, Henry John. *The South African Constitution*. Westport, Conn.: Greenwood Press, 1970.
Mazrui, Ali A. *The Africans: A Triple Heritage*. London: BBC Publications, 1986.
Neame, L. E. *The History of Apartheid: The Story of the Colour War in South Africa*. New York: London House and Maxwell, 1963.
New Encyclopaedia Britannica, Vol. 7, p. 589. Chicago: Encyclopaedia Britannica, 1985.
"Notes." *South African Law Journal* 6 (1939): 345–46.
Official Year Book of the Union of South Africa and Basutoland, Bechuanaland Protectorate and Swaziland, 1926–1927. Compiled and edited on behalf of the Department of Foreign Affairs. (Pretoria: Government Printer, 1926).
O'Meara, Dan. *Volkskapitalisme: Class, Capital, and Ideology in the Development of Afrikaner Nationalism, 1934–1948*. London: Cambridge University Press, 1983.
"Overview of Interaction in Africa." *International Bulletin* (of the Africa Institute of South Africa, Pretoria) 1, 3 (1987): 56.
"Parliament." *South African Digest* (September 18, 1987): 5.
Paton, Alan. "Indaba without Fear." *Optima* 35, 1 (March 1987): 2–10.
Price, A. Grenfell. *White Settlers and Native Peoples*. Westport, Conn.: Greenwood Press, 1972.
Race Relations News 49, 4 (December 1987): 8.
Robertson, Janet. *Liberalism in South Africa: 1948–1963*. Oxford: Clarendon Press, 1971.
Roux, Edward. *Time Longer than Rope: A History of the Black Man's Struggle for Freedom in South Africa*. Madison: University of Wisconsin Press, 1964.
Saunders, Christopher. *Historical Dictionary of South Africa*. Metuchen, N.J.: Scarecrow Press, 1983.
Schlemmer, Lawrence. *Employment Opportunities and Race in South Africa*. Denver, Colo.: University of Denver, 1973.
Simons, H. J. "The Law and Its Administration." Pp. 41–108 in *Handbook on Race*

Relations in South Africa. Edited by Ellen Hellman. New York: Octagon Books, 1975.

South African Department of Foreign Affairs and Information. *1983 Official Year Book of the Republic of South Africa*. Johannesburg: Chris van Rensburg Publications, 1983.

———. *Report of the Commission of Inquiry into Legislation Affecting the Utilization of Manpower*. Pretoria: Government Printer, 1979.

South African Department of Public Affairs, *Official Yearbook of South Africa 1986*. Pretoria: Government Printer, 1986.

South African Institute of Race Relations. *A Survey of Race Relations in South Africa 1971*. Natal: The Natal Witness, 1971.

Southern African Catholic Bishop's Conference: "Special Commission on Economic Pressures." Mimeograph. n.d., p. 12.

Spandau, Arnt. "South African Wage Board Policy: An Alternative Interpretation." *South African Journal of Economics* 40, 4 (December 1972): 377–87.

———. *Economic Boycott against South Africa: Normative and Factual Issues*. Johannesburg: Labour Research Programme, University of the Witwatersrand, 1978.

Spero, Sterling D., and Abram Harris. *The Black Worker*. New York: Kennikat Press, 1931.

Steenkamp, W. F. J. "Labour Policies for Growth during the Seventies: In the Established Industrial Areas." *South African Journal of Economics* 39, 2 (June 1971): 97–111.

———. "Labour Problems and Policies of Half a Century." *South African Journal of Economics* 51, 1 (December 1983): 58–87.

Thomashausen, Andre E. A. M. *The Dismantling of Apartheid*. Cape Town: Printpak Books, 1987.

Thompson, Leonard. "The Compromise of Union." Pp. 325–64 in the *Oxford History of South Africa* Vol. 2. Edited by Monica Wilson and Leonard Thompson. New York: Oxford University Press, 1971.

Truu, M. L. "Economics and Politics in South Africa Today." *South African Journal of Economics* 54, 4 (December 1986): 343–61.

van der Horst, Sheila T. *Native Labour in South Africa*. London: Frank Cass, 1971.

———. "Labour." Pp. 109–57 in *Handbook on Race Relations in South Africa*. Edited by Ellen Hellman. New York: Octagon Books, 1975.

van Jaarsveld, F. A. *The Afrikaner's Interpretation of South African History*. Cape Town: Simondium Publishers, 1964.

Weekly Newsletter 460 (September 27, 1948): 6. Cited on p. 163 in Eugene P. Dvorin, *Racial Separation in South Africa: An Analysis of Apartheid Theory*. Chicago: University of Chicago Press, 1952.

———. 465 (November 1948): 8. Cited on p. 166 in Eugene P. Dvorin, *Racial Separation in South Africa: An Analysis of Apartheid Theory*. Chicago: University of Chicago Press, 1952.

———. 484 (March 12, 1949): 7. Cited on p. 161 in Eugene P. Dvorin, *Racial Separation in South Africa: An Analysis of Apartheid Theory*. Chicago: University of Chicago Press, 1952.

Welsh, David. "The Growth of Towns." Pp. 171–244 in the *Oxford History of South Africa*, Vol. 2. Edited by Monica Wilson and Leonard Thompson. New York: Oxford University Press, 1971.

Weyl, Nathaniel. *Traitor's End: The Rise and Fall of the Communist Movement in Southern Africa*. New York: Arlington House, 1970.
Williams, Walter E. *The State against Blacks*. New York: McGraw-Hill, 1982.
Wilson, Francis. "Farming, 1866–1966." Pp. 104–71 in the *Oxford History of South Africa*. Vol. 2. Edited by Monica Wilson and Leonard Thompson. New York: Oxford University Press, 1971.
———. *Labour in the South African Gold Mines 1911–1969*. London: Cambridge University Press, 1972.
Wilson, Francis, and Leonard Thompson. *The Oxford History of South Africa*, Vol. 1. Oxford: Oxford University Press, 1969.
Yudelman, David. "Industrialization, Race Relations, and Change in South Africa." *African Affairs* 74, 294 (January 1975): 82–96.
———. "Lord Rothschild, Afrikaner Scabs, and the 1907 Strike." *African Affairs* 81, 323 (April 1982): 257–69.

Index

African National Congress (ANC), 11
Afrikaner: anticapitalism, 126; and Bolshevism, 61; conflict with Indians, 17, 106–9; nationalism, 11–12; opposition to apartheid, 104
Agriculture: black farmers, 88–99; conflict with whites, 90–92; exports, 137
Andrews, William H., 52, 57
Antidiscrimination laws, 4–5, 7
Apartheid: and capitalism, 125; conflicting interests, 120–21; court challenges, 34–35; criticism of, 15; defined, 7; evasion of, 100; evolution of, 7–11 *passim*; official policy, 19–20; repeal of, 128–30; special case, 145–46; tariff support for, 87, 101
Apprenticeship Act (1944), 79–80
Asians, discrimination against, 37. *See also* Indians and Chinese

Banning, 28–29
Bantu. *See* Blacks
Blacks: compared to American, 14; compared to other Africans, 133–34; defined, 30; "exploitation" of whites, 56; as farmers, 88–90; foreign workers, 147; land ownership, 129–30; voters, 24; in white areas, 112–14
Boers: defined, 2; employment of blacks, 51; trek, 5–7
Bolshevism, 60–61
Botha, Pieter W., 17–18; Group Areas Act, 113

British: concession to injustice, 25; settlement, 3; unionists, 52–53
Buthelezi, Mangosuthu, 130

Cape Town agreement, 11
Capitalism: and apartheid, 125–26; defined, 126–27
Cartels: taxicab, 148; in the United States, 47; Witswatersrand Native Labour Association, 46
Chamber of Mines, 51–52; against color bar, 54–56, 114–15; collusion against blacks, 89–91; victory, 59–60
Chinese: discrimination against, 36, 48; repatriation, 51; U.S. discrimination against, 48
Civilised Labour Policy: applied to blacks, 71; defined, 38; evasion of, 101–3
Collusion: business, 46–47; minimum wages as, 70; in United States, 47; union, 76. *See also* Cartels
Color bar, 52, 55, 62–63; early, 37. *See also* Job reservation
Coloureds: conflict with Indians, 109–10; defined, 30; discrimination against, 32, 36, 53; origin of conflict, 4; protection of, 19–20, 79
Common law: nullification of, 28; Roman-Dutch, 27, 35
Communist, role in strikes, 56–58
Constitution: entrenched clauses, 24, 26; proposed for Kwa Zulu/Natal, 139–43

Court: independence of, 40; packing of, 14, 26; ruling in Group Areas violation, 112; subordination of, 26
Creswell, Frederick, 60, 72

Discrimination: breaches in, 102–3; early, 7; illegal, 34–35; and profits, 83–86; and property rights, 85–86; U.S., 47; white opposition to, 15
Disenfranchisement: blacks, 25; Coloureds, 14, 25–26
Disinvestment, 135–36; opinion surveys, 137
Dutch East India Company, 3; rights for blacks, 4
Dutch Reformed Church: and poor whites, 49–50; view of apartheid, 13

Equality, 27
Equal pay, 53; economics of, 67–70; union demand, 71–73, 81–82; in the United States, 74–75, 81–82
Exports: minerals, 1; to neighbors, 137–38

Fagan, Henry A., 9–10
Free market, 70, 122

Gompers, Samuel, 48, 51
Government: black conflict with, 134; employment of whites, 85–87; monopolies, 127; and strikes, 57–58
Great Trek, 5, 23
Group Areas Act, 32, 111; contravention of, 112–13; modification of, 129–30

Hertzog, James B. M., 11, 25, 52, 58; Bolshevism, 60; views on race, 8

Immorality Act, 31; interracial sex, 11
Indaba, 130–31; Bill of Rights, 139–43
India, 7; trade suspended with, 108
Indian: discrimination against, 7, 10, 20, 32; emigration, 11; merchants, 106–8, 111; migration, 7; religion, 2; repatriation, 107–8; unionization of, 80–81; Zulu conflict, 109
Industrial Conciliation Act, 38; section 77 determination, 41–42, 61, 77. *See also* Job reservation
Influx control, 32–34; advocated for whites, 49–50, 102; repeal of, 128. *See also* Pass laws

Job reservation, 10, 39; business contravention, 100, 114; challenged, 59, 71, 77; determination, 41–42; erosion of, 81; exemptions to, 78–79; government violation of, 102–4; repeal of, 129; union support for, 118

Kruger, Paul, 7, 106

Labor, preference for blacks, 4, 51–52
Labour Party, 56, 60–61
Languages, 1–2
Lipton, Merle, 90
Louw, Leon, 131–32
Lynching, compared to U.S., 18

Malan, Daniel F.: anticapitalist sentiment, 126; views on apartheid, 12–14, 19–20, 58, 108
Masters and Servants Act, 35–36, 88
Milner, Sir Alfred, 10
Mines and Works Act: changes in, 118–20; of 1911, 37, 54; of 1926, 37, 62
Mine Workers Union, 51; against policy change, 115, 118; and Weihahn Commission Report, 119
Minimum wage law, 10, 39; Davis-Bacon Act, 75–76, 86; economics of, 67–70; sought for blacks, 62–63, 71, 73, 75. *See also* Rate for the job
Mixed marriage: ban on, 31; repeal of ban, 129

National Party, 60
Native Land Act, 9, 29–30, 88; beneficiaries of, 121; mineowner support, 89, 91

Pact Government, 38, 60–61
Parliament: court challenge to, 25; supremacy of, 23, 25–26, 28, 35

Pass laws, early, 4, 10–11. *See also* Influx control
Poor whites, 49–51; and capitalism, 126
Population: of Natal, 130; by race, 1–2
Population Registration Act, 30–31
Prohibition of Mixed Marriages Act, 31
Property rights, effect on discrimination, 82–85

Quotas: hiring, 37, 40, 77; violation of, 102. *See also* Status Quo Agreement

Race, classification of, 31
Racism: Australia and New Zealand, 14, 18, 22, 50; compared to U.S., and 18
Rand Rebellion, 56–58, 114
Rate for the job, nurses demand, 73. *See also* Equal pay; Minimum wage law
Reservation of Separate Amenities Act, challenges to, 34–35. *See also* Segregation
Rhodes, John Cecil, views on race, 9, 90
Riekert Report, 40, 101–2
Roosevelt, Theodore, views on race, 9
Rule of law, 24; defined, 26

Sanctions, 135. *See also* Disinvestment
Segregation, in public accommodations, 34–35. *See also* Group Areas Act
Settlement: British, 3; Dutch, 3
Slavery: abolished, 5; importation, 3–4; trade outlawed, 4
Smuts, Jan Christiaan: *A Century of Wrongs*, 126; views on race, 8, 60, 108
Socialists. *See* Communists
South Africa Act, 24, 25
Status Quo Agreement, 53–54; victory against, 58–60, 75; violation of, 55–56
Strijdom, Johannes G., 14–15
Strikes, 36, 51, 56–58

Transvaal Ordinances, 36–37, 46, 51
Tutu, Desmond, 125

Union: discrimination, 38; violence against blacks, 37, 51

Van der Horst, Sheila, 73, 86
Van Riebeeck, Jan, 3–4
Verwoerd, Hendrick F., 13; conflict with business, 104; view of apartheid, 15–16
Vorster, Johannes B., 17, 105

Wage Act. *See* Minimum wage law; Rate for the job
Wage differences, 54, 100; in building trades, 98–99; concern for, 73–74; elimination of, 149
Warfare: British-Boer War, 5, 18, 23; First Hottentot War, 3; Kaffir Wars, 5
Washington agreement, 75
Whites: defined, 30; poor, 49–51; rights of, 13; shortages of, 97–98, 102–5

ABOUT THE AUTHOR

WALTER E. WILLIAMS is John M. Olin Distinguished Professor of Economics at George Mason University in Fairfax, Virginia. He earned his Ph.D. in Economics at UCLA in 1972. Prior to his present position he taught Economics at Temple University and at California State University, Los Angeles. Between appointments he spent two years at the Urban Institute in Washington to do research on public finance, poverty, and racial discrimination.

Professor Williams is author of *America: A Minority Viewpoint*, *The State Against Blacks*, and *All It Takes Is Guts*. He has authored over 50 monographs, articles, and reviews that have appeared in many publications, and writes a nationally syndicated column carried in 80 newspapers. Professor Williams has made numerous television appearances including "Face the Nation," "Nightline," "Firing Line," "Crossfire," "Nightwatch," and has hosted the documentary "Good Intentions," based on his book, *The State Against Blacks*.